FRIENDLY SOVEREIGNTY

FRIENDLY SOVEREIGNTY

Historical Perspectives on
Carl Schmitt's Neglected Exception

Ted H. Miller

The Pennsylvania State University Press
University Park, Pennsylvania

Library of Congress Cataloging-in-Publication Data

Names: Miller, Ted H., 1965– author.
Title: Friendly sovereignty : historical perspectives on
    Carl Schmitt's neglected exception / Ted H. Miller.
Description: University Park, Pennsylvania : The Pennsylvania
    State University Press, [2022] | Includes bibliographical
    references and index.
Summary: "Explores the diverse views of Jules Michelet,
    Thomas Hobbes, and Seneca on the extralegal aspects of
    sovereign prerogative power, often associated with grace,
    favor, leniency, and pardons"—Provided by publisher.
Identifiers: LCCN 2022020023 | ISBN 9780271093376 (hardback)
    | ISBN 9780271093383 (paper)
Subjects: LCSH: Schmitt, Carl, 1888–1985. | Michelet, Jules,
    1798–1874. | Hobbes, Thomas, 1588–1679. | Seneca, Lucius
    Annaeus, approximately 4 B.C.–65 A.D. | Prerogative,
    Royal. | Sovereignty.
Classification: LCC JC389 .M55 2022 | DDC 321/.6—dc23/eng/
    20220628
LC record available at https://lccn.loc.gov/2022020023

The Pennsylvania State University Press is a member of the
Association of University Presses.

It is the policy of The Pennsylvania State University Press to
use acid-free paper. Publications on uncoated stock satisfy the
minimum requirements of American National Standard for
Information Sciences—Permanence of Paper for Printed
Library Material, ansi z39.48–1992.

For J. David Miller,
and in memory of Susan Miller

CONTENTS

ACKNOWLEDGMENTS

I have accumulated many debts while writing this book. My first acknowledgment must go to my family. Their presence has sustained me. I also wish
to acknowledge the encouragements and comments of Deborah Baumgold.
As a fellow Hobbes scholar and a friend, Deborah has been a consistently
helpful and cheerful interlocutor. Her deep insights into Hobbes and his
intellectual contexts are treasured by myself, and I know by many others.
I also wish to offer my heartfelt thanks to John Morrill. With all that John
guided me toward, I might have written a book devoted entirely to the discontents that tracked the friendly sovereigns of Great Britain in the seventeenth century. I regret that I was unable to include more. I also owe a debt
of gratitude to Markku Peltonin. His friendship and scholarship have been
invaluable to me. I also value the help and friendship of Dan Kapust. David
Sacks was an insightful resource. I am grateful for comments and exchanges
I've had along the way with Conal Condren, Gabriella Slomp, Philip Con-
nell, Duncan Bell, Christopher Brooke, Chris Meckstroth, Duncan Kelly,
Molly McClain, Annabel Brett, Ayse Zarakol, Tracy Strong, Luc Borot,
Laurnes van Apeldoorn, Matthew Kramer, John Robertson, David Dyzenhaus, Paul Cavill, and Håvard Friis Nilsen. I owe Lauren Neff my thanks
for her help in preparing the manuscript. It is a far more readable work
than it otherwise would be as a result of her assistance. All errors, of course,
are entirely my own.

I also happily acknowledge my indebtedness to Cambridge University
and to Clare Hall in particular for a visiting fellowship. I thank the conve-
ners of the Political Thought and Intellectual History Seminar and the Early
Modern British and Irish History seminar for welcoming me. The fellowship was a most rewarding experience, both intellectually and socially. I
thank David Ibbetson, who not only approved the fellowship but joined
the crew of latinists much better than myself on the vexing matter of Seneca's
use of double negatives. Liz Ramsden and Amanda Barclay at Clare Hall
were unfailingly helpful in handling the practicalities. I also owe Tony

Hooley, Evelyn Nallen, and Rosemary Luff my thanks for making my stay such a pleasant one. Chapter 1 contains a substantially revised portion of an entry published in *The Encyclopedia of Political Thought*, edited by Michael T. Gibbons et al., Wiley-Blackwell, 2014 (© 2015 John Wiley & Sons, Ltd.). I can't thank the University of Alabama enough for the sabbatical leave that made this research possible.

INTRODUCTION

Although straightforward questions about sovereignty almost never admit of satisfying simple answers, my goal in this book is to risk some corrigible oversimplifications to yield answers more adequate to the complexity of this famously tangled concept. That is, some of the more incorrigible over-simplifications of the recent past—sheltered and amplified under the ongo-ing influence of the Weimar and later Nazi theorist Carl Schmitt—have enjoyed too much sway in our understanding of sovereignty, and I hope to reveal some of the things these assumptions have been hiding. At the cen-ter of my efforts are historical analyses and interpretive arguments regard-ing three politically engaged thinkers: the nineteenth-century French historian Jules Michelet, the seventeenth-century political philosopher Thomas Hobbes, and Seneca, the ancient Stoic philosopher and the tutor and advisor of the emperor Nero. To name my own oversimplification, each of these three thinkers was particularly concerned with what I'm calling sovereignty's "friendly aspects."

THE FRIENDLY SOVEREIGN

Who, or what, is a friendly sovereign? Why emphasize sovereignty's friendly aspects, and when do sovereigns put their friendly powers to use?

First, the "what." The friendly sovereign is the person or entity that makes exceptions for friends. I use the term "friends" very broadly, to include anyone the sovereign officeholder might wish to favor, forgive, buy off, capitulate to, or otherwise engage to the advantage of one or both parties. By "exceptions," I mean exceptions to the rules, very often laws, that keep order within the sovereign's community. A sovereign's "friendly exceptions," or an exercise of friendly extralegal prerogatives, therefore involves the relaxation or outright breakage of these same rules to confer the advantages that would otherwise be unavailable under customary legal limits.

When? Today, the sovereign's community is typically assumed to be a state, but we cannot limit ourselves to modern nation-states in any discussion of sovereigns and sovereignty concepts. One reason we cannot is that the powers human beings have called "sovereign" have long predated states. These and other entities have unquestionably informed our conceptions. We have assigned monotheistic deities the exercise of sovereignty over the universe. Even after the rise of modern states, thoughts on sovereignty have been in dialogue with deities.

Christ was folded into Michelet's grand attack on all past friendly sovereigns, each guilty of distributing unmerited grace. Conversely, the representatives of deities could train their critique upon humans for their ingratitude. When Alaric, the Visigoth king, sacked Rome in 410, he allowed those gathered in basilicas to be spared. Roughly three years after Alaric's invasion, Saint Augustine begins *The City of God* by insisting that Alaric's mercy was not the product of his personal benevolence. It was a miracle. Augustine (falsely) maintains that those spared in Rome by Alaric witnessed a mercy previously unknown by either barbarians or Romans. The pagans' gods, he boasts, lacked the power to spare their worshippers in their temples in years past. However, Augustine complains, these same pagans now blame Rome's misfortunes on the Christians and accuse them of failing to imitate their "abominable sacrifices" to their "demons." Augustine considers this a betrayal. Those pagans were spared in the basilicas because they passed as Christians, and the pagans should instead be thanking the Christians and their God for his mercy. Anyone who denied that Alaric's mercy originated in God, writes Augustine, was blind; anyone who failed to give praise was thankless; and anyone who tried to stop another from giving thanks was a madman.[1]

Now, the why. I am emphasizing sovereignty's friendly aspects because debates about sovereign exception making within political theory—and along important strands of intellectual history—have become too narrow. Much has been studied, but blind spots have also developed. The conduct I'm gathering under the name "friendly sovereignty" was once more familiar territory, even in the nineteenth century, and well before. But the friendly aspects of sovereignty's extralegal powers were largely eclipsed in theoretical discourse in the twentieth. Since 2016, friendly sovereignty's unattractive head has only partially reemerged. To fully witness this aspect of sovereignty again and to understand its significance, we must overcome the habitual blind spots.

The experience of political and even administrative authority speaks in favor of broadening our theoretical perspective. We know that sovereign power has often claimed an immunity from the authorities that work on their behalf to keep and enforce law. Power, especially sovereign power, uses and indeed advertises its capacity to break, bend, moderate, suspend, or supersede those laws. Leniency is one mark of power. We also know that many of these actions redound to the favor of some over others. As with Augustine's God, earthly sovereigns convey such benefits of mercy or generosity to demonstrate their power, and want others to know and acknowledge that it was the product of their will.

Despite this knowledge, many of us in political theory and intellectual history have been operating within a framework that pulls us away from what we know about this dimension of sovereignty. That is, recent theoretical treatments have tended to obscure the favoritism or mercy of sovereign exception making, or to see it only when we consider the lethality of sovereign power. I emphasize the friendly aspects of sovereignty because when we think of sovereigns and their characteristic decisions over exceptions, we in political theory and intellectual history have been thinking too exclusively of exceptions that unleash hostilities.

That is, the debate about sovereignty has been focused on sovereigns who authorize extralegal acts of coercion by threat of harm, exclusion, or confinement. We have focused on the meaning of assertions of sovereignty in the contexts we usually associate with crises. We focus on the swift, powerful, and urgent responses of those who undertake the extraordinary measures in the name of defending a community and/or defeating its enemies. We turn first toward tumult and/or the sovereign's lethal or purposefully dangerous powers. Following tradition, we learn to link sovereigns who exercise these powers with beasts—lions and foxes, according to Machiavelli, and wolves, as Thomas Hobbes knew—because the world of animals, like the world of deities, is unbounded by human law and therefore also dangerous. But we ought to know that necessity, urgency, and danger do not always accompany the extralegal actions that mark sovereigns as sovereigns.

Let me immediately clarify: I am *not* maintaining that those who think of the hostile aspects of sovereign rule bending and breaking are simply mistaken, nor am I arguing that its friendly aspects are more essential to what sovereignty means and has meant for centuries. I am arguing, however, that these hostile or threatening aspects have tended to eclipse other, especially the friendly, aspects of sovereignty. We need to restore balance to our considerations and learn to see again what we've taught ourselves to ignore.

How, then, to restore the balance? I intend to do more than appeal to our experience and intuition. I will offer historical evidence for the significance of the friendly aspects of sovereignty. The conversation was not always so intently focused on a single, hostile, dimension. Hostile and violent exception making has not always supplanted and substituted for the whole, nor set the terms for all other exceptions: Will they live or die, be protected or exposed?

Much of the debate over sovereignty among political theorists is built upon a claim about historical forgetfulness. Although friendly sovereign prerogatives do answer to something like a commonsense understanding of what power allows, this study also makes a claim about forgetfulness. In political theory, the friendly sovereign is typically passed over, and this diminishes our understanding of both sovereignty and the thinkers who have contemplated it in the past. Yet I first will consider a rival story about sovereignty, exceptions, and forgetfulness. It is a narrative, fostered by Carl Schmitt, that is itself responsible for much of our current forgetfulness of the friendly aspects of sovereignty.

Schmitt's story of the forgetful focuses its attention on the intellectual tradition that emerged in the nineteenth century with liberalism—in particular, those strands of the ideological framework devoted to technological, scientific, and moral progress.[2] They are accused of having forgotten, or even repressed, sovereignty. His ire is directed toward those who wish to disassociate themselves from the very concept of sovereignty. Schmitt paints a one-sided picture of liberals, showing only those who no longer wished to know sovereignty. For them, the wish to be sovereign is synonymous with a violent human past, a primitive residue that must be spurned by those who would move beyond that phase of human development by means of moral and scientific improvement. Some self-appointed defenders of sovereignty concepts claim—often, like Schmitt himself—a putative return to the hard-bitten, realist wisdom of early modern state theorists like Thomas Hobbes. The past, then, speaks truths about sovereignty that must be recovered.

Hobbes is the opening wedge: his "truths" force those who want to congratulate themselves for their moral or rational progress to confront the ugly and violent habits from which they cannot truly distance themselves. Sovereignty, teaches Schmitt, makes itself known in moments of hostility, and only those familiar with such crises can truly know it. Moreover, they will know it when the sovereign "decides the exception." By this Schmitt means an exception to normal legal constraints that would otherwise limit those who govern from unleashing the state's hostile capacities. This is not a reference to the monopoly on legitimate violence referred to by Max Weber as the distinguishing mark of the state, but the unleashing of hostile capacities in a moment of crisis.[3] This hostile power is deployed against those whom the sovereign, in this crisis moment, deems the threat to the state's existence. His monopoly is over this decision and not merely over the use of force to hold members to the rules.[4] By this account, those who do not return to the allegedly Hobbesian lessons they've spurned will never understand either sovereignty or, indeed, politics. Schmitt therefore claims the special epistemology of the bellicose man in a moment of urgency: those too moderate, or simply too accustomed to the tranquility of a normal order, do not know what it takes to defend the state in such moments and therefore cannot understand.

Schmitt's implicit historical challenge can be taken seriously. We can return and explore past sovereignty concepts and the experience of sovereign exception making. I take up that challenge in chapter 3 and those that follow. In returning to this forgotten aspect of sovereignty, I'll stress that the hostile exceptions do not have a monopoly over acts that shed light on sovereignty. The past may indeed know sovereignty better than we do in the present, and there is no shortage of political persuasions—past or present—that would put sovereignty and its violence behind them. My contention is that what we need to learn from the repressed aspects of sovereignty far exceeds the limited horizon that roots sovereignty solely in the capacity for hostile exceptions.

Before I outline how I plan to proceed through my contention about sovereignty's friendly aspects, I want to consider a potential objection.

AN ANTICIPATED OBJECTION

Because I keep the focus on the connection that marks the exercise of sovereignty and the making of exceptions, but nonetheless depart from Schmitt's approach to sovereignty in other ways, I wish to anticipate a critique. One form of friendship already plays a role within the logic that informs the circumscribed Schmittian view of both sovereignty and politics. The hostility unleashed by a sovereign decision on the exception is on behalf of some and against others. It is hostility deployed against enemies and on behalf of friends. The friend-enemy distinction is crucial to Schmitt's concept of politics. If we allow Schmitt's implicit notion of political friendship to govern our understanding, it follows that it is impossible to be a sovereign without friends. In what sense, then, did Schmitt forget the friendly sovereign?

We can put flesh on this objection by assembling pieces from Schmitt's various works. Schmitt argues that certain spheres of life are defined by a distinction that uniquely belongs to it. The distinction between good and evil is the final distinction of the sphere of morality. To aesthetics belongs the distinction between the beautiful and the ugly. They can function independently. The good need not be beautiful, nor the ugly evil. The distinction that defines the sphere of "the political" is, he asserts, the one between friend and enemy. It too can function independently, but can come to dominate and color all other distinctions. Such domination is one of the hallmarks of the totalitarian rule: the distinctions of the other realms of life must lose their independence and be made to align with the valuations of the political.[5] Schmitt's sovereign, this objection would also note, is involved in the practice of making the distinction that belongs to "the political."[6]

As we've noted, the political crisis is for Schmitt a most "teachable moment." He privileges existential moments and the decisions that accompany them as golden opportunities to resolve what he deemed long-standing forms of confusion over essential concepts, including sovereignty and "the political." The crises that most interested Schmitt were the ones wherein an enemy is identified as a threat to a state's survival.[7] That is, key concepts come into focus where the possibility of war (civil or between nations) remains as a real, concrete possibility. If the sovereign decides upon the exception, then he is withdrawing the normal legal protections from those to whom he attributes the crisis. Members of the state may also have to endure sacrifices and struggles not otherwise demanded of them, or law-ful, in peacetime.

Sovereigns may not be the only truly political actors, but they are among the most important figures because the person in possession of sovereignty will have the authority to draw the line between friend and enemy. Sover-eigns mobilize and invigorate the state and its members (that is, those on the "friend" side of his distinction) against enemies. They may even craft a new political order out of the ashes.[8] Schmitt goes so far as to assert that without the possibility of war and the friend-enemy distinction, and an understanding of who in the world is "affected, combated, refuted, or negated," the concept of sovereignty is incomprehensible.[9] Schmitt's friend-enemy distinction in the mouth of a sovereign therefore doesn't merely name and make enemies; it also names, or can be said to make, "friends" by uniting a particular "us" against a particular "them."

It would seem, therefore, that Schmitt's hostile sovereign is also a "friendly" sovereign. Indeed, in terms of Schmitt's own friend-enemy dis-tinction there is no sovereign without the intense bonds that unite "friends" in defense of their state against an enemy threat. However thin the solidar-ity forged by the declaration or threat of a common enemy, there is no doubt that Schmitt appealed to the notion that communities that struggle polit-ically for themselves are united by deeper prior bonds.[10] Bonds based upon a shared history, region, custom, religion, or other factors form over time, and members distinguish themselves from others with whom they may have conflicts. When these potential collective political *selves* have conflicts and when these reach a level of intensity with some *other* that they believe to threaten their ways, Schmitt insists the fog that has obscured the mean-ing of sovereignty and politics may lift on the meaning of both concepts.

Here is what meets this objection. One can freely acknowledge that Schmitt does attempt to connect both his definition of "the political" and his concept of sovereignty with precisely this kind of solidaristic appeal to "friends" in combatting "the enemy" in a period of extremity or crisis. Schmitt's appeal for many resides in his conjuring of eye-opening moments. The friendliness to which I refer in discussing a sovereign's "friendly excep-tion" may in some instances neighbor Schmitt's hostile, crisis exceptions for the whole. It nonetheless remains distinct, and as regards sovereignty, it remains a theoretically neglected variety of sovereign exception. It may not necessarily yield, as Augustine's disappointment shows us, the eye-opening moment that can accompany active belligerence. The friendly exception may or may not be excused by claims by the sovereign (or by apologists) that the exception is in the interest of the public, is necessary, or is even an urgent requirement for the defense, or welfare, of the whole (i.e., of the Schmittian solidaristic "friends"). The friendly exception can be a crisis decision, but it often is not one. Nevertheless, it deserves our attention because it has always been an exception that has marked sovereigns as sovereigns. Our authors, among others, have known this in ways we tend to forget when theorizing.

The friendly exception that forms the center of this discussion of sovereign exceptions is in the first instance granted to individuals or select parts of the whole and not, in the first instance, for the whole. The friends of the friend-enemy distinction are called upon to understand themselves as the political whole that must unify, fight, sacrifice, and subjugate and defeat enemies without and within. That is the belletristic friendship of the whole. I write of another. The sovereign's particular "friends," the particular recipients of his mercy or generosity, are those he singles out for the kindnesses that only an entity with exceptional prerogatives can deliver. A friendly exception may, nonetheless, put the friendship that Schmitt identifies, the solidarity of a supposedly united people, to the test. It may fracture that unity.

After this favored one, few, or subset has received the sovereign's friendly exception, we may consider its benefit or detriment to the whole. Unlike the hostile/crisis sovereign exception, friendliness does not in this instance always separate an "us" from a "them." In some instances, the sovereign will attempt to exercise a prerogative or issue a command that seeks to blur such lines. From this it follows that the friendly exception instructs us regarding an important aspect of a sovereign's exceptional prerogatives without necessarily a link to "the extreme case" or a crisis. This is not to say that friendly exceptions do not sometimes cause crises. Where populations are committed to conflicts between an "us" and a "them," the friendly sovereign may find him- or herself testing the limits of their power to make exceptions. The sovereign's generosity is never more scrutinized, or at greater risk, than when it uses its friendly prerogatives to treat some of "them" as if they were members, or equals, or even particularly valued parts over against some community's understanding of itself. This may become the case when a sovereign declares hostilities to be at an end, or an amnesty, or forgiveness. The challenge may be heightened if these sovereign pronouncements forbid vengeance, retribution, or demands for compensation by the victorious "us" against their former foes.

Thus, the friendly sovereign's erasure of domestic or foreign friend-enemy distinctions is just as political, and just as sovereign, as the hostile sovereign's. Friendly sovereign assertions, however, have a significance even when they do not disrupt or reshuffle the things that members have considered fundamental to their community's unity. Schmitt's sovereign and the exceptions that he makes are always in orbit around hostilities and the possibility of killing, and only rarely plumb the depths of all the friendly things that only sovereigns can do by successfully exercising the prerogatives of their office. Neglecting this friendly aspect of sovereignty, therefore, deprives us of a fuller understanding of both sovereignty and indeed the political stakes that attach to the exercise of these prerogatives.

RECENT REMINDERS

A number of comparative historical observations informed the genesis of this book's argument. The comparisons were between the present, then only a few years into the second decade of this century, and several distant pasts. I was first struck by the contrast between the protest I shared with many others regarding sovereign abuses of discretion in my nation's "War on Terror" and some of the protests voiced against sovereign discretion in seventeenth-century Britain. We protested the creation of a prison outside the jurisdiction of US law in Guantanamo Bay and the authorization of torture. In those earlier tumultuous years, the Stuart kings were often under suspicion of not merely using the threat of hostilities to abuse established royal emergency powers to insulate themselves and/or factions from critics and constitutional checks, but favoring persons or groups that some, indeed many, of their subjects counted as enemies. Their accusers felt they had favored these few over the kingdom itself. Kings had long been expected to grant favor, distribute patronage, and exercise mercy, but when these prerogatives were perceived to serve something other than the public good, suspicions mounted. The accusers were particularly fervent in cases when they were also motivated by their pious and angry reaction to the Laudian program Charles had sanctioned for a united and more hierarchical Church, one intended to spread, amplify, and dictate lessons from the pulpit on the duty to submit to the king and his bishop's spiritual and political authority.[11]

This was a very different experience of the sovereign's capacities—especially its capacity to function outside of law—from that more recent experience. Where did the similarities and differences lay? Both eras could raise serious concerns about the spheres where the sovereign might operate, or indeed permit others to operate, outside the limits of a customary legal order. Both could, within the logic of their legal regimes, connect these abuses to violations of right. Between the two, however, it was the seventeenth-century grievances that offered a more rounded and complex picture of a sovereign's extralegal capacities.

Well before the start of the twenty-first century, Carl Schmitt's influence among political theorists had long been established. One could be unsympathetic to his politics but nonetheless impressed with his insight into the diminishing prospects for "the political," and likewise appreciate his decrial of the depoliticizing, neutralizing impulses of advanced industrial liberal polities. His was one of the more impressive rejoinders to a technocratic age.[12] After 2001, however, the utilization and adaptation of Schmitt's insights hit new heights, spread much further, and became more of a nodal point in critiques of sovereignty and the ongoing use of crisis or emergency measures.[13]

Schmitt's fixation on extralegal violence as a window onto what liberal regimes repress remained in place, even as his glorification of conflict was sometimes rejected. Scholars who followed this path to Schmitt through the Giorgio Agamben's critical repurposing of his account of sovereignty, recombined with a repurposed Foucaultian biopower, embraced a binary that further solidified the connection between crisis harms and sovereignty.[14] It would seem for some that there were only two ways to speak of sovereignty: either according to the archaic, possibly naïve, *de jure*, high abstractions of state-sanctioned narratives about the structure of its authority, or the more penetrating look at a sovereign's *de facto* powers. Within this binary these *de facto* powers—often assumed undiscerned within the formal ideologies of legality and rule—traveled in the general direction of the hostile and defensive. The *de facto* powers were, precisely, and for some in their totality "the ability to kill, punish, and discipline with impunity wherever it is found and practiced."[15]

With scholars both before and after this period claiming twin inspiration from both Hobbes and Schmitt, the urge to further disentangle these two grew stronger.[16] As chapters 5 and 6 will detail, the differences between Hobbes and Schmitt, especially on matters of sovereignty, are much larger than is often assumed, and indeed larger than Schmitt himself allowed in the phase of his career when he pursued criticisms of the philosopher.[17] Moreover, many of the most trenchant attacks upon the roughly contemporaneous Stuart monarchs' exercise of sovereign prerogatives stood in constructive contrast to critiques of the proponents of expanded presidential authority in the twenty-first century. These earlier attacks by his subjects concerned those persons or factions that these kings refused to attack or exclude, or the crown's proclivity to moderate the hostilities favored by the most martial factions.

One of the more important lists of grievances made against Charles I was presented to him by the House of Commons shortly before his rule was destroyed in civil war. It was the Grand Remonstrance of December 1, 1641. Some of the complaints will be quite familiar: the subversion of Parliament's role in advising and authorizing the king's governance, the evasion by the king of its consent over taxation, and the deprivation of the rights of subjects. But among these there are also intermingled many, sometimes lengthy, objections to Charles's use of his friendly prerogatives. The Remonstrance paints a picture of a king who had long permitted himself and his family to be surrounded and advised by "malignant parties," working for "the advantage and increase of Popery" via the "subtle practice of the Jesuits and other engineers and factors of Rome."[18] Also, "such Councillors and Courtiers as for private ends have engaged themselves to further the interests of some foreign princes or states to the prejudice of His Majesty and the State at home."[19] The Crown is here accused of exercising such a leniency against the putatively forbidden faith that the state is said to have slid from its (already detested) toleration to a positive preference for some of the false faith's members: "The Popish party enjoyed such exemptions from penal laws as amounted to a toleration, besides many other encouragements and Court favours."[20] As a result of these influences, they also alleged, Britain's international struggles against Catholic nations and regions had been subverted: they undermined or abandoned the state's military efforts against Spain in the West Indies, failed in their efforts to defend French Protestants in La Rochelle, and had essentially abandoned the struggle against the Hapsburgs in the Palatine.[21] The Crown was likewise accused of abusing its prerogative in granting monopolies, especially on everyday staples like soap, salt, wine, leather, and mineral coal, and for using the Star Chamber court as a means of further protecting and bolstering the power of monopolists to afflict, fine, and tax those engaged in what had become their exclusive trade.[22] The king had also corrupted and manipulated the nation's other courts, in part by pressuring judges to serve their selfish ends when these conflicted with the justice due subjects.[23] Revisionist historians have in some cases rightly accused Charles I's accusers of falsehoods, but this does not diminish the fear and rage that such friendly sovereigns could evoke when their subjects thought the love they were owed whole (or sometimes what they saw as the part of that whole due themselves) was appropriated and distributed to others they declared unwelcome or undeserving.[24] After the civil wars of midcentury and upon the Stuart Restoration, sovereign forgiveness itself became unforgivable to some (including Hobbes himself, and this is no small factor in explaining his wrath against the mathematician John Wallis[25]). I detail some of these controversies after the Restoration in chapter 4.

If, however, that initial comparative insight meant using the past to spur us to see the disadvantages of becoming fixated solely upon the hostile aspects of sovereign exception making, the presidency of Donald Trump (2016–2020) may help rescue us from this fixation, if little else. What had been a plea to draw attention from the all-too-familiar hostile sovereign near the start of the century must now (in 2021) address itself to a new reality. Although still shocking to many, there is today for US citizens a fresh and still jarring memory to confront: that administration's often disturbing uses of executive discretion overlap with the sovereign monarchical habits that had once seemed largely lost, outside of occasional pardon scandals.[26]

A president who both dangled and then utilized the US executive's discretionary powers over the pardon to induce or excuse unlawful behavior, undermine the foreign policy set by Congress, and thwart congressional and judicial investigations and prosecutions of constitutional and statutory transgressions constitutes a wake-up call.[27] So too that president's affinity for, and accommodation of, autocratic leaders.[28] The same can said of Trump's pardons for those who transgressed the rights of immigrants or the military code of justice to signal an affinity with those portions of the electorate hungering to satisfy their bellicose, xenophobic, and often violent and racist appetites.[29]

To insist that the friendly aspects of sovereignty demand our attention is not, I again wish to stress, a plea for turning our eyes away from the hostile, crisis-driven, sovereign exertions of modern executives. This is decidedly not an either/or. To elevate the platform so that we might further scrutinize the friendly sovereign whose winks and proddings permit lawless fulfillment of his wishes (whether those actions stoke hatreds, line his pockets, or attempt to cure a tenuous grip on power by cultivating dependents, trading favors, or subverting elections) is not to diminish the importance of warnings about the role of crises in helping to make the US executive power a colossus capable of overwhelming the branches meant to check its excesses in the US Constitution. Put somewhat differently, we can say that some of Bruce Ackerman's predictions for a crisis-driven expansion of executive powers came true (indeed, some of Professor Ackerman's predictions could be mistaken for a playbook for some of Trump's operatives).[30] Nevertheless, there are aspects of Trump's abuse of his office's extralegal capacities that went unanticipated through this characteristic focus on crisis rule, and many of these overlap with those aspects of sovereignty that I'm calling friendly.

Our original historical comparative perspective is not rendered extraneous by this change. Trump's abuse of his office is still seen from within the lens of the present, which shows us a face of corruption. "Corruption" is not an improper word for what we've witnessed, but understanding it *merely* as corruption carries its own blind spots. The corrupt is always a departure from a specific ideal, and it holds out some promise that the ideal might be restored. That is one possibility, but so is the possibility of a turn toward a fundamentally different political order. It is not the purpose of this book to assess the likelihood of these prospects. What I can offer in this analysis is an understanding of an older status quo, one in which friendly sovereigns were unconstrained by settled and sedate expectations of constitutional liberalism. The authors I focus upon were more accustomed to sovereign powers who made both friendly and hostile exceptions to law and custom. None of them can mourn the loss of a political order like the ones that have governed most of us in the West. (Michelet, the closest to us historically, campaigned to end the rule by monarchs to complete the work, as he saw it, of the Revolution of 1789.) Their assessments of friendly sovereignty, therefore, can be somewhat more clear-eyed than our own. They are not fixated on restoring that which had yet to be established. Those traumatized by the present, or those in relatively recent years enamored by a more merciful sovereign, can benefit from this shift in perspective.

It is important to understand those who were discontent with the older status quo, like Michelet; those ambivalent, like Hobbes; and those who encouraged the growth and practice of friendly sovereign prerogatives, like Seneca. They help us understand the prospect of living inside the good graces of a friendly sovereign. Recent philosophical treatments of republican liberty have resisted the suggestion that those with the discretion to reward can set limits on freedom, but it is appropriate to ask if living within the tangled web of those who grant and/or seek an arbitrary grace is compatible with the dignity due free persons.[31]

REVERSE CHRONOLOGY AND A MAP OF THE BOOK

Before describing the chapters to come, it may also be noted that our three major thinkers are presented in reverse chronological order. This has been done to counter what may be an implicit assumption. The book identifies a set of related practices that I gather under the rubric of "friendly sovereignty," and the investigation of each of these thinkers places them in historical contexts. I do not, however, claim to have written "a history of friendly sovereignty." A reverse chronology discourages that reification. Friendly sovereignty is a concept; it references a subset of all that sovereigns may do. Among thinkers of sovereignty concepts it identifies common problems confronted by these authors as they contemplate sovereign power. Some topics are passed, like batons, between generations, and addressing them may form a tradition. For all its connections to the mercy of deities thought timeless, there is no such specific tradition of *the* friendly sovereign problem in political thought. Neither is there what I would wish to call "an evolution" in thinking on these matters that can be traced over the long term. The order of the chapters and sections will help avoid those misleading impressions.

Chapter 1 begins with an extended discussion of concepts of sovereignty as they have developed among some of the theorists counted as canonical. It proceeds as far as Schmitt and will describe some further aspects of his thesis and how it stands with what came before and some of what has come since.

Chapters 2 and 3 form the first of three sections devoted to thinkers deserving of particular attention as regards the friendly sovereign. This section is devoted to the nineteenth-century French historian Jules Michelet.

If friendly sovereignty forms a blind spot in Schmittian accounts of sovereignty, then Michelet occupies two. Michelet represents something Schmitt declares impossible: a liberal who understood sovereignty, including sovereignty's hostile aspects, and a liberal keenly aware of sovereignty's friendly aspects. Of the three thinkers we focus upon, Michelet was the most resolutely hostile toward friendly sovereigns, both monarchs on earth and the sovereign said to govern the universe. He detested the king's favor, and likewise rejected the religion whose God forgave the sins of those they deemed undeserving. Along the way, I compare Michelet with Jean-Jacques Rousseau (especially on the question of original sin) and with his contemporary François Guizot.

The next section, chapters 4 and 5, are centered on Thomas Hobbes. Schmitt does much to try to link Hobbes with his own decisionist understanding of sovereignty. In the first of these chapters, I argue that Hobbes was no decisionist, nor could he have been, given the way in which law and justice were administered at this time. The chapter also explores the debates Hobbes's contemporaries had over monopolies and other friendly powers.

In chapter 5 I take up a comparison between Hobbes and Leibniz on another facet of friendly sovereigns. Hobbes's "Mortal God" (i.e., Hobbes's earthly absolutist sovereign) is accompanied by what I call a civil theodicy. Theodicy attempts to justify the existence of evil in the world created by a perfect entity. Most often this takes the form of an attempt to explain why the innocent, like the biblical Job, suffer. Another part of that theodicy is explaining why the wicked prosper. Hobbes and Leibniz take up both questions. As regards the Mortal God, Hobbes shows himself much more concerned with the damage the sovereign can do to himself, and the state, by allowing the wicked to prosper. Leibniz, by contrast, teaches the calm expectation of the best of all possible worlds. Anticipating a later conservatism, there is in Leibniz (unlike Hobbes) little sympathy for those who complain about a political order in which the wicked prosper or in which there is no cure for existing injustices.

The last of our major sections before the conclusion is devoted to Seneca and in particular his incomplete work *De Clementia*. Of our three, Seneca is the most in favor of friendly sovereign prerogatives. *De Clementia* was written as a mirror for a prince, specifically Nero. In this period long after Rome had ceased to be a republic, killing outside the law, I'll argue, was not the exclusive privilege of the prince (*princeps*). It was the ability to spare life outside the law that truly marked the prince as godlike in his powers, and

Seneca did much to encourage the very dangerous young man he was tutoring in kingship to put this privilege to use. It has been argued that Seneca's *De Clementia* was an act of recognition. The philosopher urged a community governed *de facto* by a king to stop pretending it was still governing itself as the republic it once was. I'll argue that in urging Romans to love their clement Caesar, Seneca was substituting one form of pretense for another. As Seneca well knew, one of the great privileges of sovereign power was to be able to have the false praise of subjects upon command. The reputation for clemency that Seneca encouraged Nero to seek had some basis in fact, but it was ultimately the perpetuation of a fiction well suited to a particularly vain king.

CHAPTER 1

A SURVEY OF SOVEREIGNTY CONCEPTS

A key premise of this book is that sovereignty cannot be adequately studied apart from the concrete circumstances in which those who claim sovereignty assert their authority. If we are to know what political actors expect when they make, or even witness, a claim to sovereignty, then we need to know when, where, how, and to whom such claims are addressed. We also need to know, on all these same registers, what preceded and followed them.[1] Indeed, our contentious claim against Carl Schmitt is that the inadequacies of his account of sovereignty, and of who *knows* it, are that it leaves too many historical particulars out of sight.

The dive into historical particulars, however, carries its own risk. From a conceptual point of view, the danger is that the very concept itself loses its center. No two contexts are alike, and sovereignty "itself" is oceanic. It would not be unreasonable to at least entertain the possibility that there is no single thing, or even a predictable collection of clustered moments wherein a stable entity, or stable set of actions, emerges to predictably track what we wish to call "sovereignty."

Nonetheless, we who profess an interest in the topic must take it for granted that something, or things, unites such claims. To study sovereignty at all, one must try to speak in generalities long enough to make the dive into particulars worth the effort. Reviewing and in some matters merely asserting, rather than fully defending, some of those generalities is the purpose of this chapter. The historical argument for turning our gaze back to the neglected, friendly aspects of sovereignty begins in chapter 2.

Here is how we'll start: sovereignty is often synonymous with a struggle to maintain a power that someone has believed they or some other person has possessed. For newer claimants, it can be the aspiration to grasp a power or capacity they believe they deserve, usually according to some prior conception. "Sovereignty" over something is the claimant's due; that is, they are entitled to free rein and independence over a range of decisions. For still others, the concept is a part of an effort to take such powers away from an adversary or from the undeserving. Finally, "sovereignty" has become for some the marker of deficient forms of thought about political life and power: it is a product of a species of foolishness, and a dangerous mythology of political, and sometimes personal, efficacy that fosters unfulfillable aspirations and the false hopes of those who would either flee or conquer the contingencies that necessarily attend all political relations.

Although there is no single quality that uniquely marks all sovereigns as sovereigns, sovereignty's meaning holds together in moments, in periods, in specific circumstances. It need not always hold together the same way in all circumstances, but we assume the concept survives in spite of its inherent ambiguities because so many have thus far refused to live without it. Working from these generalities, this study will avoid the temptation to speak of a sovereignty, including state sovereignty, that wanes, is stable, or is making a comeback. There is enough within any claim to sovereignty that is inherently unobtainable that convincing generalized claims regarding sovereignty's "decline" or "return"—rather than the fate of particular sovereigns—must lure readers with grand generalizations and the false promise of precision measurements of an indeterminate object.

In its most common usage, "sovereignty" suggests supremacy. Inherently aspirational, perhaps impossible, the concept compels persons to ask who or what will have the last word. Within a community, we ask whether sovereignty will be exercised by the people. Will it be rooted in fundamental laws, a deliberative body, a particular office, some combination of the above, or the decision of a particular office or individual occupying that office? Can there truly *be* sovereignty where powers are expected to function in coordination with one another? Where that coordinating community is said to encompass the world itself, the question comes to focus on the locus of decision-making from moment to moment, situation to situation.[2]

Political philosophers within the liberal tradition, such as John Stuart Mill, have spoken of a sovereign self that was no king, but the free individual who must set his own course in life in a modern society.[3] This position has raised questions about the limits and scope of human autonomy.[4] Political theorists and political participants past and present have argued over what is actually, or could be, possessed when states, peoples, institutions, or persons claim sovereignty. There are debates over the origins and future of such claims and whether these claims *ought* to be made. The purpose of some inquiries into sovereignty is to convince us that the very concept is so deeply implicated in violence, suffering, or confused thought that we ought to uproot and extricate it from our thinking as if it were a kind of poison for which we should seek political, philosophical, and historical antidotes.

This chapter's survey of concepts adheres to a roughly temporal framework. However, it is by no means a history of sovereignty. It serves to cover selective elements of notable treatments of sovereignty that allow us to contrast and compare some of the weightier, persistent conceptions of the term among prominent Western philosophers.

AN INCOMPLETE REVIEW OF SOVEREIGNTY CONCEPTS

Let us begin with one who is counted among the originators of the state-centered conception of sovereignty, understood to be coincident with the birth of "modernity": Jean Bodin (1530–1596). He defined sovereignty as "the most high, absolute, and perpetual power over citizens and subjects in a Commonweale . . . the greatest power to command."[5] Like others of this period and for some time thereafter, Bodin conceived of the sovereign as an office, a constellation of responsibilities and subordinate rights and liberties deemed necessary but over which contentions might arise. This office-centered mode of conceiving of authority manifests, Conal Condren has argued, in a world of situated and relational positions held by individuals who can be argued to live up to these responsibilities or the proper exercise of their liberties. They can also be assessed negatively against these standards.[6] God, if not his subjects, would punish a sovereign king who violates his laws, but more about this below.

Within this office-centered frame, Bodin was true to his humanist training. He seeks credit for defining sovereignty because he has harvested the learning of the past. He draws liberally from one of our three thinkers, Seneca, and in keeping with the search for the power, and limits, of an office, he thinks in a manner still resonant with ancients like Plato or Cicero in their contemplation of political authority. "In what way," Socrates asks Thrasymachus, "was the king like a shepherd?"[7] Thus a novel work of definition, from beginning to end, is rooted in the past before states: sovereignty was what "the Latines" called majesty (*maiestatem*). Although Bodin is not a part of our core focus, we find in his *Six Books of the Commonwealth* a ready familiarity with sovereignty's friendly aspects.[8]

According to Bodin, sovereignty is more than practically necessary. It must exist for metaphysical reasons. Human beings were meant to live in commonwealths, and, by definition, commonwealths are communities within which there is a sovereign. Sovereignty is, as such, mandated by natural law: transcendent rules that are thought to govern all life. Thus, even as Bodin seeks credit for advising state leaders in the search for what we today call modern state sovereignty, his thinking illustrates that for this pivotal author sovereignty per se is *not* modern. It is coincident with human association and order from its inception.[9] The study of it is the study of those aspects of law wherein its authorities are marked.[10]

In allowing human beings the things necessary to their survival, including the unified rule made possible by their sovereigns, commonwealths can be deemed "holy."[11] Conversely, people who live outside these principles of reason and justice are not merely imperfect (because they do not live as humans ought to) but "enemies of mankind." This is why, Bodin notes, there has always been a distinction between proper commonwealths and "the great assemblies of robbers and pirates, with whom we ought not to have any part, commerce, society, or alliance, but utter enmity."[12] Thus, princes have always been known to make a broad distinction. On the one hand, there are those who might count as "just enemies." The prince can make war or peace with them according to the established laws of war; he can make alliances with them as well. On the other hand, there is a fundamentally different category of persons, persons who live outside the natural laws: "from these disordered, which seek for nothing but the utter ruin and subversion of Commonweales, and of all civil society."[13] Agreements made with such groups can be broken with impunity.

Although defenders of sovereign authority like Bodin and Thomas Hobbes imagined legitimation rooted in an irreversible transfer to the sovereign from members of a commonwealth, the concept of rule by divine right appealed to the presumed sacredness of kingly authority. This reverential understanding of law and political authority was accustomed to equating resistance to commands—so long as they were compatible with God's will—with sin. When an obligation to God and an obligation to a king contradicted one another, the solution for subjects was to obey God but passively and patiently submit to the earthly sovereign's punishment. Kings were not accountable to subjects but to God alone.[14] An angry God would have to be counted upon to mete out punishment to a sovereign who violated his commands, and defenders of the sovereign power of kings were willing to reassure those concerned with justice that there would be divine retribution for such offenses even as they denied retribution to subjects.[15]

Modern state sovereignty's claim to be a necessity was not entirely rooted in metaphysical or teleological presuppositions. Sovereignty could be deemed necessary on the basis of prudential calculations. It is necessary, some argued, because life among free individuals without a supreme authority is too dangerous for their survival. In Thomas Hobbes's state of nature, for example, individuals are sovereign over themselves. They determine what is good or evil according to their own lights and are possessed with a natural right of self-preservation that entitles them to do what they feel they must to survive.[16] This unlimited freedom to determine their own actions is one of the things that makes them dangerous to one another (*Lev.*, 17.1). Without this common authority, their condition is one of war, a terrible condition "of every man against every man." Hobbes argues in *Leviathan* that if humans do not wish to live "in continual fear and [in] danger of violent death" or to live a life "solitary, poor, nasty, brutish and short," reason dictates that they must transfer their power to a sovereign. They must give him, her, or it the ability to "overawe" them. An unquestionable sovereign is necessary to protect them from one another and outside threats and make them subordinate to a common rule (13.8–9; 20.18). As noted, Hobbes's name has been prominent among those who connect the exercise of sovereignty with extralegal violence, especially in the name of security. Chapters 4 and 5 will show that Hobbes could also see sovereign legal immunities as not only a guarantee of security but also a source of trouble—especially if they were friendly.

From Hobbes's point of view, the laws of nature are in accord with reason, but they do not obligate us to keep peace with one another without the threat of force: "Covenants without the sword are but words, and of no strength to secure a man at all" (17.2). But it is not merely the covenants that allow individuals to escape the state of nature and its requiring a coercive sovereign power; the laws within established commonwealths also depend upon this coercive force (17.10). A power that can make law must also be above the law, Hobbes maintains, and the logic of absolutism demanded that a sovereign's power be unlimited. As the sole source of law and the final word on what is or is not lawful within a commonwealth, the sovereign cannot oblige himself. He can no more do so than any wholly independent person can hold him or herself to a promise, "for he is free that can be free when he will; nor is it possible for any person to be bound to himself" (26.6). The sovereign's authority allows us to bind ourselves to one another and a common rule, but it can only do so because we cannot bind the sovereign.

The alternative to a sovereign whose power is beyond appeal is not, Hobbes insists, a moderated form of power, but rather sedition, tumult, and civil war. Within this logic, sovereignty is either possessed in full or not possessed at all. There cannot be a middle ground, which means it must be unlimited: "And whosoever, thinking sovereign power too great, will seek to make it less, must subject himself to the power that can limit it, that is to say, to a greater" (20.18). However, in keeping with the basis of obedience to a sovereign in the natural right to self-preservation, allegiance to a sovereign does not trump the individual's right to self-preservation. Hobbes allows that subjects not protected or subjects facing death—including those deemed justly punished—do not owe the sovereign their obedience (21.21–23). As subjects, we may owe the sovereign our cooperation in the punishment of criminals, but the person serving a death sentence or even just a sentence of imprisonment is entitled within Hobbes's framework to struggle against or disobey the sovereign who threatens his life (14.8, 29; 21.12–17).

Bodin, among other theorists, defends a conception of absolutist sovereignty that acknowledges the constraints natural law places even upon "absolutists" and therefore acknowledges the sovereign's accountability to God, if not to his subjects.[17] Bodin's sovereign holds its power over its subjects "without appeale," but Hobbes seems to offer a more aggressive defense of the sovereign's supremacy and capacity to act with impunity across a wide variety of domains.[18] Bodin and the defenders of absolutist sovereignty stipulate that sovereigns cannot take property from their subjects without justification or the consent of a parliament; or at least, they allow that the sovereign can do so but only when an emergency renders it necessary. However, because absolutist sovereigns are unassailable by the public or by representative bodies, such limitations would be unenforceable.[19] In light of such problems, a particularly aggressive theorist of absolutism tends to appear the more honest and forthright in describing sovereign power, since the theory does not posit sovereign obedience to principles it does not actually compel the sovereign to uphold. For revisionist historians such as Glenn Burgess, however, the honesty and forthrightness of those few so-called absolutists, especially among the early Stuarts, is the product of anachronism. I consider Burgess's contribution in greater depth in chapter 4, but suffice it to say that he urges us to understand that the self-limitation of kings and the threat of divine punishments were understood differently in the early modern era than they are now.[20]

Hobbesian sovereign power implies that subjects cannot change their form of government without the sovereign's permission. Because they are understood to have authorized the sovereign's actions when they agreed with one another to make the sovereign, the Hobbesian sovereign can never be punished by the subjects or accused of having caused the subjects legal injury. Further, this sovereign has the right to judge what is necessary for both the internal and external peace and defense of the subjects; therefore the sovereign also possesses the power and right to make peace and war, to levy taxes for these purposes, and to coin money. Likewise, the sovereign can determine what shall and shall not be taught to subjects. The state church and the state's armies and magistrates are under his ultimate command. The sovereign not only possesses legislative authority but also has supreme judicial authority; such a sovereign has the last word in settling all disputes between subjects.

This power, Hobbes notes, makes the sovereign capable of settling all controversies and conflicts over civil law, natural law, and disputes over fact. In a world in which titles of honor sustain complex hierarchies of power and authority, the sovereign must be the "fountain of all honour" (*Lev.*, 18.18). All persons in lesser offices are equally subordinate to him: "And though they shine, some more, some less, when they are out of his sight, yet in his presence they shine no more than the stars in [the] presence of the sun" (18.19). Sovereigns not only have to be legally, financially, and martially unassailable, but their powers must also be integral, Hobbes declares. If they yield to arguments or forces that limit their power in one domain, it would unravel their power in others. Hobbes thinks power over the judiciary useless, for example, if the sovereign does not also possess the power of enforcement. The rights of the sovereign therefore have to be indivisible (18.16).

As theories of early modern sovereign states emerged, the West began to think of states as persons. They were, that is, taken to be individually unified wholes that could act independently, coherently, and express themselves as one voice—both to the people they govern and to participants and counterparts in international affairs, where other states and stateless actors interact. Among scholars of international relations, this condition is referred to as "Westphalian sovereignty" and is premised on a state's capacity to exclude external actors from interfering within it. The Peace of Westphalia, which brought an end to the Thirty Years' War in 1648, did not create the system of independent sovereign states, though it is today often understood to have set lasting terms by which states recognize and are recognized by other states.

These controlling visions of the state as a thing complete unto itself—later called the "monism" inherent in some notions of the state and sovereignty—were from their earliest moments challenged. Be it "the state" in full control of itself in relation to other states or the sovereign in relation to other power centers within, the will of sovereignty toward oneness, total coordination, and rule without question have always been much more aspirational than factual. Hobbes's concern to preserve the unity of his sovereign is itself testimony to the tenuousness of sovereignty. Sovereigns are frequently stricken with anxieties about the power they fear they may lack when they need it most, and these anxieties are often generative of the most aggressive and expansive assertions of power.[21] Hobbes pleads with leaders and peoples to avoid the temptation to design institutions to circumscribe sovereign power. He counts such limitations among the "diseases" of the body politic.[22] A system of checks and balances and notions of divided and shared sovereign powers are incompatible with his philosophy of sovereignty.

The delimitations and fragmentations of sovereignty—whether pleaded for or merely observed as a challenge to unitary ideals—are also a part of how we understand the concept of sovereignty. As the basis of the concept came to be rooted not in mysteries but in justifications available to human reason and the consent of the governed, the debates over sovereignty changed. If a sovereign were created by the consent of a people, could the people not then withdraw their consent? If the basis for their consent were natural law, then would not a person in authority who violated their obligations to natural law forfeit the claim to govern? Who speaks for the people in such circumstances? Would it be their representatives in the estates or parliaments, or would the ability to change governments be located, as John Locke asserts, in the people themselves and their ability to assert their rights under natural law?[23] Although Locke endorsed the necessity of unified rule under legitimate government powers, he was particularly hesitant—at least when contrasted with Hobbes and Bodin—to deploy the concept of sovereignty as a political concept. In fact, though God is said to possess it, sovereignty is hardly broached by Locke other than to deny the forms of absolute sovereignty he attributes to his intellectual and political predecessors.[24]

What this part of our very short survey of early modern theorists may illustrate, for it could not demonstrate it, is that sovereignty itself was always a claim upon something both conceptually and practically tenuous. Even those we today credit with giving modern state sovereignty its original meaning were never confident about the capacity for persons to actually exercise political sovereignty, and those who claimed credit for thinking something new built their concepts out of something old. Supremacy, in other words, is always asserting itself against an unlimited number of challenges, and its gains or losses are best understood situationally. We can, thus, acknowledge that the need or desire for the supremacy that aspirants to sovereignty claim is very old without having to lapse into the habit of presuming a uniform object of desire among those who assert this ever-tenuous power. This should make us skeptical of those who claim to find, defend, or contest "archaic" or "classical" concepts of sovereignty. Even those to whom we today attribute these allegedly staid concepts—and those political actors who grasp for these powers—reveal that they understand this perpetual tenuousness. The sovereign's last word is a convention that has sustained, constrained, and oppressed communities, but it also is fiction. Truly last words belong to the dead, not the living.

FOR AND AGAINST SOVEREIGNTY

The logic of sovereignty, in particular its tendency to demand unconditional rule, has been the basis for arguments against absolutist sovereignty and, indeed, sovereignty itself as a concept and political practice. Some have argued that "sovereignty" ought to be removed from our political vocabulary. This has generated an ongoing discussion that picks up steam in the early twentieth century. That discussion now tends to color our understanding of "state theorists" whose intellectual origins take us back to their reactions to Revolutionary and Napoleonic France, and still further back to Rousseau. I will begin this much-abbreviated account of the arguments for and against sovereignty with two prominent mid-twentieth-century critics, Jacques Maritain and Hannah Arendt. I will then return briefly to Thomas Paine, Immanuel Kant, and G. W. F. Hegel on the status of state sovereignty before turning to Harold Laski, one of the early twentieth-century critics of sovereignty and state theorizing. Finally, I will return to Carl Schmitt.

A natural law theorist, Maritain was one of those who called for sovereignty to be removed from our political vocabulary in the twentieth century. Not only did he second the political scientists and liberal legal theorists who said that the concept led to confusion, but he declared that it had always been a justification for oppressive practices. "Sovereignty" cultivates godlike leaders, persons, and entities placed above the peoples (as in the conceptions of Bodin and Hobbes). It fosters human rights violations, the detachment of the people's representatives from their fundamental responsibilities, and, he argued, it paves the way toward totalitarian rule.[25] His critique condemns not only the sovereignty defended by early modern absolutists but also popular sovereignty, especially that championed by Rousseau. The unlimited character of political sovereignty, Maritain asserts, carries over into Rousseau's demand for the sovereignty of the general will. It is akin to Hobbes's sovereign, he argues, in that Rousseau deems the general will an absolute, indivisible "monadic superior and indivisible Will," incapable of doing injustice and owed the unconditional obedience and subordination of individuals.[26]

For Hannah Arendt, who was also antagonistic toward Rousseau, the wish to make oneself sovereign, over oneself, or over others in what ought to be the political realm flows from one of the most disastrous missteps in the history of human consciousness. The desire to be sovereign, she maintains, stems from a prior misconception of freedom.[27] The freedom of the ancients, she writes, was located in a public sphere and was exercised in politics. Most important, freedom was found in action and in the conditional and conditioned free play of public life wherein such actions were witnessed and received by other free persons.[28] "To *be* free and to act are the same," she wrote in "What Is Freedom?" (153). It was no accident, she insists, that the ancients describe the exercise of their freedom as though they are performing arts, "where the accomplishment lies in the performance itself and not in an end product which outlasts the activity that brought it into existence" (153).[29] Freedom was a state of being, a virtue men cultivated outside the realm of necessity (such as the household or in matters where survival itself is at stake).

The catastrophic error in our political philosophy has, by contrast, taught us to look for freedom within withdrawn realms. This misconceived freedom was found outside of the world, by one self, and quite often in domains sheltered from politics: "Our philosophical tradition is almost unanimous in holding that freedom begins where men have left the realm of political life inhabited by the many, and that it is not experienced in association with others but in intercourse with one's self—whether in the form of an inner dialogue which, since Socrates, we call thinking, or in a conflict within myself, the inner strife between what I would and what I do, whose murderous dialectics disclosed first to Paul and then to Augustine the equivocalities and impotence of the human heart" (157). These withdrawn domains were first sought among Stoics hoping to endure the troubles of late antiquity—she singles out Epictetus—but were then bolstered and established by Christianity, and then again within philosophy (146–48, 150–51). Within these unworldly spaces, freedom is not sought through action but instead defined in terms of the will. The question becomes, "Am I able to will what I know I ought to do?" For Arendt, admirable ancient traditions among the politically active never suffered this division of the self; but among the withdrawn and those who had never known freedom before, it ultimately yielded a conception of freedom that fostered paralysis and ultimately oppression (157–58).[30] Is my (or "our") will done or not?[31] This is the question that animates the desire to be sovereign. Do I govern myself or others, or do I not?

"Politics" here also justifies itself in terms of necessity. What must be done to ensure my, or the state's, survival? This frame for understanding our options begets a sense of impotence that inevitably overcompensates. Having mistaken freedom for a condition without other persons or a diversity of views, it aspires to achieve a measure of control that cannot, in fact, be achieved (164). Wishing to be exempted from the contingencies, free play, and the virtues necessary to begin something new in the world, these paired—and for Arendt "fatal"—conceptions of freedom and sovereignty are in truth antipolitical: "The famous sovereignty of political bodies has always been an illusion, which, moreover, can be maintained only by the instruments of violence, that is, with essentially nonpolitical means. Under human conditions, which are determined by the fact that not man but men live on the earth, freedom and sovereignty are so little identical that they cannot even exist simultaneously. . . . If men wish to be free, it is precisely sovereignty they must renounce" (164–65). The domain where the virtuous practices of freedom might be exercised is evacuated by impossible dreams of a freedom where I am—or we are—independent of others. An inevitably arbitrary freedom that demands mastery, control, and certitude emerges in its place. These all stand as testimony to the impotent frustrations of humanity's divided self. Working by these lights, we therefore find human freedom not in participation but in the places where politics (or indeed those a community deems other) can be kept at bay, and find its converse in totalitarianism, where "politics" makes its attempt to swallow every last domain.

Arendt's view of sovereignty is complex, and its full implications require greater attention than I will give it here.[32] For the moment, however, let us take Arendt's and Maritain's attacks upon sovereignty as given. Their dissociation of freedom and sovereignty requires us to backtrack. We need to recollect the ways in which sovereignty had been associated with freedom before the twentieth century.[33] That association is rooted in state theorizing of the mid-eighteenth century, best represented by Rousseau's social contract. Servitude, he writes, is being subordinate to and dependent upon someone or some portion of the community that has the capacity to exercise an unjust mastery. A people that escapes this condition and lives in freedom must have a greater power at its disposal. It is the absolute sovereign power of the *general* will that guarantees the people against such dependencies. Such a will genuinely serves the general good rather than private or particular interests. Therefore, "in giving himself to all, each person gives himself to no one."[34] Obeying the general will, living in a civil state among equals, and subordinating our unfettered natural, individual independence to an institution wherein "each person necessarily submits himself to the conditions he imposes on others" means living by the laws we place upon ourselves and others.[35] This marks, declares Rousseau, a fundamental moral improvement in the human condition. Those that exchange the unfettered natural liberty for this *civil* liberty make themselves freer than they were before: "to be driven by appetite alone is slavery, and obedience to the law one has prescribed for oneself is liberty."[36]

Rousseau notably distinguishes the sovereign from the government. A government, he writes, is the minister of the sovereign. Government holds a commission from the sovereign; government exercises power on its behalf. A government that does not serve the general will undermines its legitimacy. Sovereignty so conceived sanctions revolution. Where the government's will is contrary to the general will, Rousseau insists, it must be the government that is sacrificed to the people and not the people to the government.[37] On the other hand, when the government does what it ought to do, its most critical function is to enforce the laws. Citizens of a republic are both a part of the sovereign but also subjects in relationship to the laws made by the sovereign. The "essence of the body politic," Rousseau writes, "consists in the harmony of obedience and liberty."[38] The power entitled to be called sovereign, on this view, has the capacity to use its government to compel compliance among individuals who refuse the general will. I can be "forced to be free" by Rousseau's sovereign in that it will not allow me to exempt myself from the laws that I, as a part of that sovereign, impose upon all others within the state.

The notion that there must be harmony between obedience and liberty when the people give themselves law would shape future conceptions of sovereignty. Thirty years later, in *The Rights of Man*, Paine references a sovereignty that belongs to "the nation." Hereditary monarchs, Paine says, had commanded authority on the basis of ignorance; they had convinced unreasoning peoples to believe that the government was the monarch's property. Reason revealed, in fact, that governments and sovereignty properly belong to the whole. Reason and democratization are in this moment wed. Legitimate governments, he writes, appeal to the common man's reason: "A well constituted republic requires no belief from man beyond what his reason can give. He sees the rationale of the whole system, its origin and operation."[39] The idea that human dignity demands that reason give law its authority comes to sanction a variety of positions on sovereignty. It can become a weapon in the hands of revolutionaries, or, as in the philosophy of Immanuel Kant, the limits reason imposes upon rule can be a double-edged sword.

Contrary to Hobbes as well as contemporaries such as Paine, Kant denies that we ought to enter civil society in a social contract for the external ends we call our "happiness." The correct justification for obedience to a sovereign must be, Kant asserts, duty; and, specifically, a duty rooted in principles derived *a priori*. In "To Perpetual Peace," he writes that these principles "are not so much laws set out by an already established nation as they are pure rational principles of external human rights in general."[40] One of these principles is equality. Not unlike Rousseau and Hobbes, Kant sees the need for a sovereign power that stands in a legally immune position in order to guarantee a state in which all subjects are equal before the law. There must be a ruler who "has the authority to coerce without himself being subject to any coercive law (for he is not a member of the commonwealth, but its creator or preserver)" (73). Kant's reasoning is tied to the egalitarian ideal of "the right [Recht] of men *under public coercive law*, through which each can receive his due and can be made secure from the interference of others" (72). Reason, on this Enlightenment view, legislates universally, and so the law, like our moral duties, must be made to apply to all under the social contract.

Kant asserts that his unassailable sovereign ought to rule in such a way as to recognize his own obligations under universal law. Every legislator is also obliged to "formulate his laws in such a way that they *could* have sprung from the unified will of the entire people" (77). When those in power (including the legislative power) make laws or commit acts that violate the principles of justice, they do wrong, according to Kant. Nonetheless, he denies a right of resistance to existing powers. The coercive power of the sovereign is the very foundation of citizens' rights, he asserts. Any claim to resist would thereby be rooted in a maxim, which, if made universal, "would destroy all civil constitutions, thus annihilating the only state in which men can possess rights" (79). Leaders of states that govern by imperfect rules have a duty to improve, however. He condemns those that are indifferent to this obligation. Might should not make right.[41]

Hegel also declares that might cannot make right and that freedom's realization in the world requires that individuals submit themselves to law.[42] In a less mature period of human history, according to Hegel, sovereign rule had been claimed as a matter of private right. Kings of the feudal era and others throughout that labyrinthine system claimed office as a kind of belonging. Their right to govern was a possession, a form of property. Thus, within feudal monarchies, "political life rests on privileged persons and a great part of what must be done for the maintenance of the state is settled at their pleasure."[43] Those who serve under the king do not do so out of a duty informed by reason and knowledge, but out of a duty informed by ideas and opinions about honor. Rule and sovereignty were personalized, and they needed, Max Weber would later argue, to become depersonalized to reach their modern stage.[44]

Feudal kingdoms, asserts Hegel, lacked a unifying principle. Ancient communities were unified but on a paternalistic basis often also sustained upon a religious foundation. This primitive "undifferentiated universality" of familial communities was unable to withstand the emergence of independent individuals. Liberated from the bonds of paternal and feudal authority, individuals within civil society were free to pursue selfish ends and inevitably conflicted with one another. Only the state, distinct from the civil society created among self-interested individuals, could overcome the conflicts among individuals. The mature state, in Hegel's view, integrates these conflicts within itself and restores a substantial universality (unity) to peoples.[45] This would be a community united on a higher level Hegel asserted, because it was rooted in the ethical obligations of independent individuals who have learned to listen to the voice of reason, a realization of human freedom, a reasoned self-determination.[46]

For Hegel, the unified state also has to embody its unity at the top, which means that the sovereign has to be a hereditary constitutional monarch. The Hegelian sovereign is willful and sits atop a harmoniously coordinated state apparatus. Unlike the medieval kings who did not exercise coordinated control, the single, decisive individual "reabsorbs all particularity into its single self, cuts short the weighing of pros and cons between which it lets itself oscillate perpetually . . . and by saying 'I will' makes its decision and so inaugurates all activity and actuality."[47] The institution Paine denounces in the name of popular sovereignty is in Hegel revived and proclaimed to be the real manifestation of reason that individuals ought to choose for themselves as a matter of ethical duty.[48] Those who champion popular sovereignty against monarchy, Hegel declares, fail to see how the sovereign monarch makes the people a coherent, unified whole: "Taken without its monarch and the articulation of the whole which is the indispensable and direct concomitant of monarchy, the people is a formless mass and no longer a state."[49] Hegel's ideal of the state became influential as the nineteenth century progressed. Resistance to these ideals, however, would also make its mark on conceptions of sovereignty.

The pluralists of the early part of the twentieth century were a reaction to Hegelian concepts of the state and reason. William James, for example, protests the monist prejudices he observes among his contemporaries.[50]

When Laski draws upon James, he does so in part to warrant an influential criticism of sovereignty and Hegelian state concepts. Hegel's claims notwithstanding, Laski argues that the celebrated unified state of Hegelian inspiration in effect sacrifices the convictions and consciousness of individuals to the state. It is the Hegelian state's might alone, not its conformity with morality, that becomes the basis for its right.[51] Laski urges the restoration of greater autonomy to organizations that exist on a level other than that of the state. Such organizations might be smaller or larger in scope than the modern state: labor unions, churches, and other associations such as universities. Whereas monist political thought demands that individuals grant the state absolutist privileges, pluralists such as Laski think individuals ought, instead, to give their allegiance to entities (states or otherwise) that can prove themselves. The claim to affection and obedience can only be rooted in what these entities, including the state, can achieve. States possess sovereignty by the people's consent, and that consent is contingent.

The logical, practical, and legal necessity behind more traditional notions of sovereignty is in this pluralism stripped away. Sovereignty is not a supreme power that must exist to avoid chaos or complete human destiny. In Laski's account, it is instead something considerably more fragile: "We have . . . to find the true meaning of sovereignty not in the coercive power possessed by its instrument, but in the fused good-will for which it stands."[52] When the state commands something that contradicts the majority's conscience or convictions, it should discover the limits of its power in relation to other associations: "Only with consent can the State's will win preeminence over that of other groups." When popular support is withdrawn, the State "finds its sovereignty by consent transformed into impotence by disagreement."[53]

Laski was writing in 1917 from his temporary home, the United States. Five years later—and roughly two years into the fragile Weimar Republic—the German legal theorist Carl Schmitt published *Political Theology*, his influential work on sovereignty. In it he denounces contemporary liberal legal theorists for having lost the capacity for understanding sovereignty, especially the need to use sovereign power to protect the state not merely from foreign opponents but also from forces within the state that threatened its existence.[54] Schmitt, like Laski and James, attacks the monism of his contemporaries, but he launches the assault from a different direction and upon a different set of practitioners of monist thought: the contemporary neo-Kantians.[55] Neo-Kantian monism was insisting upon a purely rational, unified, and ordered understanding of the law. Unlike Laski's critique of a unifying theory, Schmitt's does not think monism bolsters the state. According to Schmitt, monism is a habit of thought that makes liberal states and liberal state theorists blind as well as vulnerable to those who know the difference between working within—and taking for granted—the rationally unified formal system of law, and the decision to reject one legal order in favor of another. Knowing the difference includes the decision to reject one legal order in favor of another. The neo-Kantians, he maintains, had taken these fundamental "real decisions" for granted and were undertaking to purify knowledge of such systems and exclude the arbitrary decisions of real-world actors.[56] Schmitt insists upon their political and juridical relevance.

The difference the liberal theorists were ignoring was in fact known, Schmitt argues, by early modern theorists of sovereignty such as Bodin and Hobbes. Legal norms had become a fixation among neo-Kantian, and liberal bourgeois principles such as the "sovereignty of law" and "the rule of law, not the rule of men" had eradicated meaningful thought of sovereignty.[57] Sovereignty, Schmitt counters, cannot be understood as an abstract concept. Moreover, the authority the sovereign exercises cannot ultimately be derived from a norm or from the law. It comes from a place incomprehensible by liberal legal rationality. These shortcomings of liberal theory, he argues in *Political Theology*, are best revealed in moments of crisis, the "borderline case and not the routine," that is, more precisely, when the state is under existential threat.[58] Under such circumstances, states under a liberal order of law may have to suspend the protections normally afforded citizens.

But who, Schmitt asks, can decide that such actions are necessary, and what must be done to restore public order? The argument, Schmitt says, is not over the abstract notion; rather, it is instead about "the concrete application, and that means who decides in a situation of conflict what constitutes the public interest or the interest of the state, public safety and order, *le salut public*, and so on" (6). Against this background of a regular or routine order, Schmitt memorably concludes, "sovereign is he who decides the exception" (5). As such, the sovereign "decides whether there is an extreme emergency as well as what must be done to eliminate it. Although he stands outside the normally valid legal system, he nevertheless belongs to it, for it is he who must decide whether the constitution needs to be suspended in its entirety. All tendencies of modern constitutional development point toward eliminating sovereignty in this sense" (7). Among these modern constitutional thinkers, he singles out the ideas of Hugo Krabbe, who argues for the rule of law, and Hans Kelsen, who argues for repressing the concept of sovereignty from juridical theory in particular.[59]

From within the closed system of normative rules cultivated by the monist mindset, Schmitt says, "decisions emanate from nothingness" (31–32). Legal ideas do not of themselves make themselves a reality. There is always, in every such *decision*, an interposition of a person or entity with a particular authority. Sovereignty properly understood reveals this, according to Schmitt: "The legal force of a decision is different from the result of substantiation." It is not because the law is true to the most rational application of a norm, but because it issues from a person with authority that the law wields binding force. Legitimacy did not always issue from mere legality. Schmitt says it is this force and authority that becomes inexplicable within the purely rational cosmos of modern liberal constitutional theory. Thus, "in the absence of a pivotal authority, anybody can refer to the correctness of the content. But the pivotal authority is not derived from the norm of the decision" (33). It was the godlike, extralegal power that Schmitt appreciated in Hobbes's "Mortal-God."[60] Sovereign power was above the law, capable of suspending law—deciding upon exceptions—and the power to make law and therefore create new systems of law. Substantial conceptions of sovereignty were, thus, secularized theological concepts (36). (While discussions of God's, or a "Mortal God's," ordinary and extraordinary laws and powers can be a useful insight into early modern states, I will show in chapter 4 that Hobbes was by no means the "decisionist" Schmitt describes.)

Enlightenment philosophy had taught thinkers to search for and even insist upon a regular order within the universe. Although he does not posit an immediate transition, Schmitt sees in these habits of thought the germs of later ages wherein exceptions will be made to ultimately disappear. The early modern thinkers Schmitt admires allot sovereigns powers like those of the omnipotent God who gave the universe its order. The image of this God was shaped by voluntarist doctrines. Even if the creator of the universe had given laws to the world, surely his omnipotence implies that he is never bound to those laws himself. A sovereign, like God, can act outside the ordinary course of nature. He can, that is, perform miracles. "The exception in jurisprudence," Schmitt writes, "is analogous to the miracle in theology" (36). Enlightenment rationalism is opposed to the exception in every form, however, so there can no longer be miracles either in the universe or politically. And yet modern states do intervene in ways that are inexplicable within conventional legal norms. These acts become that much more inexplicable and mysterious within a system that refuses to acknowledge them. Instead, they put on a "huge cloak and dagger drama" to conceal the actions of this invisible power (38).

Schmitt's thoughts on sovereignty returned to the spotlight over the last three decades and have stimulated wide discussion. Jacques Derrida, for example, described the work of deconstruction as laying bare the cloak-and-dagger drama of a regular, rational order; it echoes the terms of Schmitt's critique of liberal mystification, although his political aims are very different than Schmitt's.[61] Derrida is in many instances critical of Schmitt's position, indeed exposing the German's own cloak-and-dagger dramas.[62] The apprehension that law and force are intermingled, that might and right may blend in ways we do not always wish to acknowledge—that their mixing indeed maintains the gap between justice on the one hand and law on the other—became a substantial topos in Derrida's last works.[63]

Schmitt plays a major part in Giorgio Agamben's thinking about sovereignty as well. Agamben finds in Schmitt's location of sovereigns outside the normal system to which their rule nevertheless belongs the jumping-off point for an analysis that combines Walter Benjamin's critique of modern state sovereignty's turning of the exception into the rule with Michel Foucault's concept of biopolitics.[64] Sovereignty, Agamben holds, politicizes life; it is continually drawing the distinction between the life that is due the protection of law and the life that can be exposed to unlimited and legally unchecked sovereign violence. This ongoing process of distinction and exception making happens not only without the state but within it, as the sovereign's law is made to withdraw from more and more categories of individuals that the state is willing to see excepted from the regular order in the name of security. This resonance of this domain of exception making with the operations of the current political climate of securing states against crisis has made the exploration of sovereignty a pressing issue. At the same time, the current exploration's emphasis on Schmitt's philosophy, by way of Agamben's, has cabined what had been the very expansive range of sovereign action into a narrower channel: that of a threatening, extralegal security apparatus that might eat the state from within in the name of its protection.

The most recent work on sovereignty is attentive to discussions of the fate of the sovereign state and the connections between the aspiration to sovereignty and unchecked violence. A great cluster of work in international relations theory centers on the question of sovereignty and what can or cannot be done to regimes that abuse human rights, on the rise of international nongovernmental organizations, on international criminal courts, and on the United Nations and the progress and fate of the European Union. In the subdiscipline of political theory, we continue to debate the characteristics of sovereignty. Especially among those who wish to understand the concept in historical context, the impulse to reject grand, encompassing theories of sovereignty is strongly felt.[65] The present research joins in the call for modesty.

This research also sustains a calculated resistance to the Archimedean redefinition of sovereignty into so-called archaic notions and new, more explicitly ethically motivated formulae. Our political endeavors, in abstract and concrete terms, are likely to bring sovereignty concepts in tow, not the reverse, no matter how we parse the malleability of this oceanic concept. My objective in the following chapters is to address the urgent need to reorient the debate about sovereignty to pursue understanding of more than the hostile exception. The waning days of the Trump presidency underscored the urgency of understanding sovereign generosity. In circumstances removed from our own, this understanding will enable a more lucid investigation of parts of political history—including liberalism's history—than our focus on hostile sovereign exceptions has allowed us to pursue. Ultimately, we will want to ask whether sovereignty's friendly aspects—even when they achieve some of what we wish—are consistent with the ideals of an egalitarian political order.

CHAPTER 2

MICHELET:

Burying the Governments of Grace

Why begin this extended account of friendly sovereignty with Jules Michelet? His work, especially his *History of the French Revolution*, offers one of the most powerful and thoroughgoing denunciations of the friendly aspects of sovereignty we can find. He also occupies a fundamental blind spot—or, one might say, erased or exorcised aspect—in the Schmittian account of liberalism and its development during the nineteenth century. In Schmitt's overly general descriptions of nineteenth-century European political thought, a prominent place is reserved for liberals who wished to do away with sovereignty. In fact, only some liberals did, among them Michelet's contemporary and early champion, François Guizot, but not, significantly, Michelet.

According to Schmitt, nineteenth-century liberals uniformly campaigned against sovereignty out of a blind or duplicitous fidelity to Enlightenment ideals. Sovereignty and the aggression it requires—that is, decisions on the exception—are things that liberals since the nineteenth century could not acknowledge. They repressed it, he declares, like the proverbial recipient of a Freudian diagnosis.[1]

Its opponents took sovereignty for a sign of retrograde sensibilities. Within the logic of liberalism, proponents of sovereignty, in any of its forms, were necessarily primitives. Insofar as liberal states performed the work assigned to sovereigns, the work was a source of shame. Arbitrary violence and coercion had to be masked and hidden beneath the veneer of an ideology that likens its state's legal order to the uninterruptible and impartial functioning of a frictionless, rationally executed machine. Again, some liberal intellectuals of the nineteenth century, such as Guizot, did wish to push aside sovereignty in all its forms. It would be inaccurate, however, to say that this opposition to sovereignty was born out of a concomitant unwillingness to engage in political or class antagonisms or to resort to extralegal measures to preserve the status quo.[2] For Michelet, the sovereignty of kings and the era of hero worship needed to be buried, and the passing of that form of sovereignty was cause for rejoicing. Yet Michelet, unlike Guizot, allowed that the future still had room for the sovereignty of the people. Indeed, the distance between the two intellectuals' liberalisms can be measured in part by their very different attitudes toward Rousseau. The following discussion of Michelet's liberalism and his persistent animosity toward sovereign generosity and forgiveness demonstrate the cost of eliding Michelet in Schmitt's history of liberalism.

Michelet's thought is best understood against the background of the complicated political landscape of nineteenth-century France, especially the events that preceded and culminated in the Revolution of 1848. Within the country's very wide ideological spectrum, Michelet came to occupy a position to the right of (pre-Marxian) socialist historians such as Louis Blanc and Philippe Buchez and to the left of the conservative liberal François Guizot.[3] Those to Michelet's left campaigned against private property; they professed their admiration for Gracchus Babeuf. They also were apologists for Robespierre and the Terror. Michelet rejected both of these positions.[4] On the other side politically was Guizot. A critical intellectual of the conservative left, he worked within the Chamber of Deputies for much of the Bourbon Restoration that followed Napoleon's defeat in 1814, and he played increasingly important roles in French politics over the first half of the nineteenth century. He was a fellow academic and a historian, and he was responsible for Michelet's early appointments with universities and the National Archives. Michelet supported the 1830 Revolution that toppled the Bourbons and replaced them with Louis Philippe, from the Orléans line, otherwise known as the "bourgeois king." Guizot, as prime minister during much of Louis Philippe's rule, became an integral part of the new constitutional monarchy's government. Guizot remained a monarchist, while Michelet grew disaffected. He also began to stress his connections to factions dissatisfied with the government. Although they did not necessarily share his views, Michelet identified with the petty-bourgeois artisans and small-time property owners. The son of an often-impoverished Paris printer, he lionized the skilled men of urban France and its struggling farmers ahead of modern factory laborers.

Yet it was the working classes in Paris who had fought for the Revolution of 1830.[5] The revolution had not ended monarchy, but those who had struggled for it in the streets expected to receive greater political rights as a result. Disappointment came to fester over the years, as the promises made in critical moments when the lower classes required their leaders' support went unfulfilled. The part of the left coalition that had supported the revolution fractured. Among those who broke further left, Michelet is credited with stoking discontent among his students in rousing lectures. The bourgeois king's monarchy was itself eventually toppled in the Revolution of 1848.

For Michelet, as for much of political France in the nineteenth century, history was an arena for contemplating the present.[6] The revolutionaries of the previous century had embraced antihistorical comportments. That is, reason alone would define the future. Devotees of that generation's abstract, enlightened plans cast those who wished to look backward in a negative light. Theirs was the revolution that would restart history in 1789 at year 0. Michelet's century sent the pendulum swinging the other way. Some who had never stopped looking to the past returned from exile, while those wishing to recover parts of the 1789 Revolution could now forgive those who looked to history—that is, as long as they drew the correct lessons from it. History thus became the field on which so many battled intensely with their contemporary rivals. Among the ideologically diverse liberals, the historical status of liberty and the struggles for it were the basis of important distinctions.[7] For Michelet and others, what to do and where to go next became a contest over which aspects of the past to preserve, to resurrect, or to bury.[8]

Michelet's political opponents, both proximate (e.g., Blanc and Guizot) and very much further to the right (Bourbon legitimists and ultraconservatives), fought over the present in historical terms. Well into the century, their various political programs were fueled by dreams of progress and honor, and of revenge and hopes of turning the clock back.[9] They wished to install a monarchy unconstrained by a constitution and bolstered by a dominant church and nobility who reinforced obedience, and they wished to reinstall the codified social hierarchies that liberalizing reforms had eroded to the advantage of the middling orders. History, however, was against them.[10] Old inequalities were too difficult to restore, and as their plans for the future implicitly attested, the *ancien régime* had suffered divisions in the nation's governing institutions. Against events and circumstances—including an empowered, enriched, and constitutionally protected bourgeoisie—they went in search of consolidated political authorities made unassailable by the forces, classes, and enlightened ideals that had defeated them in the eighteenth century.

ROMANCE, REVOLUTION, AND RELIGION

Michelet was more than a political historian; he was also a romantic. He spurned many of the mechanical ideals to which Schmitt's liberals are joined at the hip. He described and critiqued what he saw as the hubris of the enlightened, scientific revolutionaries. Their cold and dispassionate approach was a true flaw, as was their having rejected history as nothing more than the record of the errors of the past.[11] They were to be saluted for having defeated Louis XVI, the Church, and the nobility. The defenders of the Enlightenment had, according to Michelet, achieved a victory over a poisonous faith that had enslaved the people and over a regime built upon unearned merit. Their failure, however, was that they did not ultimately replace the old faith with a new one.

Alexis de Tocqueville testified to the power and popularity of the Revolution and caused it to spread like a faith.[12] As far as Michelet was concerned, the revolutionary faith had not achieved enough, nor did it have sufficient staying power. His works are an effort to inculcate a new faith. He preached that faith, his own political theology, by lauding aspects of the Revolution in his histories, and by casting other elements—including the Terror—as forces of retrograde darkness.[13] The true spirit of the Revolution had, for a time, overcome these things. With the Terror and the secret operations of the Jacobins, they had surrendered again to the lures of servitude, only resurgent in a new form. Michelet's political plea was to call upon Frenchmen to prevent those same forces, to his political right and left, from returning. It was not, however, a blanket condemnation of sovereignty per se.

Michelet's sympathies were with Rousseau and with the sovereignty of the general will. His accounts of some of the early accomplishments of the Revolution, especially the sentiments that gathered force through the Festival of Federations, were concrete praise for the realization of a general will. Yet in many respects Michelet outdid his prerevolutionary counterpart in his hostility toward sovereign generosity and original sin, the religious doctrine that made generations desirous of friendly sovereigns up and down the cosmic hierarchy. Therefore, I begin this chapter with the historical backdrop to his central conflict with the doctrine of original sin and the generous sovereigns who wielded the power to forgive. Then, because it helps to navigate the less well-known thinkers of the French canon with the better known, I will also contrast his opposition to original sin with that of Rousseau.

ROUSSEAU AND MICHELET: AGAINST ORIGINAL SIN

The Revolution of 1830, also known as the July Revolution, had been unfriendly to the Church, comporting with Michelet's own anticlericalism, which outlasted that of some of his liberal contemporaries. This position provides the first instance of his opposition toward a friendly sovereign, in this case the God of Christianity, or, more specifically, the God of Christian France. In France before the Revolution, the Church held that it was God's will that the people obey their betters, from the local clerics up through the king and those in his service and favor. In the early phases of Michelet's turn against the monarchy of Louis Philippe, his attention was drawn in particular to one of the traditional targets of anticlerical thinking: the Jesuits.

Having been "beaten down, sunken" at the start of the July Revolution, the Jesuits appeared, according to Michelet in his lectures of 1843, to be resurfacing, much to his consternation.[14] At the start of the Bourbon Restoration in 1814, France had in principle become a constitutional monarchy. According to its new constitution, the Charter of 1814, France was a nation in which everyone could profess their religion with equal freedom and worship with the same protection. Nonetheless, Catholicism was the religion of the state.[15] In the revisions of 1830, Catholicism was no longer the state religion, and censorship was forbidden.[16] Thanks in part to the

Bourbon monarchy's heavy hand in trying to reintroduce piety into the population, the middling orders and artisans, who had been on the bitter receiving end of lessons in humility, obedience, and other forms of self-abasement, were then anxious to prevent the restoration of what conservatives saw as a desirable relic of the old regime.[17] Anticlerical sentiment was sometimes manifest in physical attacks.[18] But as Louis Philippe's rule continued, the Church and the monarchy created by the revolution moved, haltingly and unsuccessfully, toward reconciliation.[19] A naïve 1840s American tourist might have witnessed signs of this attempt, gleefully claiming to have seen members of the royal family, if not Louis Philippe himself, attending church.[20]

Faced with the revolution's exclusion of the Church from its role as educator, liberal factions within the Church sought a role in a more pluralistic system. Instead of calling for a return to precedence and altered alliances, these factions declared that they were due their own liberties. They wished to oversee training their own clergy and protested the secular monopoly on university educations. Accommodations were sought, and the idea gained favor with some in the government, including Guizot.

These rapprochements between the state and Catholicism provoked a very strong response in Michelet. He pitched his criticisms at an existential level. The Jesuits, he wrote, were not merely making their way back into the education system that the state had wrested from them in prior years. They were, moreover, returning with a plan to resubordinate the French. Their ultimate plan, Michelet contended, was to undo the progress achieved in the revolutions. In the preliminary statement to the published version of his lectures, Michelet declared that the Jesuits had "risen themselves up again, without anyone suspecting it." Within ten years, he predicted, their influence would bring about "the death of liberty."[21]

Michelet's anti-Jesuitical works are trenchant and conspiratorial. He claims not to be attacking Catholicism but to be making a plea to other orders within France against the Jesuits. They had, in fact, become the order that was in the popular mind synonymous with the counterrevolution. Those suspicious of liberty's enemies were therefore well primed for Michelet's message, which certainly built upon those suspicions. He accuses them of having created a secret tyranny. Unlike a conventional tyranny, which wounds the body, Michelet declared, theirs is a willful attempt to inflict hidden wounds upon the soul:

Jesuitism, the spirit of police and of impeachment, the low habits of the scholar informer, once transported from the college and the convent into the whole of society, what a hideous spectacle! A whole people like a house of Jesuits; that is, from top to bottom occupied in denouncing each other. Treason at the very hearth, the wife a spy upon the husband, the child upon the mother. No sound, but a sad murmur, a rumbling of people confessing the faults of others, tormenting and quietly gnawing one another.

This is not, as one may suppose, a picture of the imagination. I see from here such a people whom the Jesuits are daily thrusting down deeper into this hell of eternal misery.[22]

Michelet's attacks upon the Jesuits and his assault upon the government for having attempted a rapprochement with the Church begin with his own petty-bourgeois preoccupations with the family. He spends great energy decrying what he saw as the Jesuits' strategy of undermining the bond between husband and wife and between fathers and their children. He wished to see wives subordinated not to priests but to their husbands.[23] His account might even be compared to the aggressive *political* sorting of friends and enemies. This is a form of political thinking Schmitt teaches us not to expect from a liberal thinker. Michelet's lectures spurred a public campaign against his teachings in 1845.

In his *History of the French Revolution*, the first two volumes of which were published in February and November of 1847, Michelet moves beyond some of these narrower attacks on the Jesuits. He launches an assault on original sin and weaves his opposition to Christianity into a larger historical struggle: the Revolution's triumph over the Church and Christianity was a historic victory of justice over grace. Indeed, that struggle was one of the themes that consistently fueled Michelet's writings.[24] Contrary to the hard polarities of Schmitt's existential narrative, anarchists and Marxists were not always pitted against ultraconservatives in the battle between Christianity and its secularizing opponents.[25] Here again, a liberal middle, and its precursor, is excluded at a cost, and this spurs on our look back at Rousseau.

One of Schmitt's contemporaries, Ernst Cassirer, had found a less abrupt beginning to the conflict between the Enlightenment and the Church. Mindful of the subsequent battles between the followers of Rousseau and the

Church, he argued that one of the "tragic misunderstandings" of Rousseau's life was that he "never understood the significance" of the struggle that began when he rejected original sin.[26] The Church, however, understood the significance of Rousseau's rejection immediately. Although separated by a century and several revolutions, the contrast between the better-known critic of original sin and Michelet is instructive.

Rousseau was content to declare that he knew human weakness first-hand. He said to one accuser that he was "often doing evil and always loving the good."[27] He treats virtue and vice with an earthy specificity, and his writings illustrate his own experiences wrestling with these tensions.[28] One may be drawn in personally, per Rousseau's designs, but Rousseau's conclusions follow larger, impersonal, social, and roughly historical trajectories. The latter are almost always that of decline and degradation: "Man is born free, and everywhere he is in chains. He who believes himself the master of others does not escape being more of a slave than they."[29] Having gained the objects of their debased desires, dependent persons will seek in turn to make others depend upon them. Rousseau describes this socializing cycle in terms that evoke Christian notions of fallenness.[30] He insists upon man's natural, primitive innocence, a social fall that is all the more noteworthy in light of his denial of original sin.[31] According to Rousseau, our fall takes place as we enter society and through our ill-considered and misguided judgments. These judgments, not those made in the Garden of Eden, corrupt us.[32] Redemption in Rousseau therefore takes another course. He pleads: shut out corruption by listening to the "voice of nature." In contrast, Michelet tends to associate primitive life with barbarism, though it is not a constant concept in his work. He ended his career by urging readers to take lessons from nature, but especially in his earlier writings, nature meant subjection to deterministic, often fatal forces.[33] Michelet connects his suspicions of generous power with the doctrine of original sin, but for Rousseau a God who damns all from birth was insufficiently generous.[34]

A proponent of Giambattista Vico, Michelet endorses a Promethean view of humanity: we *make* ourselves. Therefore, a romantic *return* to the primitive is not a part of his repertoire. In Michelet's view, humanity must take responsibility for improving itself. Importantly, human improvement—when and where it happens—reveals itself in history, and this obviously grants an important role to the historian who can convincingly articulate this improvement. Indeed, the historian may play a leading role. A convincing or authoritative account of the past permits the historian in this era of competing grand narratives to gesture toward the proper future trajectory. He can likewise denounce the forces and factions that hold back humanity's progress. As regards the natural, Michelet holds that humanity ought to pull itself up and out of the determinism of natural necessity: one needs to move from "fatality," as he often puts it, toward liberation. His "Introduction to World History" begins: "With the world, a war began that will end with the world, and not before: the war of man against nature, of spirit against matter, of liberty against fatality. History is nothing but the story of this endless struggle."[35] For the most part, Michelet takes the position that a people achieves liberty through human progress, which is to be measured first as our distance from nature's fatality. A *return* to liberty (as Rousseau sometimes desired) could only occur had that progress itself been reversed. The Jesuits were one such retrograde force among several, and a victory over their gains would be one not only for liberty but also for life over death.[36]

In the battle over original sin, Michelet does not fully spurn the notion of innocent origin. His is largely a negative assertion, however. It still stands in contrast to Rousseau's affirmative insistence upon natural innocence.[37] More often, Michelet goes on the offensive against a theology and a Church that assign both grace and damnation arbitrarily, though his targets are not only those who sentence the damned.[38] Worse still are those who save, sanctify, and favor, because they do so without justice. Whereas Rousseau—or even Michelet's friend Edgar Quinet—adopts a Protestant skepticism toward sovereign kings and the Church's ability to grant or withhold grace, Michelet pushes beyond that reformation offensive. He escapes the boundaries of Christianity.[39] Without fully abandoning the God of monotheistic religions past, he convicts their generous, forgiving God for putting grace above justice.

Grace, be it that of God, his priesthood, or kings who play the part of gods, is one of the grand and repeated themes of Michelet's histories. He declares time and again that grace is the *enemy* of justice.[40] It is arbitrary, and that which must be begged for in light of original sin is, for Michelet, the scene of compounded injustices. Whereas Rousseau claimed to be more Christian than the Church, more devoted to the teachings of Christ than the dogmatists, Michelet indicts both Christianity and Christ. Of his many accusations, one from the introductory chapters of *History of the French Revolution* merits quoting at length:

Let us consider this grand sight:
I. The starting-point is this: Crime comes from one, salvation from one; Adam has lost, Christ has saved.

He has saved! Why? Because he would save. No other motive. No virtue, no work of man, no human merit can deserve this pro-digious sacrifice of God sacrificing himself. He gives himself, but for nothing: that is the miracle of love; he asks of man no work,— no anterior merit. (19)

Christ himself is an arbitrary gift giver. Humanity, condemned in advance, must be saved, and only he, the sovereign, can bestow salvation. He does so because he has a will to do so. In this formula, work and merit, the vir-tues Michelet emphasizes as a petty-bourgeois artisan liberal, are now pit-ted against Christ's arbitrary decision in favor of his elect. Justice or desert have nothing to do with the deity's decision regarding who is saved. Salva-tion depends solely upon the deity's generosity, and this dependence makes its anxious recipients slavish. Michelet continues:

II. What does he require in return for this immense sacrifice? One single thing: people to believe in him, to believe themselves indeed saved by the blood of Jesus Christ. Faith is the condition of salva-tion, and not the works of Righteousness.

No Righteousness without faith. Whoever does not believe is unrighteous. Is righteousness without faith of any use? No.

Saint Paul, in laying down this principle of salvation by faith alone, has nonsuited Righteousness. Henceforth she is, at most, only an accessory, a sequel, one of the effects of faith. (19)

The unjust God merely requires loyalty, not that his dependents be just. If they withhold their faith, or especially if they are just, they face a terrible consequence. For Michelet, arbitrary grace and arbitrary force are two sides of the same coin. In contrast with Schmitt's formulation of exception-deciding sovereigns, Michelet's is a more balanced and complete picture. His arbi-trary, and therefore miraculous, sovereign is lamb *and* then also wolf:

III. Having once quitted Righteousness, we must ever go on descending into Necessity.

Believe, or perish! The question being thus laid down, people discover with terror that they will perish, that salvation is attached to a condition independent of the will. We do not believe as we will.

Saint Paul had laid down that man can do naught by good works, but only by faith. Saint Augustine demonstrates his insufficiency in faith itself. God alone gives it; he gives it even gratuitously, without requiring anything, neither faith nor justice. This gratuitous gift, this grace, is the only cause of salvation. God gives grace to whom he pleases. Saint Augustine has said: "I believe, because it is absurd." He might also say in this system: "I believe, because it is unjust."

Necessity goes no further. The system is consummated. God loves; no other explanation; he loves whom he pleases, the least of all, the sinner, the least deserving. Love is its own reason; it requires no merit.

What then would be *merit*, if we may still employ this word? To be loved, the elect of God, predestined to salvation.

And *demerit*, damnation! To be hated by God, condemned beforehand, created for damnation. (19)

Rousseau told his Church accusers that no matter their false claims, they could not exclude him from the "ranks of the elect" if he were inscribed there.[41] Michelet, as we have seen, condemns the very idea of an elect and here also attaches his attack on monarchy. Both the God of monotheism and the kings who proclaimed themselves God's lieutenants on earth have only ever governed for the good of those who enjoy their favor, not for the whole of their peoples. So people were governed for centuries, absent the regular rule of justice and equity: "The iniquity of conquest confirmed by decrees from God, becomes authorised and believes itself just. The conquerors are the elect, the conquered are the damned. Damnation without appeal. Ages may pass away and conquest be forgotten; but Heaven, devoid of justice, will not the less oppress the earth, though formed in its own image. Necessity, which constitutes the basis of this theology, will everywhere reappear with desperate fidelity in the political institutions, even in those wherein man had thought to build an asylum for justice. All monarchies, divine and human, govern for their elect" (22).

The reaction is tardy, Michelet writes, but Justice does eventually answer the centuries of Grace and its many abuses and attempts to swallow, subordinate, or impersonate it (3, 22, 23). His romanticism in full flower, Michelet asserts that the Day of Judgment upon the unjust, who ruled with the aid of the Church, was the Revolution (26).

In light of this long history of injustice and the relief that had arrived only recently with the Revolution of 1789, what was to follow the disappointment of Louis Philippe's monarchy? In the 1847 volumes of the *History of the French Revolution*, Michelet writes: "Let us bury, and forever, the dreams in which we once fondly trusted—paternal royalty, the government of grace, the clemency of the monarch, and the charity of the priest; filial confidence, implicit belief in the gods here below. That fiction of the old world—that deceitful legend, which was ever on its tongue—was to substitute love in the place of law" (48). The resistance toward generous and forgiving sovereigns speaks to another useful point of contrast with Rousseau. Here, the way that each spurns the love a tyrant offers brings them somewhat closer to one another.

THE SUSPICION OF GENEROUS POWER: ROUSSEAU'S *SPARSIO*

The suspicion of generous power has a long-standing place among thinkers gathered under the name "republican." James Harrington, Algernon Sidney, Niccolò Machiavelli, and even Lord Bolingbroke trained their ire on the malign influence of power and riches within courts and capitals. They share the conviction that free peoples wish to avoid the corruption and vice cultivated by the lure of a tyrant's riches or favor.[42] At present, more recent republican theorists tend to focus upon the tyrant's threats; in some cases, they seek to avoid definitions of unfreedom that link it with the temptation to accept rewards, rather than with the fear of suffering punishments or cruelties.[43]

In a twist not uncharacteristic of the history of ideas, some moneyed elites in today's Western liberal democracies build narratives of freedom and power around configurations of those who give and those who receive. In these political narratives, the world divides between "makers" and "takers." The wealthy and industrious "make," and the masses, driven by a seemingly insatiable appetite for taxpayer-funded welfare-state programs, "take." This army of democratically enfranchised masses, they say, impinges upon the wealthy's "economic liberty."[44] However, the moral economy of the relationship between those with the resources to give and those who accept their gifts looked otherwise in the context that gave rise to French republicanism.

Mindful of the tax exemptions for the aristocracy and the happy relations between the July Monarchy and the growing industrial classes, the takers rested much higher on the socioeconomic ladder. By contrast, the makers were found among the laboring classes, who were least welcome in the halls of power. Some indeed resented the exclusion and reserved their most vociferous assault for those they saw as parasites occupying the top echelons of society.[45] In this milieu of class antagonism, those at the top who described themselves as generous did not find a uniformly welcome reception. In other words, the suspicion of generous power was very much alive in nineteenth-century France. They already had ample reminders from the restored Bourbons to believe that such powers also demanded that those they oppressed should beg their forgiveness.[46] For many of the more radical and romantic contemporary political thinkers possessed of such resentments, the place to turn was, again, Rousseau.[47]

Rousseau condemned the "happy slaves" among his contemporaries and predecessors.[48] The civilized had fostered societies in which persons made themselves dependent upon one another. Proud of their progress, they had in fact followed a path toward mutual degradation. The most powerful or fortunate members, noted Rousseau, were inclined to turn those who needed their favor into their creatures—persons who would abandon their principles to please their betters. Generous power made a false promise of dignity. Real dignity required that one spurn these worthless trophies, especially those paraded by decadent masters or their underlings.

That was Rousseau's challenge to individuals, but he reserved harsher treatment for the communities that worship the false virtues, for they pave the way toward a grand ethical collapse.[49] From our condition as independent natural primitives, he argues, we slide into a collective life that diminishes us by the pervasive inability to do without others. Persons come to believe they must trick others into serving their individual purposes.[50] By this point, there is no going back from the present to a state of primitive independence. Rousseau pleads instead with his readers to contemplate recovering the dignity of exemplary republican citizens and their institutions.[51] Their virtue, he tells us, has made them wish to avoid becoming dependent upon particular persons. As members of virtuous communities, they depend instead as one equal among all others. Each depends upon the whole of their virtuous society, and each gives himself to all.[52] With no friends in high places and no favors to grant, no individual seeks to put themselves ahead of others or escape their responsibilities to the whole. When duty requires it, particular wills give way to the general will.[53]

How are these aspects of Rousseau's thought relevant to our subject? Rousseau praises generosity as a virtue, but he distinguishes it from a vicious, dependent-making generosity.[54] The distinction comports with his animus toward those who use what they possess to dominate others, although it was a temptation Rousseau could not always avoid. In *Reveries of the Solitary Walker*, for example, he tells us that he was himself lured into a momentary act of vicious generosity. He then felt compelled to perform a virtuous generous act to compensate.

These events occurred, Rousseau recalls, at the saint's day fair held at La Chevrette, the chateau where he lived for a time by the grace of the wealthy and high-stationed Mme. d'Épinay.[55] From his description, we see that the fair was a public event, an ostentatious benefit provided to the people by his patron. After attending a supper (almost certainly restricted to his host's more distinguished guests), Rousseau writes that a young man in the diners' company opted to purchase some gingerbread from a vendor. He did not consume it himself. He instead threw pieces of it, one after another, into the crowd of common fairgoers. The fortunate watched as the poor scrambled for the food. The hungry were falling over one another. Men were fighting and knocking one another down. "Everyone found this charming," Rousseau observes. Others then bought gingerbread and tossed it to the hungry mob as well. Gingerbread was flying everywhere. In a moment of *mauvaise honte*, Rousseau did it too. This unkind generosity did not sit well: "Inside," he writes, "I was not having as much fun as they were."[56]

He then reports wandering off into the fair. He there saw half a dozen famished Savoyard boys milling about near a little girl selling apples. Each had a problem. They wanted the apples; she wished to be rid of her remaining stock. The boys could not scrape together enough money. This "comedy" amused Rousseau for a period, but then he took action. He purchased her remaining apples and gave them all to the children. Their joy made him glad, and in the text Rousseau discusses the specific layers of his delight. With moral and intellectual precision, he isolates the specific elements that compounded his joy in the moment. People near the scene witnessed his generosity and were pleased by the spectacle. Seeing the witnesses' pleasure, he notes, increased his own. It increased yet again when he reflects upon the fact that all this joy was his own doing. It was the work of his own sovereign will. Finally, this generous act improved his mood that much more because it helped erase the stain of the last: "In comparing that amusement with those I just left, I felt with satisfaction the differences between healthy tastes and natural pleasures and those produced by opulence, which are only the pleasures of mockery and the exclusivist tastes engendered by contempt. For what sort of pleasure could one take in seeing herds of men, debased by poverty, piled up, suffocated, and brutally maiming one another to grab greedily at a few pieces of gingerbread that had been trampled underfoot and covered in mud?"[57]

The gingerbread flingers and Rousseau when he distributes his apples bring to mind the self-aggrandizing theatrics of Roman emperors and lesser imperial officials. According to Jean Starobinski, an ancient gesture, the *sparsio*, is duplicated in each of these scenes. It was a moment all too familiar among the subordinated ancient Romans, who would cheer their benefactors when they sprayed the crowds with candy, coins, and sometimes more valuable things. Those who were ruled by emperors, who no longer truly lived in a republic, would sing the praises of those who gave such ostentatious gifts.[58] In the painting Cardinal Richelieu commissioned of himself accompanying Louis XIII, the king and his adviser are transplanted into ancient Rome. They reappear as the emperor Titus and his loyal assistant, tossing coins to his happy, prancing subjects whose faces show only gratitude or their anxiousness to receive.[59] Louis had done the same upon his coronation in Reims in 1610, putting the dominant and the subordinate on display.[60]

By contrast, those known to defend republics and their ideals would distinguish themselves by a pointed counter-gesture. Yet whereas Rousseau made amends by offering up his own, more virtuous forms of generosity, they made their mark by openly refusing the generosity of tyrants.[61] Some refused in the most aggressive way possible, as when the conspirators who killed Caligula chose the day of the emperor's ritual *sparsio* to kill him. It was a tit-for-tat exchange between a tyrant, offering gifts to those he expected to show gratitude, and his rebellious subjects, who preferred the risk of attempting the murder of the emperor to accepting his generosity.[62]

Although he at times denies it, the satisfaction that comes from being known as the one with the benefits to share was a temptation Rousseau could temper but not obliterate in himself.[63] For those less modest, especially those who occupied sovereign office, the logic was more straightforward: good fortune came from above. A higher power—the gods and later the God of monotheism—bestowed it. To make one's primacy known to those the higher power did *not* choose to seat in the throne—including (or even especially) those near the source of good favor—the sovereign shares the wealth. Power wants all to know that its avatars punish and reward, especially when these distributions are *exceptions* to the norm or the law.

Thanks to Schmitt's overbearing influence, our present framework for understanding sovereign exceptions and the unimpeded power of rulers makes us think of extraordinary violence. We should not stop doing so. Bellicose nations, including our own, salute their violent saviors. We might correctively note, however, that whatever else divine right meant over the centuries, it also contained the idea that the benefits God intended for the people and lesser authorities flowed from him through his earthly conduits. Violent sovereign prerogatives were feared, but the sovereign's generous prerogatives were loved, at least by some, and indeed prayed for by the many. Deciding the exception was the *generous* sovereign's power to effect miracles, because he could grant a subject what others could not. This form of largesse was a critical instrument in the creation of grateful and dutiful people, and the more complete picture of sovereignty takes into account that generous sovereign exceptions were very welcome among the servile and corrupt. The friendly sovereign's critics took it upon themselves to cast doubt, blame, and suspicion upon those who gave, received, and requested such love.[64]

MICHELET'S GOVERNMENTS OF GRACE

We are unlikely to surpass Rousseau in the exploration of the psychological dynamics that attend a dominating generosity. Perhaps his tortured hypocrisies are the secret to his insight. Michelet, on the other hand, gave us one of the most robust critiques of situated and particular generous sovereigns. More so than even Rousseau, Michelet detested power that ostentatiously gave and, in the case of the Church, sovereign powers that generously forgave. In these he saw instruments of domination and the cultivation of servile ways among subjects and followers. For this, he denounced them. Reflecting on preceding monarchies, for example, he speaks of Louis XIV's "strange divinity." He was worshipped by both common persons and the "gilded beggars" of the court: by the first for the false promise of revolutionary justice—a resonant complaint among those dissatisfied with the July Monarchy—and by the second for his generosity among the elect.[65]

Michelet is impelled to stronger action than Rousseau. He does not seek to compensate for cultivating dependency by finding a more virtuous generous act to perform. Not unlike Caligula's assassins, he instead aspires to systematically deny sovereigns of their generous powers, undertaking to bury the "governments of grace" as dead relics of the past that France and Europe should leave behind.[66] He wishes at the same time to resurrect the sovereignty of the people in whom he would resurrect revolutionary sentiments through his writings.

In Michelet's narrative of persistent challenge to human progress, "governments of grace" is not a reference to a single regime. Grace's war upon justice was, according to Michelet, centuries old; its roots were in the Middle Ages, the time when human beings bowed their heads and resigned themselves to living with neither liberty nor justice. In the *History of the French Revolution*, Michelet likens the lengthy period of oppression to a natural rock formation, thrust up from the center of the earth. It rises up from the primitive center to impose tyranny upon men with a crushing weight: "a mountain of dogma upon her heart."[67] In his parlance, such governments are a recurrent historical form of "fatality," imposing a resistance to the historical change Alexis de Tocqueville declared inevitable but that Michelet thought endangered. This fatality was a means for Michelet and his contemporaries to identify the dividing lines between classes and even the political factions within camps, including liberalism. Fatality always accompanies those who would stand in the way of human progress.

Like his rock formation, Michelet's governments of grace have striations. The formation of these layers spanned the Middle Ages to his present, and Michelet describes and battles each in turn. He complains to his readers of the sympathetic pain he feels for the oppressed whose struggles he resurrected in his multivolume *History of France*.[68] I won't be reviewing all those governments of grace, some of which, such as Louis XIV's, are already well known. Because complaints against governments of grace in the mid to late 1840s resonated with complaints against the contemporary governments, I will instead focus in this section on the governments of the brief constitutional monarchy following Napoleon's defeat.

It is fair to say that the *ultraroyalistes* (the "Ultras") and aspects of their propaganda during the reigns of Louis XVIII and Charles X taught many Frenchmen to detest boasts of sovereign generosity. An important factor in this was that the Bourbons returned to power in a France that had already been made more modern by the Revolution and Napoleon. Those who defeated Napoleon made their return possible, but the social and political transformations that had occurred had an inertia. They could not be reversed in spite of the wishes of many aristocratic and noble exiles who returned to France with the Bourbons. These circumstances compelled the

Bourbons to offer a written constitution, the 1814 Charter; they would not have been able to return without the promise to solidify some of the Revolution's gains for previously subordinated classes. First in line for these guarantees were the newly wealthy post-revolutionary and Napoleonic bourgeoisie.

Some of these gains were decidedly concrete. Many "notables" possessed claims on Church lands sold off by the state during the Revolution and had long since become influential in French society. Without their support, the Bourbons could not return from exile. The returning Bourbons were likewise dependent upon France's conquerors (in 1814, its occupiers), especially Great Britain. That nation desired to see the country they had helped wrest from Napoleon remain closer to themselves. They wished for a nation that joined with the more liberal, constitutional side of European divisions, not a nation that might join with the holdovers from the age of absolutism, specifically Russia and Austria.[69]

The Charter of 1814 dictated that Parliament would now meet regularly, and its consent would be required for legislation (art. 18). It made property inviolable, including the Church lands (*biens nationaux*) whose purchase by the people to relieve its debts had been dictated by the revolutionaries. Thereby the charter made good the promise to protect the gains of those who had profited by the issuance of notes backed by confiscated lands (*assignats*), as well as other transfers from the ancient regime made possible by the Revolution and subsequent events. Restoration would not mean a return to old ownership prior to the Revolution.[70] Press protections as well as freedom of religion were made constitutional principles (if not necessarily facts), and offices were declared open to all on the basis of merit.[71]

These were not insignificant gains for French liberals. However, a Bourbon claim to generosity posed a symbolic challenge to these gains. The first of the two restored Bourbons, Louis XVIII, declared in his preamble that the charter was something *he had granted* to France (*une charte octroyée*).[72] The new constitution was, so he declared, his gift to his people, akin to the gifts of earlier monarchs (including absolutists) to their subjects. Later excised in the July Revolution by the Orléanist monarchy of Louis Philippe, the preamble implied a threat, however unrealistic, that the king might take away that which he had granted.[73]

Here, contrary to the Schmittian script, we have an example of the liminality of the sovereign on a different register. Louis XVIII asserts that he is outside the rule of law that he establishes, but he places himself there not by acts of extraordinary violence and not through the declaration of enemies or a crisis. Instead, he stands alongside and not under the constitutional order by claiming that he has acted with extraordinary kindness and wisdom. To be sure, France's defeat had placed him there, and the restored Bourbons could never live down or obliterate the fact that they returned at the hand of France's former enemies and post-Napoleonic occupiers. Louis XVIII nonetheless claimed for himself a generosity in the name of his newly reestablished sovereign latitude. It was a ray of hope to Ultras and a point of anxiety for liberals and others who had stakes in the status quo.

The restored Bourbons were bound to make everyone mindful of the lure of selective memory and attention and the limited power of wishful thinking. They were anxious to obscure the fact of their compromise with the reality of France's post-revolutionary social order. Not only were the liberal institutions they assented to enduring *by their grace*, but their return to power on these terms was also the work of the Almighty, a gift from above. The preamble includes this passage: "Only the supreme authority can give to institutions which it establishes the strength, permanence, and the majesty with which it is itself invested; that thus, when the wisdom of the King freely coincides with the wish of the people, a constitutional Charter can be of long duration; but that, when violence wrests concessions from the feebleness of the Government, public liberty is not less in danger than the throne itself."[74]

When he reached the shore in 1814 from his exile in Britain, the king's brother (and successor), the Comte d'Artois, arranged to have his corpulent older sibling greeted by virgins dressed in white.[75] Even in its willful mis-recollection, the message was clear enough: France always was, and yet was again, a royal possession. She was giving herself back to her long-lost hereditary king. This was not the only love story that the restored Bourbons told about themselves, their providential fate, and the nation they in moments pretended to have been ruling even when they were out of power after the Revolution.[76]

When the Comte d'Artois was crowned Charles X in 1825, he held an elaborate neo-Gothic coronation ceremony in Reims Cathedral, the traditional location of their absolutist and divine-right ancestors.[77] "Providence" had made him king as well, so he shared his blessings. France had already begun the process of building railroads, and yet the dead past would not relent. Charles X made himself the last monarch to employ the royal touch to cure the scrofula of the grateful diseased poor—although less ostentatiously than his early modern predecessors.[78] To many it appeared that legitimacy was running on fumes, and even monarchists of a tepid liberal persuasion, like Chateaubriand, disliked what they perceived as desperation in the Bourbons' theatricality. Those given to more progressive perspectives simply found it comical in its anachronism.[79]

The next regime, the July Monarchy, celebrated itself on different terms. Guizot and others, such as Adolphe Thiers, cheered the installation of the Orléans line. It was England's Glorious Revolution resurrected in France. A regime that had defied the constitution and become tyrannical had been replaced with a constitutionally limited regime. Kingship itself, however, remained a part of the well-governed, constitutionally limited state: Louis Philippe was their William III.[80] Michelet, however, viewed the Revolution from a different perspective. The 1830 Revolution, he asserted, was the product of a popular force from the bottom. It was not a second Glorious Revolution, but the second French Revolution. Moreover, he further claimed, it distinguished itself in a manner that reinforced his views regarding the way history ought to be written. From the egalitarian perspective that attached itself to what we now call "social history," Michelet praised the event this way: "It is the great singularity of the July Revolution to be the original model of a revolution without heroes, without proper names; no individual in whom the glory might have lodged. Society did it all."[81]

Shortly after the Orléanist regime began, thinkers more radical than Michelet began to lament their early tentative support for the new monarch.[82] Honoré Daumier's cartoons are among the most famous fruits of this opposition. He too was mindful of what he disliked about generous power. One of his best-known works is a sketch of Louis Philippe, already possessed of the infamous pear-shaped head, sitting atop a commode-throne in the guise of Rabelais's Gargantua.[83] Daumier was not the first artist to borrow this image to discredit a king, but he added his own touches.[84] In Daumier's cartoon, Louis Philippe dines in public on a feast of France's wealth. He placidly receives the substance of the state through the taxation of the beleaguered masses; then he distributes his largesse to his elect in two places. Coins collected by the tax gatherers reach his mouth by a steep ramp from the ground to the royal pear head's wide-open lips. Some coins dribble from his mouth to the elect below—a kind of passive *sparsio*. Largesse issues with greater intensity from his seated posterior. On the underside of his toilet throne flows a current of honors, titles, and other grants of privilege, received by men on their way to the Chamber of Deputies.

One need not have been a member of the radical or republican left at this time to hold the sentiments illustrated in Daumier's cartoon. Although he held the left's press in low regard, de Tocqueville offered the following summary of the transition he had witnessed:

> All that remained of the Ancient Régime [after the restored Bourbons were removed in 1830] was destroyed forever. In 1830 the triumph of the middle class was decisive and so complete that the narrow limits of the bourgeoisie encompassed all political powers, franchises, prerogatives, indeed the whole government, to the exclusion, in law, of all beneath it and, in fact, of all that had once been above it. The bourgeoisie . . . settled in every office, prodigiously increased the number of offices, and made a habit of living off the public Treasury almost as much as from its own industry.[85]

By the time Michelet had joined the opposition, Louis Philippe's monarchy was already in jeopardy. Political societies had been banned since 1835, but a campaign of reform banquets—a legal dodge of prohibitions against the meetings of political societies—were hosted. They were thrown with relatively low ticket prices, and while not exactly a popular revolt, they became a notable public symbol of resistance inspired by the monarchy's reputation for corruption.[86]

In power since 1840, Guizot's government for Louis Philippe had for years ignored proposals for electoral reform. Widely believed to have actively subverted the electoral results, it won votes through patronage and the manipulation of small districts.[87] The monarchy's favor was not limited to helping sympathetic legislatures secure their electoral successes. While members of the Chamber of Deputies were not paid a salary, a growing number were given some form of paid public employment. From 1832 to 1847, the numbers increased from 142 to 193 out of a total of 459 deputies. (In 1847, 160 of the government's 230-seat majority were salaried by the state; in other words, not all of those with public employment received a state salary.)[88] Guizot was accused in 1847 in the press by a deputy (Émile de Girardin) of corruption, having subsidized sympathetic newspapers, and of having sold peerages for 80,000 francs. Also said to be for sale were titles of honor, theater licenses, and access to parties with ministers. When Girardin was made to answer for his claims in the Chamber of Peers, a majority in the Chamber of Deputies declared themselves satisfied with the Guizot government's explanations. They were mocked for having done so.[89] Such were the tensions over the July regime's generosity and its power over dependents as Michelet amplified his opposition by issuing the first two volumes of his history of the French Revolution this same year.

BURYING THE GOVERNMENTS OF GRACE: TEARING DOWN
THE BASTILLE, RESURRECTING THE *RED BOOK*

The corrupting generosity of a friendly sovereign is such a strong theme in Michelet's writing that it penetrates even his account of the classical grievances regarding the violent powers of French kingship. For example, as a historian, Michelet is anxious to catalog the injustices associated with the Bastille, the traditional symbol of the arbitrary power to imprison and exercise violence against a regime's enemies. (In fact, the Bastille was a system of prisons with more than the one famous location in Paris.) It embodied for Michelet the subjugation of the people to arbitrary power without protection of law or a proper judicial hearing. Of equal urgency to Michelet is linking this symbol of violent and coercive power with the complaint lodged against an all-too-friendly sovereign.

While the Bastille is given its own chapter in the lengthy (February 1847) introduction to his *History of the French Revolution*, another moment of extended treatment requires consideration if we are to understand the link between the arbitrary power to harm and generous power. Michelet devotes a chapter preceding his account of the Bastille to the *Livre rouge*, or *Red Book*. Though less well known among the events leading up to the end of Louis XVI's reign, the *Red Book* was a scandal indicative of a too-generous monarch. Michelet was therefore determined to keep it center stage in an era when the July Monarchy's generosity toward its elect was a matter of contention.[90]

Published in April 1790 against Louis XVI's wishes, the *Red Book* was a ledger of the king's and queen's gifts to courtiers. That April was a momentous month: the monarchy was becoming more desperate in its conflict with the Constituent Assembly; meanwhile, the Church lost, by vote of the Assembly, its status as France's state religion.[91] The Constituent Assembly, building upon prior determinations in 1789 by the National Assembly, made April 1790 the month in which it most fully appropriated Church lands. It had been determined that the wealth of the Church, including its lands, were merely held by the Church for the state in a stewardship relation. The Church served the state, and so the Church's wealth might be put to service in redressing the state's enormous debt. In April 1790, therefore, the Assembly authorized the Treasury to issue 400 million notes (the aforementioned *assignats*) for Church property. These were sold to the public to meet France's national debt.[92] According to Michelet, the monarchy and the Church then reacted in 1790 by attempting to rally the people around historic and habitual sympathies, most successfully those of the rural and devout populations.

Michelet subtitled this chapter "The Passion of Louis XVI," naming, in fact, a pamphlet distributed by the Revolution's clerical opponents.[93] This attempt to turn the not-yet-executed king into a martyr was working with some when damaging news leaked. King Louis, who had at that point sworn his fidelity to the Assembly's constitution, was using state wealth to pay emigrants raising troops abroad.[94] The *Red Book* emerges from the backlash, surfacing when the Assembly demands a more thorough accounting of the king's expenses. Michelet assigns great significance to its publication: "This impure book, defiled at every page with the shameful corruption of the aristocracy, and the criminal weaknesses of royalty, showed whether people had been wrong in shutting up the filthy channel through which the substance of France was flowing away. A glorious book, in spite of all that! For it plunged the revolution into the hearts of men" (347). The significance of the *Red Book* chapter is more than introductory, because Michelet is able to extend its themes of sovereign generosity into the subsequent account of the Bastille. For example, he begins the chapter by rehearsing what has become a familiar refrain, that the tax exemptions of the nobility were resented by the peasantry and other subordinate orders, who were shouldering the burden of sustaining the state, including the splendor of Versailles and courtiers resident there:

> When Queen Anne of Austria was regent, there remained, says Cardinal Retz, but two little words in the language: "The queen is so good!" [*La Reine est si bonne!*]
>
> From that day France declines in energy; the elevation of the lower classes, which notwithstanding the harsh administration of Richelieu had been so remarkable, subsides and disappears. Wherefore? Because the "queen is good;" she loads with presents the brilliant crowd besetting her palace; all the provincial nobility who

fled under Richelieu return, demand, obtain, take, and pillage; the least they expect is to be exempted from taxation. The peasant who has managed to purchase a few acres has the sole duty of payment; he must bear all—he is obliged to sell again, and once more becomes a tenant, steward, or a poor domestic. (58)

A few years later, de Tocqueville would famously link the resentment to the effects of centralization. A ruling class whose exemptions accorded with their role in governance in earlier periods had become, as centralization and absolutism grew, useless appendages.[95] Whereas de Tocqueville would have preferred, as he preferred after these events, the resurrection of a medieval democracy he claimed to have discovered, Michelet found redress in a plea for a more punitive, more rigorously centralized solution.[96] There could be no place in it for an aristocratic class deemed parasitic.[97] The Revolution had done right in eradicating the nobility and eliminating kingship.

Michelet declares a historical pattern in the formation of generous sovereigns. Kings begin severe, he notes in his discussion of the *Red Book*. Like Louis XIV, they allow "no exemptions" at the beginning of their reign. Colbert rolls back 40,000 such exemptions from taxation, and the country thrives. Then the king grows more good-natured: "He is more and more affected by the fate of the poor nobility." Suddenly, "everything is for them," and the nobility flourishes anew. He distributes "grades, places, pensions, even benefices, and Saint-Cyr for noble young ladies," while France is driven to "her last extremity" (59). The reign of Louis XVI follows the same pattern. He is severe under Turgot, but he finally yields to the nobility and the pleas of Marie Antoinette in 1778. "The most amiable man in France," de Calonne (Necker's replacement), becomes comptroller-general. Nothing the queen demands is refused. She buys the Château de Saint-Cloud. The king then treats himself to the Château de Rambouillet. The count d'Artois sells his lands in America for millions, and receives them back and keeps them. The *Red Book* reveals the queen's lover, Coigny, and the enormous pensions he received. He even dared to refuse the king's request to take less.[98]

This, Michelet happily notes, is what the Revolution spoiled. Daumier's tax gatherers vaguely recall the labors of Sisyphus as they trudge up the ramp to the monarch's mouth. Evoking another fruitless task from mythology, he writes that the Revolution "roughly tore aside the graceful veil that masked the public ruin. The veil, being removed, revealed the [perpetually leaking] vessel of the Danaides," and like those punished in the myth, the French were seemingly condemned to an eternity of refilling the vessel (59).

These familiar complaints regarding the French state and monarchy take a more particular turn in Michelet's writing when he draws connections between waste and excess and his suspicion of grace. While the throne is condemned as profligate and overly generous toward its favorites, generosity itself is isolated as a false virtue in a sovereign. Listing off the expense of another 500,000 francs to allay the threats of a potentially troublesome courtier, Michelet returns again to his assault with dripping irony: "France is in good hands. Everything is going on well. So good-natured a king, such an amiable queen" (60). Then from irony to apostrophe: "O, heaven! O, earth! O, justice! If it were through conquest, or by a master's tyranny, that the people were perishing, they could endure it. But they perish through good nature! They would endure the hard-heartedness of a Richelieu; but how can they endure the good nature of Loménie and Calonne, the tender-hearted financiers, and the philanthropy of the farmers of the revenue! Suffer and die: be it so! But to suffer *by election*, to die through mere necessity—so that *grace* for one is death and ruin for the other!" (61–62).

When Michelet shifts to his account of the Bastille, he does not then cease to speak of a king the nobility calls good or of the sovereign's claim to control grace (62, 64, 68–69). It is not an objective good that persons were locked up in the Bastille. As Michelet is quick to note, the Bastille is not the usual prison. One arrived at the Bastille by means of a *lettre de cachet*, and it was only nominally a place supervised by the police. In point of fact, Jesuits administered the prison and made it also the place for convents for forced conversions (63). Regular justice was not its domain, for the Bastille was the possession of a dynasty. Châteauneuf had passed it to his son and grandson, who were in control of the department of state prisons. The "magistrate was ignorant of everything," writes Michelet, even though it was he who gave an account of the prison to the government's minister. The minister would then distribute blank *lettres de cachet* to intendants, bishops, and the people in administration.

In other words, imprisonment for what may have been no cause at all was the *gift* of the king, administered to his servants, courtiers, and Church within this unaccountable prison system. "Never," writes Michelet, "had man's dearest treasure, liberty, been more lavishly squandered." The *lettres de cachet* were "the object of profitable traffic." They were given to fathers who wanted to "get rid of their sons" and to wives "inconvenienced by their husbands" (63). If the "government of grace" reigned because the king had the grace of God and his servants and favorites stood in the king's good grace, then those in the Bastille receive through these letters the "the king's excommunication" (64). The king did not kill at the Bastille, because killing required a decision and a judgment. This particular prison was instead a realm of oblivion: a "middle term between life and death." One was neither free nor executed, but rather assigned to the realm of the forgotten.[99]

For our purposes, what is remarkable is the length to which Michelet goes to cement the relation between the Bastille and the Crown's sovereign generosity: "And all through good-nature. The king was too good to refuse a *lettre-de-cachet* to a great lord. The intendent was too good-natured not to grant one at a lady's request. The government-clerks, the mistresses of the clerks, and the friends of these mistresses, through good-nature, civility, or mere politeness, obtained, gave, or lent, those terrible orders by which a man was buried alive. . . . Thus, the *government of grace* . . . disposed, according to caprice or fancy, of liberty, of life" (64). We shall see that this is not the limit of Michelet's persistent suspicion of sovereign generosity. His obsession with grace, forgiveness, and sovereign acts of generosity exceeds the bounds of monarchical government. These concerns continue to preoccupy him even when he turns to the sovereignty of the people. They remain his concerns when he attempts to articulate a new faith by recounting the formation of France's general will during the Revolution.[100] The sovereign will of France's people may not have replicated the corruption of its monarchs, but it too was culpable in his eyes. This suspicion of the people's sovereign generosity is the subject of the next chapter.

CHAPTER 3

MICHELET:

Sovereign People, Political Theology, and Liberal Exclusion

POPULAR SOVEREIGNTY, THE REVOLUTION, AND THE FRIENDLY SOVEREIGN

Not all the friendly sovereigns Michelet condemned were "governments of grace," nor were they all monarchical. Moreover, Michelet's approach to sovereignty was not merely adversarial. Against friendly sovereigns, he remained a proponent of popular sovereignty. As does any such proponent, he grappled with the key political questions about popular sovereignty. Who are "the people"? How do they make their will known? How does this will, when expressed, come to hold sway and exercise its sovereign power? Who, if anyone, may speak for the people? Even in attempting to persuade his readers of his answers to these questions, Michelet is critical of those moments when France's sovereign, the people, became in his view too friendly.

Michelet was a nationalist and a proponent of what could be described as French chauvinism. France's revolution was a gift to all humanity, and it was the leading light in the progress of the species.[1] According to Michelet, France had long been Europe's spiritual leader, its true pope. Thus it was not to the pope of Rome, to emperors, or to kings that Europe turned to for justice. It had always been France: "Who could disown the theological popedom in Gerson and Bossuet, the philosophical popedom in Descartes and Voltaire, the political and civil popedom in Cujas and Dumoulin, in Rousseau and Montesquieu? Her laws, which are but those of reason itself, force themselves upon her very enemies. . . . This is not an accident of the latter ages . . . it is the legitimate result of a particular tradition . . . for two thousand years. No people has one like it."[2]

Such passages need to be framed in terms of Michelet's claims to having become disappointed with France and what it had become. France, in the nineteenth century, was now in jeopardy. "She," as he would put it repeatedly, had forgotten herself.[3] He meant with this rhetorical strategy to drive Frenchmen to ask: How could this "people"—how could France— recover herself? This was also a project, in no small measure, of claiming credit for himself and his historical methods. Upon the completion of his forty-year, seventeen-volume *History of France*, he declared retrospectively that he had been the first historian to truly bear witness to the Promethean processes whereby *France* had created herself. Other historians, he wrote, had been too narrow in their focus. They allowed some part of the whole, or early components, such as the particular races (as the concept was then propounded), to render their histories deterministic.[4] One of the great totalizers, Michelet laid claim to having captured the whole, including the processes whereby factors such as geography and climate had long since superseded matters of race in the creation of France.[5]

This refusal to allow parts to determine the whole also manifests in his political works from the late 1840s, *Le Peuple* (1846) and his multivolume *History of the French Revolution* (*Histoire de la Révolution française*, 1847–53). He would teach France to "find herself" again.[6] Earlier, I referenced Michelet's distance from the socialist historians Buchez and Blanc, who had celebrated Robespierre and the Jacobins and excused the Terror. He draws these distinctions with particular intensity in his history of the Revolution, especially when it comes to the question of who could speak the words or issue the commands that would unify the revolutionaries.[7]

We see this in his assertions regarding the Revolution's ideal of *fraternité*. He argues that the Jacobins had perverted and misconstrued *fraternité*:

> Fraternity! Fraternity! It is not enough to re-echo the word—to attract the world to our cause, as was the case at first. It must

acknowledge in us a fraternal heart. It must be gained over by the fraternity of love, and not by the guillotine.

Fraternity! . . . Do you imagine it was first coined by Robespierre or Mably? . . .

"Fraternity, or *death*," as the reign of Terror subsequently exclaimed. Once more a brotherhood of slaves. Why, by atrocious derision, impart to such an union the holy name of liberty?

Brethren who mutually fly from one another, who shudder when they meet, who extend, who withdraw a dead and icy hand. O odious and disgusting sight! Surely, if anything ought to be free, it is the fraternal sentiment.[8]

It was a regression, a brotherhood of slaves, because its claim to fraternity and solidarity was rooted in coerced choice. One could not form a free people or claim a fraternal heart if one professed one's fidelity to the whole out of servitude. Along with the fear of being put to the test by the Revolution's self-appointed censors, servitude undermined the claim to liberation for adherents to the brotherhood.[9] A fraternity that was exclusive (continued admission or ejection from Jacobin society could mean life or death) was inhuman. Michelet echoes his friend Edgar Quinet in likening the Terror to a return to the Inquisition and the ways of the Middle Ages.[10] He goes further to declare that Robespierre had made himself first pope (national popes were to be celebrated; individual popes were retrograde) and then divine king (complete with a Trinity) during the Terror. This regime bolstered itself with the uses of grace as well and even the protection of the Church.[11]

True fraternity only becomes possible in the eighteenth century, writes Michelet in *History of the French Revolution*. Philosophy had at that time "found man without rights, or rather a nonentity." From the inhumanity of the Terror, Michelet's language works a remarkable transformation. Its inhumanity issues from its own "nonentity."[12] That is, having been debased and having the habits of servile persons, the oppressed remain incapable of fraternity. They lack the liberty to exercise the choice to unify by their own lights. When the choice is fraternity or death, there already is no possibility of fraternity. Likewise, the prerevolutionary individual was "disarmed, bare, unprotected, confounded, lost in a system of apparent unity, which was no better than common death" (7). The Enlightenment and the

Revolution, at least before the Terror, freed these nonentities from their demeaned status. Those living before the Enlightenment had been "entangled in a religious and political system, of which despotism was the base" (6). With the liberty briefly created by the Revolution and the philosophies that guided it, there was a sudden ontological change from nonentity to entity: "And she said, 'Let us create man, let him *be*, by liberty'" (7).

Speaking to his nineteenth-century contemporaries regarding "our age," he declares that they had to be "awakened and recalled to its true tradition." They had, in fact, to "commence its work" again. The temptation felt by some to revive the Jacobin fraternity had to be resisted: "It will no longer inscribe amongst its laws, 'Be my brother, or *die!*' But by a skillful culture of the best sentiments of the human soul, it will attain its end in such a manner that all, without compulsion, shall wish to be brothers indeed. The state will realise its destiny, and be a fraternal initiation, an education, a constant exchange of the spontaneous ideas of inspiration and faith, which are common to us all" (6–7). Education was the solution that would allow for this voluntary return of France to itself, and Michelet considered his work *The People* [*Le Peuple*] an early attempt at such an effort.[13]

He would not, however, repeat the mistakes of the eighteenth century. The revolutionaries and their *philosophe* predecessors mistakenly believed that the education had to be philosophical. They had too little use for history and too little use for the spiritual. Michelet declares it the advancement of his own century and his own work to realize that unity has to be achieved on the level of sentiment, instinct, and inspiration.[14] These are the things unearthed and known by history. The Revolution would have to become its own religion, but not, as some of the left had claimed, the fulfillment of Christianity.[15]

The Revolution had instead to be or become the faith that would replace Christianity. Insofar as Christianity united more of humanity than had pagan religions, the Revolution—which unites so many more—was its heir. In that the Revolution was founded not upon grace and not upon the deceitful doctrine of original sin, but upon right and justice, it was Christianity's adversary.[16] As he writes in the later volumes of his history: "Nullifying an arbitrary religion which favored the elect should have implied the *affirmation of a religion of equal justice for all*: nullifying the possession of property through privilege should have implied the *affirmation of property without privilege, available to all*. . . . It had to smash the scholastic kernel of doctrine and bring forth living fruit. With that, the Revolution might have survived. Then it could have said, I am, life and affirmation are mine. . . . But the Revolution set aside the two very questions which contained the germ of life."[17]

A few years before de Tocquevillle, in 1856, instructed his readers that they should understand the Revolution as something that functioned and spread like a religion, with its general appeal across nations and peoples, Michelet had already formulated his complaint.[18] The Revolution had failed to become enough of a religion. It may have spread like one among some, but its failing had been that it had not done enough to know itself as a rival religion, a new creed that would supplant the religions of old.

MICHELET'S POLITICAL THEOLOGY OF DEMOCRACY

What were they to worship in this new religion? Michelet calls for an education to solidify the bonds between citizen and nation. His histories would supply the lesson, and his history of the Revolution would even enact the moment of the nation's modern resurrection with the demise of the *ancien régime*. Particularly important in his narrative is his account of the Festival of Federations, held in Paris in July 1790. Michelet's power as a romantic historian has led some to describe him as the prophet of "the religion of democracy."[19] His account of the festival may be that religion's most sanctified moment. The event and the year leading up to it are described as the remaking of man and society.[20] The expression of the general will in these moments was, according to Michelet, humanity's rebirth.

The Festival of Federations (now commemorated as Bastille Day) was for Michelet the grand expression of humanity's determination to be free and united, unfettered by the "fatality" of the ancient regime. With the Revolution, France had become a federation of democracies, but it was not enough to celebrate this freedom locally. The nation undertook to salute the taking of the Bastille and to celebrate fraternity on the national level with delegations from every Department. The transformation, in Michelet's romantic account, reverberated around the world. His account of the event's impact upon Kant is noteworthy. Radiating east, the news shattered what had been the otherwise impenetrable stone encrusting the philosopher's heart:

> In a remote region of the northern seas, there then existed an extraordinary, powerful creature, a man, or rather a system, a living

monument of scholastic science, callous and impenetrable,— a rock formed by adamant in the granite of the Baltic; on which every religion, every system of philosophy had struck and been shipwrecked. He alone remained immutable, and invulnerable to the outward world. His name was Emmanuel Kant; but he called himself Critic. For sixty years, this perfectly abstract being, devoid of all human connection, had gone out at precisely the same hour, and, without speaking to anybody, had taken precisely the same walk for a stated number of minutes; just as we see in the old town clocks, a man of iron come forth, strike the hour and then withdraw. Wonderful to relate, the inhabitants of Koenigsberg (who considered this as an omen of the most extraordinary events) saw this planet swerve and depart from its long habitual course. . . . Was not that a surprising and wonderful change? Why, no; no change at all. That expansive intellect was following its course. What he had, till then, in vain sought for in science, *Spiritual Unity*, he now beheld forming itself by the heart and instinct.[21]

It was during this same period, between July of 1789 and July of 1790, says Michelet, that France itself, its people in unity, dictated events. The National Assembly may have described itself as leading: in fact, it was following. It merely recorded the will of the French nation. During this event, the Assembly was grudgingly overpowered by the infectious spirit of the gathered masses. They were inspired to abolish titles of nobility and to disassemble the system of exemptions and privileges. Thousands of new magistrates were appointed all at once. They were, according to Michelet, replacing the old from the bottom up. A community without law spontaneously gave itself order (382–89). Bound by its own obligation to provide itself with security—in response to the brigands roaming the countryside, a criminal life not that far removed from the old regime's aristocratic tax collectors. France thereby supplanted the ineffectual and corrupt governance of the old order. Those officials, he tells readers, slinked out the back doors of their communities, leaving its souvenir, debt (384–85). France was spontaneously organizing itself. From July 1789 until the festival, writes Michelet, France was giving the world the example of its path forward: a "worn-out society" that was undergoing its "crisis of resurrection, [one that] affords us a spectacle of the origin of things" (383). In his account, an apotheosis of the general will, all prior divisions of class, religion, and region melted away. All the people of France became one: unified, loving one another in the true spirit of fraternity, and reconstituted. "France" had "united with France," and it was a prophetic moment for the world, a "symbol of the future alliance of nations, of the general marriage of the world" (402–3).

At this stage, however, the unification had to be national. Within it, Michelet's popular sovereign is—like the sovereigns seen by today's dominant tradition—outside the law. The aristocracy, he notes, had told the French people that tearing down the old order would only yield chaos. Instead, in this "formable crisis, she becomes her own law; and without any assistance, springs, with a powerful will, over the chasm between one world and the other" (389). What guides the nation, according to Michelet, is no longer "the vague love of liberty," as it was at the start, in 1789, "but a determined object, of a fixed and settled form." This new motivation leads the entire nation, "transporting and captivating the heart; at every new step, it appears more delightful . . . and France beholds distinctly what she had loved and followed, without ever having been able to attain it—the unity of the native land" (390).

Regional attachments, writes Michelet, give way to an attachment to the nation as a whole. Fixed identities of region, race, and religion, the handholds of "fatality," soften their grip and merge. The people are then one, he pointedly notes, not according to the geometric abstractions "emanating from the brain of Sieyès," but instead from a miraculous moment when previously divided peoples recognize each other as a naturally united whole (391).[22] Michelet's political theology of the Revolution is on full display. It is a conversion experience—a secularization of enthusiast and evangelical sentiments—that promises the transformation of old, outmoded identities rooted in region, race, and religion. These identities are to be abandoned, and persons reconstituted as *French*: "But lo! The native land appears to them on the alter, opening her arms and wishing to embrace them. . . . And they all rush towards her and forget themselves, no longer knowing on that day to what province they belong" (390). The love particular to fraternity crafts this new identity in superseding the old divisions (398).

The anti-heroic stance in his praise of the 1830 Revolution resurfaces and is elevated into a rough ontology. It emerges just after Michelet gives a detailed description of the counter-revolutionary failures of the nobility and clergy. Before moving toward the Festival of Federations, he declares that these two moments, of seemingly different orders of being, could be known in two distinct ways. The religion of democracy has its own enthusiasm. Because the general will is indeed general, it may be known with an immediacy independently of the detailed accounts of the many squirming, if fruitless, efforts of the counter-revolutionaries. It is, moreover, the general, *not* the exception, that accounts for France's new spontaneous generation:

> That is real history, the real, the positive, and the durable; and the rest is nonentity. . . . Evil, precisely because it is nothing but an exception, an irregularity, requires, in order to be understood, a minute narration of particulars [i.e., in his account of the counter-revolutionary efforts]. Good, on the contrary, the natural, which springs forth of itself, is almost known to us beforehand by its conformity to the laws of our nature, by the eternal image of good which we possess within us.
>
> The sources whence we derive history have preciously preserved the least worthy of preservation,—the negative accidental element, the individual anecdote, this or that petty intrigue or act of violence.
>
> The great national facts, in which France has acted in concord, have been accomplished by immense, invincible, and, for that very reason, by no means violent, powers. They have excited less attention, and passed almost unperceived. (382)[23]

This is the Michelet who would inspire Walt Whitman[24] and who stands almost in diametric opposition to the Schmittian view. Instead of a decision on the exception, Michelet's sovereign is immense and "invincible." This sovereign is not indefeasible because of its violence but because of its generality.[25] Thus, in his own treatment of the revolution sovereignty, the realization of Sieyès's *pouvoir constituent,* Schmitt looks away from claims to a general will and toward the violent exceptions of the Revolution of 1793. Precisely those parts of the Revolution Michelet condemns as a regression to kingship and the Middle Ages—the Terror and the Committee on Public Safety—were the Revolution's sovereign expression according to Schmitt.[26]

The only fitting monument of the Revolution, writes Michelet in his 1847 preface to *History of the French Revolution,* is the Champ de Mars in

Paris, where the Festival of Federations took place. The open space there was prepared by voluntary labor from all classes, working together out of a common love for the nation reconstituting itself. These new French people gathered from around the nation to declare an invincible but non-violent will:

> The Champ de Mars! This is the only monument that the Revolution has left. The Empire has its Column, and engrosses almost exclusively the arch of Triumph; royalty has its Louvre, its Hospital of Invalids; the feudal church of the twelfth century is still enthroned at Notre Dame: nay, the very Romans have their Imperial Ruins, the Thermae of the Caesars!
>
> And the Revolution has for her monument—empty space. . . .
>
> For in that soil is profoundly mingled the fruitful sweat of their brows who, on a sacred day, piled up those hills . . . aroused by the cannon of the Bastille, France from the North and France from the South came forward and embraced. . . . Three millions . . . in arms rose with the unanimity of one man and decreed eternal peace. . . . How confidently . . . didst thou invite the world to love and peace. "O my enemies," didst thou exclaim, "there are no longer any enemies!" (2)[27]

France extended its hand to the world on the day of its rebirth and offered love and peace, but the world, Michelet asserts, was not yet ready to take it. His too-optimistic, too-anxious France inverts a passage attributed to Aristotle by Montaigne: "O my friends, there is no friend."[28] The historian pours a bit of cold water on the celebration and insists upon a temporal dynamic. Worldwide marriage among fellow humans, as Michelet himself put it, was for the future. The world in 1790 was then harboring the Revolution's enemies and still harboring them in 1847. Other nations and factions within France were not yet ready to make peace, regardless of France's initial pacific intentions.

MICHELET'S TOO-FRIENDLY POPULAR SOVEREIGN

It is here that we begin to see Michelet's critique of a too-friendly popular sovereign. In a complicated maneuver, Michelet attempts to draw a line between the bellicosity to be condemned in Napoleon or the Terror and that of France's defense of its liberty as he saw it. He asserts the innocence of the Revolution's origins, but he simultaneously makes two demands upon his contemporary audience. This France, the one that was reborn on the Champ de Mars and has since forgotten itself, must now reacquaint itself with the innocence of its origins. It must abjure the bellicose legacy that it developed subsequent to its earlier efforts (i.e., during the time of the Terror) to defend itself from those who conspired against it. Triumphal Bonapartists were likewise criticized.

At the same time, it must know itself now in the nineteenth century as still under an immediate threat. The Revolution's true legacy, its deeper and now too-forgotten commitment to liberty, remains embattled. Moreover, the cause for this peril lay at the Revolution's own feet. France, Michelet insists, has become corrupt. Correcting the corruption requires that the Revolution's original legacy—rather than the false glory of a conquering (Napoleonic) or terrifying (Jacobin) nation—be resurrected. That was what must be guarded and even defended against, Michelet insists, and the defense has to be fitted to these now-neglected, more pacifist origins.

In Michelet's view, France would have to reverse course before it could rediscover itself. In the years following the Revolution, the nation had befriended the enemies of liberty. It would now have to be a less-friendly popular sovereign than some would prefer, but not unfriendly to the bellicose degree of the Terror or Bonapartism. Indeed, Michelet observes, some of those given over to the bellicosity of the Terror and Napoleon or to the servitude cultivated under monarchies were the very ones responsible for making friends with liberty's adversaries. Too many Frenchmen, out of admiration for Robespierre or Napoleon, had learned to adore force instead of worshipping liberty and justice and right, the true ideals of the Revolution (4). Still claiming that their cause was liberty, these Frenchmen were mistaken, having been misled by false prophets. As a result, the "party of liberty [has] evinced, of late, two sad and serious symptoms of an inward evil." France was now navigating by the wrong star. The right star, Michelet pleads with his readers, is not victory but "the sun of Justice and the revolution" (4).

Michelet laments that France is not guided by the Revolution, which extends its hand of peace and justice toward the world. Instead, France now grasps a "perfidious, an odious hand,—the hand of death." That hand has been "offered and stretched out to them, and they have not withdrawn their own" (4). Michelet refers here again to the reconciliation between France's governments and the Church: "They believed the foes of religious liberty might become the friends of political freedom" (4). Whereas some Catholics were pursuing a new strategy wherein the faithful might seek rights within a liberal system, rather than the bulwark of the ancient regime that opposed that system, Michelet sees only the old threat disguised as a plea for liberty.

Michelet asks, "Why have the sincere friends of liberty formed a league with the party of religious tyranny?" His answer perceives a cause besides the outstretched hand of the old Church. He attributes the alliance to a weakness that had developed among those committed to the Revolution's cause, an alliance that emerged because the friends of liberty "had reduced themselves to a feeble minority" (4–5). They had lost the courage of their Enlightenment predecessors, such as Rousseau and Voltaire, who dared to confront those who endorsed religious tyranny. Why did they lose their nerve and become a "feeble minority"? In part, Michelet holds, they had divided against themselves. They no longer followed the example of unity exhibited at the Champ de Mars. They had instead revived the fatal factiousness of the later phases of the Revolution, devolving into irreconcilable sects and opting to invent "a system of progressive refinement, of minute orthodoxy, which aims at making a party a sect,—a petty church. They reject this, then that; they abound in restrictions, distinctions, exclusions. Some new heresy is discovered every day. . . . The sects which are the offspring of the Revolution annul the Revolution itself; people become Constituants, Girondists, Montagnards; but the Revolutionists ceased to exist. Voltaire is but little valued, Mirabeau is laid aside. Madame Roland is excluded, even Danton is not orthodox. What! Must none remain but Robespierre and Saint-Just?" (5).

Fraternity had been thus annulled, in Michelet's view, by sectarian infighting among those who fought for liberty, while the hand of friendship had been extended to those who did not share the Revolution's mission. In his history of the Terror, Michelet finds the precursors to the reconciliation with the Church. He describes Robespierre as a king and a pope, intending more by the name calling than merely figurative accusations.[29] Robespierre's efforts to spare the religious, including the Jesuits, signal the tyrant's natural sympathies with those who would undermine free institutions and have the weak depend upon grace once again.[30]

Although his rejection of the July Monarchy's reconciliation with the Church is his most fervent denunciation of an alliance with the enemies of freedom, Michelet expands his assault upon those he deemed to be building bridges with France's false friends. Fraternity could not be imposed. It had to be the voluntary action of individuals to unite with fellow Frenchmen and revive, on a more spiritual basis, the basic challenge Sieyès issued in *Qu'est-ce que le Tiers-État?*[31]

As Lionel Gossman has noted, Michelet's willingness to hive off some who did not belong to his revolutionary nation was tempered but not exhausted. The voluntary character of fraternity precluded violence. The "other who has to be seen as a brother" could be appealed to, encouraged to rejoin the fold, and praised for a relative willingness to do so; but this other could not be coerced Jacobin style or as governments and religions of grace had done. An aspect of the larger self, France, each *other* needed to be reconnected to the whole.[32] Bellicose methods created, or re-created, a servile rather than a patriotic population.

Consequently, division within France needed an alternate explanation. It would be laid, writes Gossman, "on the foreigner or the parasite, the outsider or the alien or traitor within." Indeed, Michelet is often quite pointed in identifying these nonfraternal others: "Englishmen, Jews, Jesuits, Jacobins and Catholic priests were obstacles to the realization of the complete national unity and identity." In Michelet's cosmos, these antagonisms become "legitimate objects of hatred in a paranoid vision of history."[33] They are very much on display in his anti-Jesuitical writings, in *The People*, and in his *History of the French Revolution*. In spite of exceeding and in many ways standing as an example of what Schmitt fails to discern, these aspects of his thought make Michelet a *political* thinker and a participant in the Schmittian mold.

These tensions are noteworthy in other regards. While devoted to the Enlightenment, Michelet was a self-declared enemy of what he calls the "machinism" of the Industrial Age, and his ideal state is anything but the frictionless machine that Schmitt finds in the visions of his liberal contemporaries.[34] Instead, Michelet's ideal state is rooted in the "Justice" a people discovers for itself, in what it finds, or should find, legitimate based on a renewed commitment to the religion of the Revolution. It requires the sovereign will of the people to be behind it, and Michelet views his purpose as a historian to be the union of the people with the ideals they would rediscover—and feel—in reading his works. Thus, Michelet's endorsement of the Enlightenment does not lead him to depoliticize or neutralize the political realm.[35] His more radically conservative or hard left contemporaries were no more clear-eyed in their identification of critical political choices and decisions.[36] Michelet's romanticism does not make his political commitments flighty; he was willing to sacrifice for them personally. He knew sovereignty and sovereign exceptions, and he was willing and able to describe their inner workings in intimate detail.

Michelet is significant because his quarrel with sovereignty evidences more than the omissions in Schmitt's picture of liberalism and its history. His histories take us back to a moment in the theorization of sovereignty that exposes Schmitt's understanding of sovereign exceptions to be incomplete. Even when indulging in his greatest hostilities, Michelet often couches them in terms of those who are engaged in acts of friendly sovereignty. That is, he tells "the French people" that emerged after the Revolution that they have made friendly exceptions for those they ought to have either excluded, forbidden, or outlawed:

> When young French Liberty first opened her eyes to the light, and uttered that earliest cry which transports every new creature,— "I am!" even in that moment her thoughts were not confined to *self* . . . "I am!" she exclaims to all nations; "O my brethren, you shall be also!"
>
> In this lay her glorious error, her touching and sublime weakness: The Revolution, it must be confessed, commenced by loving everything.
>
> She loved even her enemy,—England.
>
> She loved, and long she strove to save, royalty—the key-stone of the abuses which she had just demolished. She wanted to save the Church; she endeavored to remain Christian, being willfully blind to the contradiction of the old principle,—Arbitrary Grace, and of the new one,—Justice.[37]

France had been guilty of extending her sympathy too easily and of an "indiscriminate benevolence," and she was again so among Michelet's contemporaries.[38] The wish to unseat the friendly popular sovereign extends beyond his rejection of a renewed friendship with the Church. The Anglophilia of the July Monarchy and restored Bourbon monarchies were an ongoing sore point with Michelet.[39] Although a liberal, Michelet was against the impact of industrial capitalism and indeed the place of credit in the French economy. In *The People*, he whips his anti-English, anti-banking, and anti-Semitic sentiments together into a plea to change France's laws (so as to disempower creditors) and to diminish the sway of both England and the Jews.[40] Still later, and long after his disassociation from Paris academia, Michelet issues a plea to the Western nations to aid France against Germany in the Franco-Prussian War. There Michelet describes the Prussian region especially as the barbaric, tyrannical East (allied with czarist Russia and servile in its habits) the advanced nations need to hold back in much the same way that Germans, such as Schmitt, would describe Soviet Russia and the communists within Germany in the twentieth century.[41] The antagonism in his turn against Germany is Michelet at his most "Schmittian," but despite Schmitt's formulation, Michelet was not in denial of the power of sovereign decision-making.

CONCLUSION

This chapter and the last's review of some aspects of Michelet's political and intellectual contexts affirms that some nineteenth-century liberals did consciously work toward sovereignty's obliteration, as Schmitt charges. François Guizot, for one, did so even as he often outwardly strove for class and regime domination while in office. Marx never found Guizot wanting in matters of antagonism. It is noteworthy, however, that Schmitt fails to register this element of Guizot's work; the omission shows us the incompleteness of Schmitt's account of nineteenth-century liberalism.[42] Beyond Guizot, a thinker such as Michelet occupies a substantial Schmittian blind spot.[43] A proponent of progress defined in terms of the growth of liberty, Michelet held political commitments and concepts of sovereignty that Schmitt excludes from his framing of the liberal worldview. Among these commitments was his opposition to vicious generosity, which exceeded even that of Rousseau.

Michelet's understanding of sovereign exceptions not only captures much of what Schmitt declares inaccessible to liberals of this period, but also broadens the contemporary conceptions of sovereignty. In addition, his substantive understanding of what I've called friendly sovereign exceptions illustrates even greater deficiencies in Schmitt's account of sovereign exceptions. If it does not fight, die, or kill in the name of the protection of the state, for Schmitt it is not sovereign. Michelet, however, mounts an all-fronts war on friendly sovereignty, the friendly exceptions of grace, and a too-welcoming popular sovereignty among revolutionaries. Not only did he experience the sovereignty Schmitt declares rediscovered in his own works, but he in fact knew, contemplated, and in some cases denounced aspects of sovereignty Schmitt fails to discern.

Casting himself as a stranger in the land of liberalism, Schmitt offered himself up as the antidote to liberalism's antipolitical spirit; birthed in the Enlightenment and solidified in the nineteenth century, liberalism's comportment was fundamentally incapable of acknowledging the hostility that, he argued, defines "the political." The foregoing account of Michelet's thinking, however, suggests the need to peel back the layers of contrariety in Schmitt's self-portrait.

In light of what we've shown regarding Michelet's understanding of sovereignty, it is not too much to assert that Schmitt's alleged distance from liberalism as a historical phenomenon was overdrawn. This is a point that was stressed by his contemporary critics and among later writers.[44] If a champion of liberal democracy like Michelet could muster this much hostility while remaining committed to the historical cause of liberty as he understood it, if he could know sovereignty's exceptional ins and outs this well, then Schmitt's picture of liberalism must be deemed far too selective. If we historicize Schmitt, his opposition to aspects of liberalism may emerge as a feature of liberalism's twisting historical course.[45] What had been an element of liberalism's particular internal historical development—the ongoing disaffection for its own weak grip upon legitimacy, the shallow and sometimes dispassionate attachment meant to link individual to community—makes him less of an exception to liberalism than a part of the unfolding of more liberal and democratic developments on the continent. Thus Schmitt, on the basis of what now emerges as more parochial criticisms, may be seen as having declared himself largely *other and outside* a solar system whose sun he nevertheless continued to orbit. Rather than see Schmitt as an antidote to liberalism, we might see him in a long line of thinkers, like Vilfredo Pareto, who began in a liberal milieu and allowed their disaffection to blossom into fascism.[46]

French liberal history can also help us see the connections and capacities within liberal politics that Schmitt denies. It reminds us of some of the possibilities that Schmitt's polemics, combined with our particular amnesia that confuses abstract principle with history, tend to obscure. This includes the fact that liberalism (as was the case in the Weimar era) was also in many cases given over to nationalism.[47] It could be willfully and self-consciously exclusionary and hostile, and it could draw upon its memory of sovereignty to either exalt in the irresistible power of the people or condemn the twin habits of arbitrary power and subservience to "governments of grace." Michelet's liberalism was all these things. Even if Schmitt's political *philosophy* is not liberal, his antithetical comportment toward liberalism's ongoing problems may have to be seen as an aspect *internal* to liberalism's ongoing, complex historical course, rather than—as he preferred—the dawning of something new.

Does Michelet, warts and all, offer us something we can use today beyond a correction to Schmittian perspectives?[48] Where he resembled Schmitt most—where he campaigned for the exclusion of those deemed alien or too retrograde for the France that would lead his charge forward into history—he must today be spurned. His anti-Semitism and his chauvinism, his opening toward assigning nations and peoples world-historical missions and destinies, are one reason, in addition to the methodological objections, why later-twentieth-century thinkers were content to see grand narratives buried under the weight of a million micro-physical or linguistic details. While it is inevitable that we must see the development of democracy within specific historical circumstances and raise again, in light of recent history, the question of what allows citizens to find themselves as equals within a common community, Michelet's own boundaries fall far too short of the pluralist hopes that must animate the states and communities we live within today. Liberalism in the United States—once thought insuperable—has now, at least in egalitarian commitments, shown itself to be quite fragile. Now it too falls short of those same pluralist hopes, and today we need few reminders of the politicians in the United States, Europe, and Latin America who have attached themselves to the brash rejection of such visions.

Although we cannot take lessons in pluralism from Michelet, can his sense of liberty, and his resistance to those who depend upon a vicious generosity, find some new resonance? Michelet and his contemporaries were aware of the possibility that liberty can have false defenders. Those who could not accept any but their own vision of liberty and equality were too parochial. Their purity tests, their admiration for Robespierre, signaled a lapse into the past religions of grace, favor, and forgiveness even as they claimed to be marching toward the future. Michelet would have never accepted that the defenders of liberty could be true to their professed cause while operating as the dependents of individuals or elite factions with largesse to distribute. Today we find public institutions more and more captive to the whim of private wealth. Some of the self-appointed defenders of liberty at present are, as often as not, their paid thought laborers. Michelet's suspicions about the patron's generosity, the strings-attached inducements a patron supplies desperate academics and academic institutions, may be overdue for a resurrection. Who in academia today dares defy the masters?

Finally, to return to an earlier theme, Michelet's example might suggest that another form of denial was afoot in Schmitt's account of sovereignty and liberalism. In addition to the likenesses between Schmitt and his liberal contemporaries, including the common neo-Kantian frame that informed his early legal theory,[49] there is something else. The flaws he later diagnosed among liberals, such as the lack of substantive commitments,[50] the fickleness of political romantics, and the same search for solutions from a position of liberal disaffection, like his teacher Max Weber, have been among the most prominent of these claims.[51]

The connection with Weber has, of course, spurred some of the most intense controversy. It has coincided with the notion that there was a particularly German glide path from weak and dissatisfying liberalism into plebiscitarian dictatorship and worse. Today, where it seems that pathways from liberalism toward fascistic politics are being trod by more nations than Germany, our most urgent task may not be to consider how far the Schmittian apple falls from the *Weberian* tree.

Liberalism's critics, and liberals themselves, may have to resign themselves to the fact that their persuasion seems to learn the most about sovereignty from within, rather than from without, as Schmitt insisted. Sovereignty, sovereign exceptions, sovereign violence, exclusion, as well as friendly sovereign grace, favor, and forgiveness, are not utterly alien to liberalism's long and complex history. They are rather the Mr. Hydes to Schmitt's derided Dr. Jekyll, and whereas Schmittian criticism has suggested the unavailability of this knowledge from within liberalism, a fuller picture of liberalism's development across nineteenth-century Europe suggests that liberalism's history is filled with both the antagonisms that Schmitt declares lacking in his liberal contemporaries and an awareness of sovereignty's characteristic generosity, which Schmitt neglects. "Liberalism," understood not as a tightly defined philosophy but as a loose and necessarily contingent historical moment in Western history, would then perhaps admit of a new dialectical view. Although it did not produce its own gravediggers among those who labor with their hands, it may nonetheless develop within itself internal antagonists among head laborers. That is to say the disaffection with liberalism experienced by Schmitt, by Weber, and in his own way, by Michelet are best folded into a larger history of liberalism's internal development. The common characteristic may be to remind the more tranquil, pacifist, or complacent side of the liberal spectrum that a world of felt political passions and convictions exists. The factions and trending ideas are noted as having made rival demands that must be better understood by those too accustomed to the cool, decadent, reason of the satisfied. Sly, seemingly objective warnings then are issued: the complacent who lack the antagonistic will to defend the liberal state, or indeed the legacy of liberal revolutions, risk demise.

We can draw a more complete picture of both sovereignty and liberalism from these two sometimes insightful, sometimes repellent, liberals. We've uncovered some of what is missing from Schmitt's monotone account of the varied liberalism in the nineteenth and twentieth centuries. While the inclusion of Michelet allows liberalism to escape some of Schmitt's overly general condemnations, especially regarding its capacity for politics or its resources for understanding of sovereignty, it does not necessarily leave us with a more flattering picture of liberalism.

My purpose in returning to the elided aspects of Michelet's liberalism has not been to rescue liberalism from all criticism. The more Schmitt himself—by virtue of the way he is truly at home in liberalism's varied milieus—is seen to share with liberalism, the less flattering our image of both him and liberalism may become. In the ways in which he and the liberal Michelet resemble one another, the paint we find behind Schmitt's relief might make him all too recognizable in a liberal setting and perhaps too familiar for either his admirers or his detractors.

CHAPTER 4

HOBBES, DECISIONISM, AND THE

FRIENDLY EXCEPTION

This chapter and the next focus on Thomas Hobbes and his ambivalence toward the sovereign's friendly prerogatives. As we did with Michelet, Hobbes's thoughts on the matter will be compared with some proximate contemporaries. This chapter considers Hobbes's concept of sovereignty in the context of England's seventeenth-century legal culture. I will show that Hobbes was not, as Carl Schmitt has argued, a "decisionist." Hobbes's sovereign is unquestionably capable of working outside the law, but in these contexts that did not make him decisionist. Fitting Hobbes to Schmitt's decisionist mold introduces serious anachronisms. It generates an image of Hobbes defending a sovereignty concept that he, and his contemporaries, could not have appreciated.

The next chapter expands upon Hobbes's ambivalence about friendly sovereignty by drawing contrasts with Gottfried Wilhelm Leibniz. Leibniz is best known among political philosophers for the term he coined, *theodicy*. Often with an eye on the biblical Job, theodicy questions frequently take this form: Why does an omnipotent, omniscient, and loving God permit the innocent to suffer? Theodicy, however, is also generative of other questions. Why does this same perfect being allow the wicked to prosper? This second question touches on the rule of friendly sovereigns and speaks to what could be called the "civic theodicy" of Hobbes's "mortal God." The divergences between Hobbes and Leibniz on the prosperity of the wicked are illuminating, and these will be taken up in the next chapter.

When Schmitt declares Hobbes a model decisionist, he associated him with his own decisionist definition of sovereignty: "Sovereign is he who *decides* the exception" (emphasis mine). Like many of his contemporaries, Hobbes was concerned with legal exceptions, but because of Schmitt, he has been associated with the wrong century's exceptions. Having yet to experience the idealization of a clockwork universe, or a clockwork state, they could hardly champion the irrationalist and/or decisionist plea for relief from the constraints of a legalistic machine-state. They also could not have a corresponding hope for a return to the convictions of the truly "political." Hobbes and his contemporaries did indeed think of sovereign exceptions but, when they did so, were just as likely to think of the transgression of the sovereign's *friendly* exceptions.[1] They thought specifically of the Crown's capacity to pardon, suspend laws, grant monopolies and patents, and to give some in the commonwealth de facto immunity from punishment.

PART I

I begin with what Hobbes was, rather than what he was not. Thomas Hobbes was a political philosopher interested in holding British subjects to a new set of rules. His intent was to reinvent. He would build the state's rules systematically, from the bottom up, with his own geometric method. He claimed to provide a more reliable foundation than had existed previously. His reconstructed state consolidated control of law making and adjudication, the nation's educational establishments, its army, and its church. He would be, as he put it, the state's new "able architect."[2]

A true sovereign, according to Hobbes, can never share his powers, nor could those powers be less than absolute (*Lev.*, 16.4; 29.3–5; 20.18; 22.5; 30.3). "It is the office of the sovereign to maintain those rights entire"; to fail in this aspect of sovereignty is, for Hobbes, a form of desertion. Sovereign officeholders who acknowledge themselves subject to civil laws and who renounce supreme powers of adjudication, war- and peace-making powers, power over all appointments in the courts, the armies, the universities, and the power to tax or raise armies make themselves incapable of this office (30.3). There can only be one sovereign (even if the sovereign will is discovered by finding a majority vote in a sovereign assembly). As long as subjects were protected, they owed their sovereign obedience.[3]

To use Hobbes's words, subjects have to "own" the sovereign's judgments, especially on matters of controversy.[4] They should act as if the sovereign's judgments were their own, for their consent had made them so. They have "*authorized* all the actions and judgments of that man or assembly of men, in the same manner as if they were his own, to the end, to live peaceably amongst themselves" (18.1).

Those who attempted to assemble or rally independent authorities, realms, institutions, or factions were either enemies or in need of a profound reeducation in their civic responsibilities.[5] He would not tolerate what he saw as the prominent excuses to bolster independent authorities. There was, therefore, no need to counter or limit the sovereign officeholder. There could be no justification for self-initiated violations of the publicly known law—by persons of sound mind—detached from the need for self-preservation (27.22–26): not constitutional balance (28.16), nor the accusations that the ungodly were in power—even in or atop the Church (26.40–41; 47 passim). Neither could one undo the sovereign's powers by claiming either a superior understanding of the ancient constitution or the authority of Common, statutory, or natural law (26.9–11). None were sufficient justifications to resist or rebel. They were also unacceptable excuses for favoring the myriad malevolent or merely deficient political or politico-religious doctrines that declare in favor of rules that might limit or compete with the sovereign's absolute or indeed arbitrary powers.[6] The sovereign needs these powers to keep the peace. Through such strict insistence upon sovereign power, Hobbes distinguishes himself among political philosophers of Stuart England. Revisionist historians who have been anxious to reveal a bevy of false absolutists in England make a notable exception for Hobbes.[7]

Exceptions to the Sovereign's Rules

Yet even this absolutist, this stickler in matters of obedience and compliance to the order the sovereign kept and imposed upon his people, knew and expected that there would always be exceptions to his sovereign's rules. We ought not to be surprised. Hobbes lived in a context where it was commonly understood that proper governance often meant departing from the letter of the law. Not all of these departures involved the extraordinary hostility that a sovereign might use his discretion to unleash in response to a crisis. Judges, especially the judge who possesses sovereign power, were expected to be just but also merciful. Arbitrary grace and favor were a part of the sovereign repertoire. Jean Bodin, whose thought might inform numerous positions (Richard Knolles made an English translation in 1606), made pardon the fifth mark of sovereignty in the *Six Books of the Common-wealth*,[8] but England did not need Bodin to make them aware of the pardon's power. Even before Portia lectured Shylock on the subject, Tudor kings had consolidated their control over England by making clemency *their* prerogative over and against that of local residual feudal authority. As Krista Kesselring has shown, they would use this power in the context of defeated rebellions to stage and demonstrate their authority by the ostentatious, if sometimes risky, theater of mercy begged and granted.[9] The rebel, criminal, or convict who begs for his life and forgiveness, typically augments the power from whom that mercy must issue.[10]

Among Stuart kings, mercy and generosity, especially those that involved legal exceptions such as monopolies and patents, were subjects of ongoing controversy. James I spoke often of his prerogative and duty to be not merely just but also merciful. For fear of ruining the finances, he tried in the *Book of Bounty* to make regular the expectations of petitioning subjects.[11] The logic of clemency even became part of John Donne's attempt at legal diplomacy: in the *Pseudo-Martyr* (1610), the poet and lawyer deploys an elaborate logic of clemency graciously granted and accepted among princes to defuse the Reformation struggles inflamed by Jesuits and hard-line Protestants. The pope, Donne proposed, should and could grant James clemency for having rejected the faith, and James might graciously accept it. It would free English Recusants to take their oath of allegiance.[12] Following the Stuart Restoration, the sovereign capacity to make exceptions was again at the heart of Britain's controversies.[13] Beginning with the Act of Indemnity and Oblivion, it then continued in successive royal negations of Parliament's Test Acts and in the pardoning of impeached servants of the crown, notably the Earl of Danby.

Important for our purposes, Hobbes shows himself acutely aware that sovereigns often granted liberties and used prerogative powers of mercy, patents, and monopoly grants to make legal exceptions. There is every reason to think, Hobbes tells us, that his sovereign would find and use such exceptions and that these exceptions would remain an integral part of the sovereign's prerogative powers. As we find in Michelet a near total hostility toward friendly exceptions, we will find in Seneca quite the opposite.

Hobbes occupies a middle ground. Here the sovereign's friendly prerogatives can't be denied. Some were unavoidable and indeed others necessary. This acknowledgment, however, did not stop Hobbes from expressing considerable ambivalence about many of them and the way they can undermine the legal and political order of the state.

What exemplifies his ambivalence? Examples can be found in his discussion of "crimes, excuses and extenuations," chapter 27 of *Leviathan*, which begins with a distinction between sin and crime. All crimes are sins, according to Hobbes, in that crimes consist in "committing (by deed or word) of that which the law forbiddeth" (27.2). Not all sins are crimes, though. It is sinful to intend an unlawful act, but merely intending to do an unlawful act, like stealing or killing, without a visible or "outward act" makes "no place for human accusation." Crimes cannot happen where there is no sovereign to make or maintain law; they are, therefore, decidedly *human* accusations (27.3). An all-knowing God may know our bad intention if we sin, but we humans must witness some act before we can charge someone with a crime. For example, a high official commits a crime when he instructs a subordinate to quash a lawful investigation of an appointee. He commits a mere sin if he does nothing more than inwardly wish for that official to escape the legal consequences of his misdeeds.

Having made the distinction between crime and sin, Hobbes goes on to discuss a special class of liberties granted subjects by the sovereign. It is a case that in some ways troubles Hobbes's own framework. He writes: "If that man or assembly that hath the sovereign power disclaim any right essential to the sovereignty, whereby there accrueth to the subject any liberty inconsistent with the sovereign power (that is to say, with the very being of a commonwealth), if the subject shall refuse to obey the command in anything contrary to the liberty granted, this is nevertheless a sin, and contrary to the duty of the subject" (27.28). Because of the sovereign's mistake, those granted these liberties escape being classed as criminal. This exercise of freedom that should have been forbidden remains "nevertheless a sin."

Hobbes does not take this sin lightly. Unlike the repressed desire to do wrong, this sin concerns outward actions. It is sin because the subject "ought to take notice of what is inconsistent with the sovereignty, because it was erected by his own consent and for his own defense, and that such a liberty as is inconsistent with it was granted through ignorance of the evil consequence thereof" (27.28). An action the sovereign permits but should not have permitted raises questions. Hobbes carves a space for the liberty of subjects when he writes in *Leviathan* that the liberty of subjects depends upon the silence of the laws: "Where the sovereign has prescribed no rule, there the subject hath the liberty to do or forebear, according to his own discretion" (21.18). Is Hobbes referring to areas where the law stays silent but should speak?

The passage quoted above contemplates more than the laws' silence. It references something more affirmative: liberties erroneously "granted" and accrued.[14] Here it may seem reasonable to begin with Curley's intuition. He asserts that Hobbes was referencing his disappointment in Charles I's concessions to subjects at the start of the Long Parliament, that is, the liberties he granted on the basis of the Magna Carta and the Petition of Right (*Lev.*, 21.20, 144n26). In fact, Hobbes is even more open ended in his description. He is aware of another class of liberties that were not necessarily the product of either the silence of the laws or the general concessions to Charles I's resistant Parliament and petitioners.

As noted, Hobbes knew that particular subjects were able to accrue special rights, liberties, and privileges—benefits denied to others by law. Sovereigns made, as we sometimes say, "special exceptions." He knew of monopolies, of charters, of patents, and of their role as sources of revenue, especially for monarchs deprived by Parliament of the revenues they needed or desired (22.5–8). He goes so far as to describe monopolies as one of the diseases of the commonwealth relating to the deprivation of revenues: "Again, there is sometimes in a Common-wealth, a Disease, which resembleth the Pleurisie; and that is, when the Treasure of the Common-wealth, flowing out of its due course, is gathered together in too much abundance, in one, or a few private men, by Monopolies, or by Farmes of the Publique Revenues; in the same manner as the Blood in a Pleurisie, getting into the Membrane of the breast, breedeth there an Inflammation, accompanied with a Fever, and painfull stitches" (29.19). If Hobbes is arguing that subjects sin when they enjoy these legal indulgences, he might be described as having secularized a Protestant impulse in an era obsessed with "Popery in government."[15] Just as clergy ought not to offer indulgences to sinners, Hobbes's sovereign, the "mortal god," ought not to offer legal indulgences, and subjects ought not to exercise them when they threaten the commonwealth itself. Indeed, Hobbes insists that resisting a civil officer who acts to thwart one's exercise of these liberties is a crime (27.28). There is a noteworthy tension here: the privileged may do what is or ought to be forbidden to the many; but if the magistrate thwarts these bad acts, they must comply with the magistrate. If they resist, they are subject to criminal penalty in spite of their privilege.

Sovereignty Permissive and Weak

Hobbes was stricter than most in this resistance toward an indulgent sovereign, but he was also discerning with regard to the friendly exceptions he opposed. Here I wish to make a distinction between the problem of "the foole" and the permissive sovereign. Research in recent years has focused on the challenge that "the foole" creates for Hobbes, the fool being the man who does not honor his covenants with all the others. The fool says "in his heart, 'there is no such thing as justice.'" He knows that covenants such as the one that creates the commonwealth and absolute sovereign exist, but he also knows that "they are sometimes broken, sometimes kept, and that such breach of them may be called injustice . . . but he questioneth whether injustice . . . may not sometimes and with that reason which dictateth to every man his own good. . . point him in the direction of potentially successful, grand, disobedience. Says the foole, 'The Kingdom of God is got by violence, but what if it could be gotten by unjust violence?' were it against reason so to get it, when it is impossible to receive hurt by it[?]" (*Lev.*, 15.4). Kinch Hoekstra has argued that the challenge of the rational rebel is one that Hobbes felt he needed to meet, but there is a neighboring problem that is not quite the same.[16]

The neighboring problem is the absolute sovereign who, by virtue of the absolute and arbitrary power attached to his office, willingly and publicly permits parties to operate outside the law. It is the permissive sovereign who frightens Hobbes, especially the permissive weak sovereign. Here the fault is not entirely with the man who wishes to skirt his obligations to the covenant—although Hobbes does wish to convict him of that sin—but rather with the sovereign who makes the friendly exceptions and encourages both a disregard for law and a belief in the beneficiary's impunity from law.

Hobbes fears a contagious belief in legal impunity wherein the very conditions required for a law-bound commonwealth seem to melt away. This problem is not one of a dishonest covenanter who plans on breaking his promise when he savors the prospect of gaining his own kingdom by wicked acts, but of a sovereign who in some instances seeks to preserve his position by making the powerful exempt from laws and rules he would see imposed upon the multitudes. For example, after warning against the vain-glorious and foolish who reason "as if differences of worth were an effect of their wit, or riches, or blood," there tends to arise a "a presumption that the punishments ordained by the laws, and extended generally to all subjects, ought not to be inflicted on them with the same rigour they are inflicted upon the poor, obscure and simple men" (27.13).

This friendliness spawns a problem of justice that goes beyond the mere daring of fools. Persons who "value themselves by the greatness of their wealth adventure on crimes, upon hope of escaping punishment by corrupting public justice or obtaining pardon by money or other rewards" (27.14). That is to say, "public justice" is itself sometimes corrupted. Hobbes's "foole" is a person who believes that the legal impunity he enjoys may be the result of criminal daring, having outfoxed or overpowered the sovereign. Hobbes shows that he believes that an indulgent, overgenerous, or too-forgiving or pliable sovereign can give rise to threatening "great men" by other means. By virtue of the impunity granted them by the poor judgment of sovereigns, such persons come to believe that the laws that apply to others do not apply to them. It is therefore possible to pave a path toward such attitudes out of something less than those individuals' Machiavellian daring, arrogance, or cynicism. Merely enjoying the sovereign's extralegal favor may be sufficient to nurture the presumption, as are the advantages of a lofty position in a class-stratified system accustomed to punishing the poor but more hesitant to harm even the guilty among the upper orders.[17]

For Hobbes, examples of such behavior include the petty skirting of justice by bribing judges. Pardons, either by the sovereign or by those officials who serve the sovereign, are also at issue. Hobbes also makes clear that the problem of impunity seekers and impunity granters goes further: weak punishments are a problem. If a punishment inflicted for a crime is "less than the benefit or contentment that naturally followeth the crime," then, says Hobbes, it is not actually a punishment. It is instead merely "the price, or redemption . . . because it is of the nature of punishment to have for the end the disposing of men to obey the law; which end . . . it attaineth not, but worketh a contrary effect" (28.9). He returns to this topic when addressing pecuniary punishments, some of which are nothing more than means of gathering revenue at the cost of undermining lawfulness: "And in case the law that ordaineth such a punishment be made with a design to gather money for such as shall transgress the same, it is not properly a punishment, but the price of privilege and exemption from the law, which doth not absolutely forbid the fact, but only to those that are not able to pay the money" (28.18).

Hobbes professes to argue from definitions, and as the price of privilege, pecuniary punishments do not satisfy the prohibitive requirement of *punishment*.[18] They are rather de facto taxes payed by the rich to remain exempt from the law. Hobbes also defines *reward* and similarly disqualifies other forms of favorable treatment from classification as such. A true reward, writes Hobbes, may take the form of a contract for wages or a gift of grace, but it must be done "to encourage or enable men to do them [the sovereign] service." By contrast, "benefits which a sovereign bestoweth on a subject for fear of some power and ability he hath to hurt the commonwealth are not properly rewards" (28.24–25). Sovereign powers, says Hobbes, ought never to suffer extortion. When the sovereign grants such benefits out of fear, he writes, the act must not be considered a public one, but rather a private act of the weak officeholder. There are "sacrifices which the sovereign (considered in his natural person, and not in the person of the commonwealth) makes for appeasing the discontent of him he thinks more potent than himself, and encourage not to obedience, but on the contrary, to the continuance and increase of further extortion" (28.25). The king has two bodies; one of them may be extorted.

When describing the "office of the sovereign representative," Hobbes directly addresses the dangers of indulging the powerful and wealthy in their desires for impunity. Justice, he writes, "must be equally administered to all degrees of people, that is, that as well the rich and mighty as the poor and obscure person may be righted of the injuries done them." The great, especially when they injure the poor, "may have no greater hope of impunity when they do violence, dishonor, or any injury to the meaner sort" (30.15). Hobbes's egalitarianism here dovetails with his wish for a strong sovereign.

He maintains that sovereigns are within their rights to pardon persons, but he keeps to the Common Law tradition in this regard. An injury done to the public is pardonable, but an injury done by one subject to another is not pardonable.[19] This distinction violates the principle of equity: as Hobbes defines it, equity does not allow pardon without the consent of the injured or if reasonable satisfaction is offered (30.15). When "the great" are favored with impunity, especially before the lesser, it also inspires dangerous reprisals: "The consequences of this partiality towards the great proceed in this manner. Impunity maketh insolence; insolence, hatred; and

hatred, an endeavor to pull down all oppressing and contumelious greatness, though with the ruin of the commonwealth" (30.16). The sovereign
who applies equal justice to the great avoids the internal dissension that
arises when the resentments the great foster beget the hatred of those less
fortunate, who suffer from their indulgence.[20]

There is good reason to believe that Hobbes and his contemporaries
had firsthand experience in the ill consequences of bad friendly exceptions. Leaving aside the larger question of whether resentment toward the
granting of monopolies was a cause of the English Civil War, historians
have in some cases readily imagined how this aspect of the Crown's friendly
sovereign prerogatives created animosity.[21] The Stuarts and those courtiers
and privileged interests who were advantaged by this form of sovereign
grace and favor turned themselves into objects of animosity. Lacking an
administrative arm by which to distribute and enforce its monopolies, the
state had to rely upon courtiers whose self-interest was often imperfectly
aligned with the public purposes professed by the Crown. In a striking set
of passages, Christopher Hill records:

> Often there were good reasons for protecting new industries by
> giving them a guaranteed market for a period of years. . . . But too
> often selling monopolies became a means [however ineffective] of
> solving the government's fiscal problems. . . . Monopolies were
> obtainable only by those with court influence. Thus the pinmak-
> ers, of humble origin, had to bribe courtiers to get a charter of
> incorporation. The courtiers in consequence acquired real control
> of the new company. In 1612 the Earl of Salisbury was receiving
> £7,000 a year from the silk monopoly, the Earl of Suffolk £5,000
> from currants, the Earl of Northampton £4,500 from starch.[22]

The list goes on. Hill reports that the number of monopolies in 1621 were
"alleged to be 700." On the basis of some of the better-known monopolies,
Hill paints a dismal picture of what results from the exercise of this friendly
sovereign prerogative:

> In 1601 a member of Parliament asked, when a list of monopolies
> was read out, "Is not bread there?" His irony exaggerated only
> slightly. It is difficult for us to picture to ourselves the life of a man
> living in a house built with monopoly bricks, with windows (if any)

of monopoly glass; heated by monopoly coal (in Ireland monopoly timber), burning in a grate made of monopoly iron. His walls were lined with monopoly tapestries. He slept on monopoly feathers, did his hair with monopoly brushes and monopoly combs. He washed himself with monopoly soap, his clothes in monopoly starch. He dressed in monopoly lace, monopoly linen, monopoly leather, monopoly goldthread. His hat was of monopoly beaver, with a monopoly band. His clothes were held up by monopoly belts, monopoly buttons, monopoly pins. They were dyed with monopoly dyes. He ate monopoly butter, monopoly currants, monopoly red herrings, monopoly salmon, and monopoly lobsters. His food was seasoned with monopoly salt.[23]

The passage unquestionably puts meat on the bones of the Grand Remonstrance's complaint. Subsequent historians have pushed back to a certain degree on the negative impression left by disputes over patents and monopolies, but we need not maintain that the Stuarts were treated fairly on this score to acknowledge that they were the subject of bitter complaints.[24]

The Place for Mercy

It is not that Hobbes or his likely resentful contemporaries thought there was no place for friendly prerogatives. Mercy in particular was valued. Hobbes was able to reconcile his fears of a weak or indulgent sovereign with his recognition of the need for mercy by making pardon a law of nature: "A sixth law of nature is this *that upon caution of a future time, a man ought to pardon the offenses past of them that, repenting, desire it.* For PARDON is nothing but granting of peace, which (though granted to them that persevere in their hostility be not peace but fear, yet) nor granted to them that give caution of the future time is a sign of an aversion to peace; and therefore contrary to the law of nature" (*Lev.*, 15.18). As a law of nature, pardon might be expected for all persons required to live together in peace, but Hobbes understands that for sovereigns in particular, pardon is a balancing act. Echoing the logic of past kingly practice, Hobbes writes, "The punishment of the leaders and teachers in a commotion, not the poor seduced people, when they are punished, can profit the commonwealth by their example" (30.23). Hobbes was likely mindful of the ways that the Tudors helped secure their power over Britain by engaging in theatrical acts of public forgiveness of those willing to plead for it and repent. Rebellion leaders suffered death, but their followers received pardons with some regularity. Punishment and pardon, retribution and remission "worked together as strategies of rule."[25] Defeated rebellions gave the sovereign the opportunity to put these powers on display when and where the two parties (forgiver and recipient) could and often did cooperate to set the terms of the subjects' subordination. Condemned men—be they rebels or merely criminals—who are made or even pleased to ask forgiveness and mercy were a chance for sovereigns to make themselves lovable in the eyes of their subjects. The kingly action was to arrange matters, as best he could, to make a show of clemency.[26] As Kesselring notes: "Mercy was considered an essential part of sovereignty, both a necessary and legitimate adjunct to justice. While particular pardons on occasion prompted criticism, the power to pardon remained an unquestioned component of the royal prerogative through the sixteenth century. A pardon had no intrinsic meaning: its significance depended on its proper presentation. The supplicant had to show humility, repentance, and above all submission; the grant had to appear a benevolent gift, an act of grace."[27]

Therefore, mercy also had its uses in more pacific contexts. Strong sovereign keepers of law and order could afford to grant forgiveness, even as they might by their discretion have to withhold it.[28] A Weberian monopoly on the legitimate use of violence defines this sociological understanding of the state, which underscores that we should not overlook the quest for monopoly on the uses of forgiveness, mercy, and pardon as a key aspect of state consolidation.[29] The right of arbitrary magnanimity might offend republican sensibilities, but kings understood that it made one an attractive sovereign to the throngs of the servile and the willingly subordinate elite. Denying the power to pardon to local feudal elites was likewise a part of the process of consolidation. Tudor and Stuart kings flexed their muscles and satisfied their subjects with grand acts of generosity, including annual pardon of entire classes of convicts to mark the opening of Parliament or other spectacular events during a king's reign.[30]

If the advantageous use of public acts of mercy helped build up Tudor kingship, the mismanagement of public acts of mercy, grants of favor, or pardon were often at the center of subjects' discontent under the Stuarts. I will return to some of these discontents as well as other aspects of Hobbes's concern with dangerous friendly exceptions at the end of the chapter. First, I wish to address why political theorists have allowed Carl Schmitt's mischaracterization of Hobbes to distract us from his important concern with sovereign friendly exceptions.

PART II: DECISIONISM AND EXCEPTIONS IN AND OUT OF CONTEXT

What has made us look past Hobbes when it comes to friendly exceptions? I've already noted the tendency among political theorists to focus on "the exception" in their discussions of sovereignty, and how this reflects the influence of the Weimar and Third Reich juridical and political theorist Carl Schmitt.[31] Arguing that periods of peril teach us who is sovereign—and teach the naïve what sovereignty truly *is*—Schmitt's sovereign makes himself known by the power to "decide the exception."[32] In the same book, *Political Theology*, Schmitt famously declares Hobbes the "classical" decisionist thinker.[33] This will be a somewhat extended exercise to think through what Schmitt, and many of us, don't consider in Hobbes's milieu when we contemplate exceptions to law.

According to Schmitt, Thomas Hobbes recognized and understood the primacy of the existential threat for the sovereign's authority to unleash extraordinary violence in ways that others—especially Schmitt's own liberal contemporaries—did not. Schmitt's reading of Hobbes's concept of sovereignty is both anachronistic and, in some instances, misleading. Before returning to some relevant aspects of Hobbes's legal and political contexts to make this case historically, I will make the argument both conceptually and by way of a necessarily brief description of aspects of the historical context that produced Schmitt's decisionist comportment.

To state it bluntly, "classic decisionist" thinking is something we cannot find in the seventeenth century. Its classical form resides only with Schmitt and some of his contemporaries. Schmitt's writings on Hobbes's concept of sovereignty are a part of a past he constructed to possess what he said was lacking in the present: specifically, a sensibility filled with political purpose and robust antagonism. Schmitt's account converts Hobbes into a heroic victor in his own late modern battles. This includes the fabrication of twentieth-century opponents in the seventeenth century.

As I reviewed in chapter 1, we find Schmitt in strong opposition to some of the trends he believed gained dominance in the nineteenth century and into the early twentieth. Echoing elements of Weber's understanding of modernization, Schmitt observed in "The Age of Neutralizations and Depoliti-zations" (1929) that "in the nineteenth century technical progress proceeded at such an astonishing rate, even as did social and economic situations as a consequence, that all moral, political, social, and economic situations were affected. Given the overpowering suggestion of ever new and surpris-ing inventions and achievements, there arose a religion of technical prog-ress which promised all other problems would be solved by technological progress" (84–85).[34] Schmitt was determined to expose the "religion of tech-nological progress." Declaring it a religion was a partial act of defiance. The label stood against the self-understanding of many proponents of techno-logical progress. According to Schmitt, many were the product of the nine-teenth century's romanticization of the prior century's Enlightenment creed: they believed that accomplished, modern thinkers such as themselves had long surpassed the metaphysical theories and dogmatic religious convic-tions of their predecessors. He described the twentieth century as having, thus far, suffered an "overwhelming technicity" (85). From its origins in the nineteenth century, the ethos of technicity had formed, according to Schmitt, a central intellectual domain—a vanguard with weight in determining pub-lic thought—that forced itself onto other spheres, including matters of moral-ity and public intellectual leadership.

Helping to fuel this transition was a second European intellectual trend: the urge to escape controversy, and more specifically, to do so by prefer-ring transitions from the contested, or partial, to the neutral. Schmitt traced this urge to the seventeenth century but says it achieved its classical form in the nineteenth. He also declared it a process that held out a false prom-ise, and this meant that it tended to repeat itself.[35] In spite of scientific think-ing's failure to bring the peace that neutrality seemed to promise, "the widespread contemporary belief in technology is based only on the prop-osition that the absolute and ultimate neutral ground has been found in technology. . . . Technology serves everyone" (90).

Technology's capacity to serve everyone, however, meant that the over-whelming technicity that had informed hopes of economic, moral, and other forms of progress were merely reflective of a psychology determined to avoid a decision. Since technology, and especially the technologies that improve war making and propaganda, can serve everyone, they will serve all sides in any matter of conflict. And, since the quest for neutrality is never actually achieved, decisions over who or what will settle questions of "leadership or direction" will eventually have to be confronted. In short, there were truly political questions, and political answers, that could not be "derived from purely technical principles and perspectives" (91–92).

It was, writes Schmitt, the previous generation, including Max Weber, that had grasped and learned to truly lament "the irresistible power of technology." They had come to recognize it "as the domination of spiritlessness over spirit or, perhaps, as an ingenious but soulless mechanism" (92–93). This fostered a feeling of helplessness. "Soul" or "spirit" could not, seemingly, recover its position in an age in which technology had become dominant. Moreover, it was the sociological perspective, working from this legitimate anxiety, that feared mass enthusiasm for things technological. It was right to doubt its vacuous moral and spiritual concepts of improvements and progress. They feared that these forces were going to ultimately extinguish "culture itself." "Everything had been abstracted," from religion, theology, metaphysics, and even the state, "ending in the neutrality of cultural death" (93).

While remaining sympathetic to the prior generation's animosity toward the neutral, Schmitt declares that a new day is coming in which antagonists with political convictions will indeed use technology to pursue victory over their spiritual rivals. In fact, argued Schmitt, cultural reinvention is always experienced by those invested in the status quo as the prior generation had experienced technicity: as a shift toward "nothingness." The way the twentieth century would end was in his view yet to be determined, but it would not be through a recovery of the lost status quo or its culture. How the century will be understood, wrote Schmitt, "will be revealed only when it is known which type of politics is strong enough to master the new technology and which type of genuine friend-enemy groupings can develop on this new ground" (95).

Decisionism grows in the soil of this comportment, of persons weary of neutralizations and depoliticizations and hungering for something that knowingly defies the unexamined rationality of the hyper-rationalized state and society. It is not demanding a return to the magic of old, but its appetite for magic, for the extra-rational, creedal conviction, is pronounced. The decisionist feels what the previous generation thought of as the soullessness of the technological present and, like that generation, demands a reprieve.[36] Schmitt was looking for the emergence of a new set of spiritual commitments upon which new political and spiritual struggles would be launched. Like the sociologists, this framework recognized the extra-rational roots of these sentiments, and the religious functions, however secularized, that these deep convictions would necessarily play.

I will not attempt to fully contextualize Schmitt's decisionism here, but we can unearth a telling aspect of his political philosophy's historical moment. Decisionism had become fashionable in Schmitt's Germany. Its attractions were such that it even became a part of the Franke & Heidecke corporation's 1938 campaign to promote the advantages of their new camera, the Rolleiflex. This consumer product's brochure was titled *Success Alone Decides*, and in this booklet decisionism penetrated beyond the title. It was used to illuminate the camera's distinct design: theirs was no "soulless instrument" but something that "becomes alive as if by magic."[37] Although the comparison may seem trivial, it illustrates a useful point: decisionist thinking only occurs where enthusiasts declare their wish for relief from "soulless instruments," be they industrial or political.

The Rolleiflex brochure can help highlight another contrast. If the Rollei overcomes its status as mere soulless instrument by becoming alive as if by magic, this may also remind us that decisionism does not seek to replace mechanisms with magic, but to add magic on top of mechanism. The decisionist sovereign is, as it were, a magical force—an extra-rational, passionate actor that supplements an already mechanized state. The decision rescues, but also preserves, a state at risk of being indicted by disaffected political thinkers for its soullessness, late-modern decadence, or political complaisance. Schmitt's sovereign can speak and mobilize the people's deepest convictions. As he insists in the opening pages of *Political Theology*, sovereignty is a "borderline" concept. By "borderline" Schmitt means to stress the distinction between it and "the routine" case (5). Thus, a borderline case is defined against the routine and, most importantly for Schmitt, against the legally routine. He who decides the exception, says Schmitt, makes "a decision in the true sense of the word. Because a general norm, as represented by an ordinary legal prescription, can never encompass a total exception." This kind of contrast informs his assertion: "The exception in jurisprudence is analogous to the miracle in theology. . . . The idea of the modern constitutional state . . . banished the miracle from the world" (36).[38]

Although there is no seeming peril in the case of the camera, it becomes clear that for Schmitt the age of technicity has yielded the success of Germany's legal positivists (notably the neo-Kantian Hans Kelsen and Hugo

Krabbe). For Schmitt they are part and parcel of the "tendencies of modern constitutional development [which] point toward eliminating the sovereign in this sense" (7). They have put forward a vision of the state that is, according to Schmitt, thoroughly soulless and which inclines to substitute technicity's neutrality for decisions "in the true sense."[39] Thus, they allow the mechanical application of norms—the routine application of law provided by, or under, the constitution—to elide the necessary decisions. These decisions must precede and be, according to Schmitt, the fundamental basis of the state's existence. In so doing, Germany's legal positivists have contributed to the obliteration of sovereignty. They have, as we've reviewed, substituted technicity's preferred understanding of the state, as if it were a machine that ran on nothing more than neutral, scientifically known and applied legal standards. Its basis in political convictions or decisions that belong outside the stipulated legal norms is erased from consciousness. Against this we can witness Schmitt's bitter complaint: "Today nothing is more modern than the onslaught against the political. . . . There must no longer be political problems, only organizational-technical and economic tasks. The kind of economic-technical thinking that prevails today is no longer capable of perceiving a political idea. The modern state seems to have actually become what Max Weber envisioned: a huge industrial plant. . . . The core of the political idea, the exacting moral decision is evaded" (65).

In defending his concept of sovereignty, Schmitt was putting forward his own cure for the soulless machine-like state. It is the sobering force of the borderline case or crisis and the sovereign's call to arms against the enemy that threatens its prior, seemingly placid, existence. Some magic therefore is added to the machine, and those who live day to day within the stultifying confines of the ordinary and regular application of the rationalized state's and rationalized society's dictates will be shaken. They will be compelled to realize that their entire common membership in the state is rooted in a choice that the age of technicity had convinced them they did not need to confront. Miracles and magic may be at last restored to their seat at the head of the table.

The question we must ask with regard to Hobbes and sovereignty, however, is: Could any of these sentiments have ever been experienced by this so-called classic decisionist in the seventeenth century? Other political theorists have suggested that Schmitt gets Hobbes wrong, that he is somehow in error in his interpretation of Hobbes's political theory. Let me suggest that one of the driving forces behind Schmitt's misrepresentations of Hobbes is the way in which he substitutes his own context and struggles for Hobbes's. Was Thomas Hobbes struggling against a vision of the state that had already turned into an industrial plant? He was not, and therefore he cannot be a decisionist. He lacks the decisionist's opponent: the soulless world, its already-built institutions, and its proponents. Hobbes could have no struggle with technicity and its consequences for his contemporaries. He was not, and for many of Hobbes's readers, Hobbes himself was responsible for giving us a vision of the industrial-plant state, not seeking relief from a world without miracles and political antagonisms.[40]

Schmitt, however, can't help but recruit Hobbes for his crusade against the soulless state as if he had been in training for this fight from his own struggles in the seventeenth century. Nowhere is it more evident than in his misreading of his most favored passage from *Leviathan*. In book after book, Schmitt uses the passage to register both Hobbes's so-called decisionist credo and his agreement with it: "*auctoritas, non veritas facit legem.*"[41] According to Schmitt, "*veritas*" references an ideal or rational quest for the truth that takes the form of a plea that Hobbes rejects: an attempt "to substitute an abstractly valid order for a concrete sovereignty of the state."[42] This specific construction authorizes Schmitt's identification of Hobbes, above all others, as the "classical representative of the decisionist type."[43]

In fact, Hobbes's use of "*veritas*" is not a reference to this kind of norm-affirming verification. The passage in Latin that Schmitt references so frequently is in chapter 26, "Of Civil Laws," which was first written in English.[44] Hobbes is referencing a verification of fact, not a norm. The passage occurs where Hobbes wishes to make his readers mindful of a potential devious scheme to break the law: "Private men (when they have, or think they have, force enough to secure their unjust designs, and convoy them safely to their ambitious ends) may publish for laws what they please, without or against legislative authority."[45]

Hobbes uses *veritas* to reference verification for those who share his suspicions of the devious lawbreakers, not for the idealistic or rationalist person. Neither was it a *veritas* for someone hoping to affirm that a judge's ruling conforms with the rational application of law. Those who suspect a misrepresentation, Hobbes notes, will attempt to verify whether the law is, in fact, as it has been represented by such "private men." They will compare the published representation against a trusted, official record. Hobbes recommends that they do exactly this; they should seek this verification.

In the passage Schmitt repeatedly quotes, Hobbes is simply adding a qualification. Why, he asks, was the written record law? What, in other words, *makes it* law? Is it the law because it was written? His answer is "No." It is law because it issued from the sovereign's authority. Hobbes draws a conclusion consonant with his larger theory's source of the law's authority, but against an opponent erased by the Schmittian worldview. Schmitt invites us to imagine an impossible neo-Kantian on the receiving end of Hobbes's "No."[46]

It is safe to assume that Hobbes adds this qualification because he is thinking of the weight Common Lawyers assigned to custom. They sometimes pitted established, recorded, or judge-known law over and against the will of the contemporary sovereign officeholder. Such arguments were developed as a part of the Common Lawyer's strategy to retain control through jurisdictional disputes. Hobbes wanted to guard against this conservative habit, because it assigned authority outside of the present sovereign's control. Hobbes was certainly aware that the Common Lawyers claimed that the wisdom of centuries that is sometimes called England's judge-made constitution was a part of their argument for limiting the sovereign's prerogatives, but it would be a very odd way to describe this contest as one between a political philosopher attached to a concrete understanding of authority and the partisans of an abstractly valid order.

Indeed, had there been a contest between Hobbes and his contemporaries for the most concrete (or the least abstract) jurisprudence, it is not at all clear that Hobbes would have had the advantage. His Common Law opponents were the ones speaking on behalf of a specifically *English* tradition; they thought it a transcendent, impersonal authority, but one also firmly rooted in England's experience and needs.[47] Moreover, it was an authority that always had to be manifest in the ruling of a judge, which at this time and for some time in the future was an intensely personalist moment between the judge, as embodiment of the law of the land, and those receiving judgment. This sensibility has been called Gothic for its connection to the mystical Germanic Saxon past.[48] Hobbes was struggling against the weight and authority of that local tradition in favor of his personalist yet also geometrically perfected system.

Consider the ways in which Schmitt leaves us with the impression that Hobbes overcame the same challenges as he did. In spite of being "one of the most consequential representatives of this abstract scientific orientation of the seventeenth century," Schmitt tells us that Hobbes nonetheless remained "personalistic" in his understanding of sovereignty. Why, according to Schmitt, was this the case? "This is because as a juristic thinker he"—like Schmitt himself—"wanted to grasp the reality of societal life." Happily, "in those days," juristic thought "had not yet become so overpowered by the natural sciences that he, in the intensity of his scientific approach, should unsuspectingly have overlooked the specific reality of legal life inherent in the legal form."[49] This is the kind of fantasy conflict that only anachronism can supply. Hobbes had no conflict with empty legal formalism, and Hobbes's happy escape from the dangers of natural science's intellectual vanguard seems far too much of a near miss. Nor, of course, did Hobbes's nonexistent legal positivist rivals try to squeeze out the nonexistent sociological insights that informed his vision for a truly legitimate constitution.

Hobbes could not have struggled against a future he, or any of his contemporaries, had yet to create. Much less could he have declared that those future forms—the purely normative legal apparatus, or the autonomous machine-like state—must acknowledge the magic of the passionate creedal convictions that must confront the sleepwalking denizens of these overly technologized states. In short, Hobbes could no more be a decisionist thinker of sovereignty than he could have been a Rollei enthusiast.

CHAPTER 5

HOBBES'S CIVIC THEODICY:

Leibniz, Suffering Innocents, and Prosperity of the Wicked

The previous chapter reviews several aspects of Hobbes's political and social context that illustrate one of the challenges of his theory of sovereignty. The sovereign possesses extraordinary power to afflict his subjects if he deems them a threat to his rule or the state. As kings in the past have done, he can forgive or pardon rebels or the convicted. He likewise has it in his power to favor other subjects, in some cases (far less extraordinary than Hobbes might have preferred) through the granting of patents or monopolies, and in other cases by making them essentially immune from criminal or civil laws. How can persons be made to willingly consent and submit to the rule of a sovereign who might, through his unwelcome kindness, harm those the subjects understand to be their friends? How willingly will they remain obedient to a sovereign who seems to favor those they understand to be their enemies, or those they deem worthy of legal punishments or other harms? For Hobbes and his contemporaries, these were more than theoretical questions.

Hobbes has been shown to be a jealous guardian of his sovereign's power. His insistence upon the sovereign's rights, however, creates its own set of problems. Hobbes worried that the latitude afforded sovereigns—especially with regard to their friendly prerogatives—might alienate subjects. Stuart kings were often at risk of alienating subjects by virtue of the persons and monopolies that they favored. In the prior chapter I considered specific aspects of the historical record regarding sovereign powers that favored or immunized some of the kingdom's subjects. This chapter's purpose is to shine a light on this problem for sovereigns from a comparative philosophical perspective. In keeping with our view that Hobbes remained ambivalent about the sovereign's friendly prerogatives, the contrast between Hobbes and that of his late seventeenth- and early eighteenth-century critic Gottfried Wilhelm Leibniz shows the former to be far less complacent in face of such dissatisfactions.

Leibniz is best known for having coined the term "theodicy": a justification of the ways of God to man. As Hegel knew when he declared that he had superseded Leibniz, theodicy's task was to reconcile men to the existence of evil in the world. For Leibniz's contemporaries, this reconciliation meant showing that the universe is, despite the existence of evil, consistent with reason. How is the very often miserable world, in other words, consistent with "eternal wisdom?"[1] What could possibly justify the suffering of so many? Philosophical theodicy often attempts to show that this evil must be accepted because human events and indeed the world itself are consistent with a higher principle: be it God's choice of the best of all possible worlds, as Leibniz maintained; the belief that events are providential; or, as Hegel dictated, that events are ultimately reason's historical manifestation. All is in accord with the plans of the rational force that governs the universe, and it is the philosopher's task, in offering a theodicy, to make persons see and recognize that ultimate rationality.

Leibniz, of course, did not invent this form of argument. Anyone confronted with doubts about the justness of the universe, including Hobbes himself, was cognizant of the need. This need also extended to the rule of kings, who so often justified their absolutism by identifying themselves as God's lieutenants on earth and by likening themselves to God.[2] Did Hobbes supply his sovereign, his "Mortal God," with what amounts to civil theodicy? There were evils that early modern subjects were expected to endure. Those who submitted to a master, be it God or an earthly sovereign, had to know that their subordination came with a duty to honor, even worship, the master's authority.[3] And, of course, the refusal to endure the authority of masters who clothed their authority in providential design became one of the great emancipatory comportments over the centuries.

Hobbes is better known for his reminder that subjects in his commonwealth are authors of their own punishments, that any injury they ascribe to their sovereign must be attributed to themselves, or that the misery of living under "lusts" and "irregular passions" of a sovereign "is scarce sensible" when compared to "the miseries and horrible calamities that accompany a civile war" or world of "masterless men" free to engage in "rapine and revenge."[4] He was also aware that they would be forced to endure the pains that came with the friendly side of his sovereign's latitude, and this will be our focus.

The foremost challenge for a theodicy is to offer justification for a world in which the innocent are made to suffer. Both Leibniz and Hobbes knew that this was not the only challenge. One also had to confront the inverse: What justifies a world in which the wicked are allowed to prosper? This challenge afflicted earthly sovereigns and their subjects as well, especially when their friendly prerogatives favored those that some subjects may have deemed wicked and/or undeserving of the sovereign's grace. In the following pages, the two philosophers' answers to these questions will be contemplated and compared. Hobbes will show himself to be much less willing to tolerate a Mortal God that favors the wicked, even as he is steadfast in allowing that same Mortal God to afflict the innocent.

HOBBES AND THEODICY

In chapter 31 of *Leviathan*, "Of the Kingdom of God by Nature," Hobbes sets out to confront a conundrum: "Why evil men often prosper, and good men suffer adversity, has been much disputed by the ancient, and is the same with this of ours, By what right God dispenseth the prosperities and adversities of this life; and is of that difficulty as it has shaken the faith, not only of the vulgar, but of philosophers, and which is more, of the Saints, concerning Divine Providence."[5] It was not many years later that Leibniz labeled this problem "theodicy."[6] The problem has numerous aspects, but I will focus on the two that preoccupy Hobbes and their ultimate meaning for his earthly sovereign.

Because it appears to capture most of Hobbes's attention in *Leviathan*, I begin with human suffering, and in particular the suffering of innocent persons.[7] Especially when choosing to reference the woes of Job, God's sovereignty, and the suffering a divinity may choose to distribute in his universe, Hobbes repeats and emphasizes his sobering, even brutal, answers to these questions. I'll also consider if this answer had a civic counterpart with an equally brutal answer for subjects of their earthly sovereign.

SAINTS IN THE HANDS OF AN ANGRY GOD

Regarding the question "by what right God dispenseth the prosperities and adversities of this life," Hobbes was drawn to God's answer to Job's friends (*Lev.*, 31.6). "This question, in the case of Job," Hobbes writes, "is decided by God himself, not by arguments derived from Job's sin, but his own power."[8] What does it mean to say that Job's "case" was decided by God's "own power," rather than by arguments derived from Job's sin? Hobbes explains, "For whereas the friends of Job drew their arguments from his affliction to his sin, and he defended himself by the conscience of his innocence, God himself taketh up the matter, and having justified the affliction by arguments drawn from his power, such as this, 'Where was thou, when I laid the foundations of the earth?' (Job 38:4), and the like, both approved Job's innocence, and reproved the erroneous doctrine of his friends" (31.6). Sin, therefore, is not the cause of all affliction, as *Leviathan*'s printed marginal guide emphasizes. Hobbes argues much the same in the case of Adam. He notes that Romans 5:12 states "that death entered into the world by sin."[9] One might therefore conclude that had Adam not sinned, humanity would not experience death. That is, no apple, no death. Yet Hobbes rejects this conclusion. Were Adam to have remained utterly innocent, he writes, God might have still have "afflicted him," and for the same reason that God "afflicteth other living creatures that cannot sin." God afflicts because He can: His power is the only justification we are offered. Indeed, for Hobbes, the doctrine of original sin sometimes looks like a God too ready to offer excuses.[10] Regardless of how we assess the sincerity of Hobbes's faith, the political relevance of such conclusions is evident.

As sovereign over the universe, Hobbes's God is unanswerable to us. However, God is a law giver, and this complicates the question. If God legislates and we violate the law, we are due punishment. Thus, our punishment may be due to our sins and transgressions, though, as Hobbes observes, God has no need of our sin to render his afflictions. In anything that He does, God owes us no explanation. He is infinite; we are finite. The latter can't measure the former (3.12). Nevertheless, the relationship between lawmaker and law breaker does entail justification, explanation, investigation, and thoughts about extenuating circumstances. The difficulties of applying law to particular cases predictably arises. God may not owe us his reasons, but that does not mean that reasons are not sometimes offered. Hobbes himself puts some of those reasons to use when they serve his purpose.

Using passages in 1 Samuel about the ancient Hebrews' decision to cast off God's earthly kingdom when they themselves asked God for a king, Hobbes defends the slavish obedience due even cruel kings.[11] A God who does not need to give reasons, Hobbes acknowledges, very often offers them.

Moreover, even the most absolute master (human or divine) must make his will known if he wishes to be obeyed rather than merely supplicated to and worshipped. Once the master declares what he wants—or better, why he wants it—or speaks of rewards or punishments, questions follow. We see Hobbes himself grappling with this difficulty in *Leviathan* where he takes up the history of God's delegation to his earthly sovereigns among the ancient Hebrews, notably Moses and Abraham (40.1–8). Only those who spoke with God in this bygone era of prophesy, Hobbes insists, were permitted the earthly authority to answer questions concerning the meaning of what God requires. If sovereignty is typically associated with a will that won't be questioned, being truly and concretely unquestionable is too difficult even for God. Hobbes's divine sovereign sometimes solves this problem with violence, as when "his sole messenger" Moses is challenged (40.7). Within his absolutist state, Hobbes's effort to distinguish between counsel and command testifies to his efforts to police the boundary between the questionable and the unquestionable (25.1–5).

Although God and human sovereigns are both lawmakers, real differences between Hobbes's Mortal God and the immortal God emerge on this score. God has a "triple word" in announcing his laws (rational, sensible, and prophetic); man has only one. God's insuperable power makes him ruler over the universe and over men (31.5).[12] Among men, Hobbes argues, sovereign power arises from a pact. Having created a Mortal God and having promulgated its laws by voice, there are parallels between the immortal God's omnipotent rights by power and a human sovereign's. Hobbes's sovereign is a law giver but is not himself subject to laws. Not unlike God's commands, this is a matter of power and its prerogatives:[13] "For having power to make and repeal laws, he may, when he pleaseth, free himself from that subjection by repealing those laws that trouble him and making of new; and consequently, he was free before. For he is free that can be free when he will; nor is it possible for any person to be bound to himself, because he that can bind can release" (26.6; cf. 29.9). The parallels between the Mortal God and the immortal are mere parallels, not indicative of complete identification. Hobbes instructs that there are indeed things the immortal God does that the Mortal God ought not to do, and here we see a somewhat diminished brutality in Hobbes's civic theodicy.

It is a violation of the law of nature to punish the innocent. In fact, Hobbes states that it is a violation of three laws of nature and of logic. He takes the last of these first. Punishment can only be for the transgression of law. The innocent man does not transgress. Therefore, the innocent can't be punished, although they can, like Job, be afflicted by the sovereign's capacity to do harm. Hobbes acknowledges that innocents may suffer by the hand of his sovereign, even where their actions may not have merited the sovereign's hostility (28.22, 5, 7, 10–11). Logically, he might have been content to tell the innocent that their suffering was merely "affliction," not punishment. He was, however, not content to resolve this problem by means of such a cruel distinction. According to Hobbes, a human sovereign who takes this logical escape route will not find grounds for escaping God's "natural punishments," whereas Hobbes's God doesn't ask our forgiveness or need to make excuses.[14]

Does the Mortal God need such forgiveness? Not from his subjects, but Hobbes was willing to give his sovereign not merely divine but concrete and terrestrial reasons for regret if he punished the innocent or allowed others under his authority to do so. Hobbes's sovereign may not need forgiveness, but he does need to exercise caution and must be mindful of how actions may contradict natural laws. All logical contradictions aside, punishing the innocent is a violation of the seventh law of nature, "which forbiddeth all men, in their revenges, to look at anything but some future good."[15] The seventh law teaches that revenge ought never to look at the "greatest of the evil past, but the greatness of the good to follow" (15.19). It is vainglory to pile on punishment without respect to the end or profit aimed at by punishment, and "to hurt without reason tendeth to the introduction of war" (15.19).

The sovereign's office is to keep peace, to punish not retributively but with an eye to creating rules that influence the prospective actions of potential offenders; it is not to foment war against his own subjects.[16] Punishing the innocent is also identified as a violation of the fourth law of nature, commanding gratitude: "All sovereign power is originally given by the consent of every one of the subjects" for the sake of their protection (28.22). Finally, punishing the innocent violates the eleventh law of nature: equity. It contradicts the principle that those who judge ought to "deal equally" between persons (15.23–24). Justice under such circumstances is not given its due "equal distribution" (33.22).

This would seem to make Hobbes's sovereign more accountable than God, who stands above both human sovereigns and subjects. Even if there is little to stop an earthly sovereign from harming his subjects, if the sovereign listens to reason, natural law tells him he shouldn't harm the innocent.[17] That said, it is not legally or practically possible for subjects to hold Hobbes's sovereign accountable. Any person or entity held accountable to a subject is not, according to Hobbes, a proper sovereign. None within the state's authority can judge a sovereign, "because it setteth the laws above the sovereign, [and] setteth also a judge above him, and a power to punish him, which is to make a new sovereign" (29.9).[18] Hobbes's subjects will have great difficulty finding either the means or the justification to enforce the laws of nature against their sovereign so long as he provides protection.

Sovereigns who harm, even kill, individual innocent subjects are guilty of iniquity—a sin against God—but have committed no injury against their subjects. Sovereigns generally have this capacity to punish because "every subject is author of every act the sovereign doth, so that he never wanteth right to anything (otherwise than as he himself is the subject of God, and bound to observe the laws of nature)" (21.7). Moreover, it is not against the law of nature for sovereigns to harm those who are not subjects; to do so is no different than harming enemies. If subjects witness him punish the innocent and thereby see their sovereign violate the laws of nature, they might wish to hold him accountable. For Hobbes, this desire is an attempt to throw off the sovereign's authority, at which point subjects cease to be subjects and become enemies. If they are enemies, then there is no limit to what the sovereign may inflict on them: "In declared hostilities, all infliction of evil is lawful. From whence it followeth, that if a subject shall, by fact or word, wittingly and deliberately deny the authority of the representative of the commonwealth, (whatsoever penalty hath been formerly ordained for treason) he may lawfully be made to suffer whatsoever the representative will" (28.13). The laws of nature may be available to both a sovereign with an army and a subject who is threatened with his life, but they strongly favor the party with an army. Only those already within the state of nature or those willing to return to it can try to hold an unwilling sovereign accountable to the laws of nature.

We have been discussing punishment, harm, and the nearly but not quite godlike powers of Hobbes's sovereign and how he might exercise them over those he afflicts. Both divine and human sovereigns will have their Jobs, but Hobbes argues that his human sovereign ought to resist these temptations of the powerful. This brings us to Hobbes's view of David.

HOBBES AND LEIBNIZ ON DAVID, THEODICY, AND THE PROSPERITY OF THE WICKED

As Hobbes quotes it, David made a complaint against God's governance of the universe: "'How good,' Saith David, 'is the God of Israel to those that are upright in heart; and yet my feet were almost gone, my treadings had well-nigh slipt; for I was grieved at the wicked, when I saw the ungodly in such prosperity.'"[19] The guilty or the unchosen seemed more fortunate than the innocent or the chosen.[20] It was almost enough to make him "slip," or lose faith. David's complaint continues: "Behold, these are the ungodly, who prosper in the world; they increase in riches. Verily I have cleansed my heart in vain, and washed my hands in innocency."[21] Questions of cosmic justice were never merely concerned with why a just God would allow the innocent to suffer.[22] There was always this other side, which would be especially disappointing to those who suspected that they had "cleansed their hearts in vain." Witnessing the wicked prosper was all the more disappointing when that same God had been counted upon to "break the teeth" of the ungodly and wicked.[23] Here I will bracket the very interesting differences between the prosperity of the wicked and David's reference to the chosen and unchosen. Prosperous David's own wickedness will be addressed last.

Now let us start the comparison with Leibniz. Both Hobbes and Leibniz preferred philosophies that discouraged rebels, although for differing reasons, and each would encourage those who cannot make sense of God's dictates to blame the flaws in their own reasoning, but the two differed on the question of how far our reason comprehends God.[24] For Leibniz, some of what God does may be beyond our comprehension, but this elusiveness does not mean that we cannot grasp with our reason that there is a pre-established harmony in God's creation. Through the principle of sufficient reason and our knowledge that God is a perfect being, we may conclude that he could not possibly have made the world any better than it is.[25] To suggest otherwise is to accept God's imperfection. Hobbes's God and his human sovereign often rule by fear;[26] Leibniz disapproved.[27] God, notes Leibniz, commands us to love Him.[28]

For Leibniz, the duty to love God inverts the logic of the old phrase used to praise a worthy person: "To know him is to love him." Leibniz argues from the understanding that "to love him is to know him." In fact, to love God is to incur a duty to know him.[29] Love is that mental state which makes us take pleasure in the perfections of the object of our love. Since there is nothing more perfect than God, there can be no greater delight than in loving him. Most important, God's perfections could and should be known by means of our own highest faculties, beginning with the acceptance that God can never disappoint reason.

Contemplating God's perfections is easy, according to Leibniz, because we find the ideas of these perfections within ourselves.[30] His God's perfections are so much "within ourselves" that this God is now said to operate in conformity with human reason. Three times three is always nine, and not even God, says Leibniz, can prevent this from being so. As Patrick Riley emphasizes, Leibniz's theodicy is an element of a "universal jurisprudence," one that not only binds men but also God himself to mankind.[31] Hobbes holds that "there be many things in God's word above reason (that is to say, which cannot by natural reason be either demonstrated or confuted), yet there is nothing contrary to it; but when it seemeth so, the fault is either in our unskillful interpretation or erroneous rationalization."[32] Whereas Hobbes will find divine leeway by insisting upon God's standing above human reason, Leibniz makes it his mission to close the gap between the seemingly irrational and reason. God and man must live under a single rational law. If God seems to do wrong, it becomes incumbent upon philosophers to show why His will is right. Although Hobbes was happy to correct philosophers and theologians that what they thought of God must be wrong or impious, he was not convinced of the need to take on this burden.

The difference between Hobbes and Leibniz on the prosperity of the wicked becomes clearer in hard cases where they have to cope with the dramatic deviation of human fate from reason. Hobbes leans heavily on God's omnipotence, and he argues that this reality must in many respects drive us into silent, unquestioning submission toward God. God's might makes right, in Hobbes's accounting, and where we cannot comprehend His word, we must swallow the "wholesome pills" of religion whole, rather than chew and "labour in sifting out a philosophical truth by logic."[33] Leibniz pursues a different course. Insisting on the immutability of certain truths, Leibniz reconciles the divergence not by committing humans to reverent silence but by committing us to ongoing inquiry into the incommensurate. Whereas Hobbes tells us to avert our scrutinizing gaze from the cruel Almighty (to swallow the pill whole, so to speak), Leibniz insists we look harder to rediscover the divinity that is due our love and devotion.

This priority on reason is why Hobbes's negative theology—his discussion of praise for God by declaring our inability to know his perfections—is rejected outright by Leibniz.[34] So too is Hobbes's doctrine of necessity.[35] He groups Hobbes with the materialists who were destroying a sense of moral duty.[36] Leibniz, unlike the less cosmic Hobbes, counsels that we should start with the assumption that the most perfect order—our world, which must be the best of all possible worlds—can and must be grasped with our reason. The world includes evil. We must, therefore, assume that this evil, including the suffering of the innocent and the prosperity of the wicked, is a part of God's larger and most rational design. It is all done with God's foresight, using these things "for his ends, since superior reasons of perfect wisdom have determined him to permit these evils" and to even "co-operate therein."[37] Wishing for a better world would require the alteration of a plan that cannot be improved upon. To ask for any such change would therefore be to insult the God we are meant to love. Yet were we to have our "improvement," it would make the world less, not more, perfect. We can see why it was Leibniz, and not the ambitious Hobbes, whose thought came to be associated with a certain conservatism that counsels the downtrodden or disadvantaged to smilingly accept the fate determined by higher powers.[38]

Only Leibniz could have won Voltaire's mockery in *Candide* with the figure of Dr. Pangloss. The doctor's descriptions of human and natural catastrophes are always part of the best of all possible worlds. Having traced the source of Pangloss's venereal disease—by which he is horribly disfigured and about to die—through several generations to a companion of Christopher Columbus, Candide offers reassurance: "Oh Pangloss, cried Candide, that's a very strange genealogy. Isn't the devil at the root of the whole thing? Not at all, replied that great man [Pangloss]; it's an indispensable part of the best of worlds, a necessary ingredient; if Columbus had not caught, on an American island, this sickness . . . we should have neither chocolate nor cochineal."[39] Here Voltaire derides Leibniz's doctrine with still worse human tragedies: "Nothing could have been so fine, so brisk, so brilliant, so well-drilled as the two armies [one of which, the Bulgars, had just impressed Candide into service]. The trumpets, the fifes, the oboes, the drums, and the cannon produced such a harmony as was never heard in hell. First the cannon battered down about six thousand men on each side; then volleys of musket fire removed from the best of worlds about nine or ten thousand rascals who were cluttering up its surface. The bayonet was a sufficient reason for the demise of several thousand others."[40]

What of those who, like David, complained of the prosperity of the wicked? Leibniz borrows from his interlocutor Bayle to make his response.[41] The rejoinder to these doubts about the justness of the universe folds the complaint into the same category as those who would relieve the suffering. Here it comes in the form of a fairly aggressive, even moralizing, inversion. Those who demand that God do better in preventing the wicked from prospering are told to consider the error they have made:

> They who are stagger'd at the prosperity of the wicked, have very little meditated on the nature of God, . . . they contract the administration of a cause which governs the universe, to the size of a providence purely subaltern; which betrays a littleness of mind. What! Wou'd they have Almighty God, . . . manifesting the wonders of his infinite wisdom, establish Laws . . . so little fix'd, that the first fit of spleen or ill humor in any one, might intirely subvert 'em to the destruction of human liberty in general? The governor of a small town must expose himself to contempt, if he chang'd his rules and orders, as often as any of the corporation [townspeople] thought fit to grumble: And shall God, whose Laws are calculated for so general a design, that perhaps what we see of the universe is only an underplot in the great action, be oblig'd to derogate from these laws, because they don't hit one Man's fancy today, and another's tomorrow; because at one time a superstitious votary, falsely imagining that a Monster presages a reverse in human affairs . . . [42]

Leibniz approved much of Bayle's answer. A deity who appears arbitrary, even by tinkering with creation to prevent the wicked from prospering, is not in conformity with human rationality or morality. He especially could not be made to deviate from the universe's regular order to remedy the moral dissatisfactions of those who were distressed by the prosperous wicked person, the successful swindler, or the world's many other villains.

Unlike Leibniz's God, Hobbes's God could always interfere when he wished to depart from the normal course of nature. So could Hobbes's sovereign:

> There are occasions when kings cannot manage affairs . . . or even when they can, they judge it more correct to content themselves with choosing ministers and counsellors, and to exercise their power through them. When right and exercise are separated, the government of the commonwealth is like the ordinary government of the world, in which God the first mover of all things, produces natural effects through the order of secondary causes. But when he who has the right to reign wishes to participate himself in all judgments, consultations and public actions, it is a way of running things comparable to God's attending directly to every thing himself, contrary to the order of nature.[43]

As regards the suffering of the innocent, subjects within a protected commonwealth lack the power to rectify the violation of the law of nature. Nevertheless, Hobbes is willing to identify a violation of the law of nature and is not as willing as Leibniz to excuse or rationalize such transgressions. There are many "inconveniences," as Hobbes puts it, that subjects must inevitably suffer—including the sovereign enriching his, her, or its favorites and flatterers—to avoid the worse alternative of a slide back into the deadly state of nature, and they must be made to recognize the prudence of avoiding this slide.[44]

Where an inconvenience might be remedied by a more just policy on the part of the Mortal God, the worshipful have greater responsibility than merely recognizing an inconvenience as part of either God's, or the human sovereign's, inherently rational master plan. Because the subjects have authorized the absolute sovereign, any inconvenience they might suffer at the hands of their sovereign should be described as part of their own less exalted but nonetheless rational plan.[45] It is not providence, but necessity that should encourage them to endure these problems. Escaping the evil of the state of nature should be their first thought when they contemplate the inconveniences of the sovereign's absolute rule:

And though of so unlimited a power men may fancy many evil consequences, yet the consequences of the want of it, which is perpetual war of every man against his neighbor, are much worse. The condition of man in this life shall never be without inconveniences; but there happened in no commonwealth any great inconvenience, but what proceeds from the subject's disobedience and breach of those covenants from which the commonwealth hath its being. And whosoever, thinking sovereign power too great, will seek to make it less, must subject himself to the power that can limit it, that is to say, to a greater.[46]

In short, Hobbes can acknowledge that the state that protects us and to which we owe our obedience may not be the best of all possible states. It must first not be the pathway to the worst of all circumstances. Unlike Dr. Pangloss, standing in for Leibniz, the Hobbesian subject experiences afflictions, shrugs his or her shoulders, and says, "Things could be worse."[47] As a philosopher, Hobbes dares to remind sovereigns—human and divine—that things could be better. The Leviathan, the artificial man, is a creature of greater "stature and strength" than the man God made.[48]

The differences in the two philosophers' cosmic theodicies can help us better grasp Hobbes's civic theodicy. Having remade the political world so as not to decline into the worst possible, Hobbes allows himself to think of improvements. We may say that, in spite of demanding obedience in exchange for the Mortal God's protection, Hobbes is less fearful of insulting his Mortal God than either he or Leibniz is of insulting the immortal one.[49] For example, one well-known improvement Hobbes proposes consists of telling his sovereign that he ought to construe the "safety" he guarantees rather broadly. Thus, the sovereign's duty to make us safe is not a concern merely for our survival but also for making good man's design "to live as pleasantly as the human condition allows [within the commonwealth]. Sovereigns therefore ought to legislate to ensure that the citizens are abundantly provided with all the good things necessary not just for life but for the enjoyment of life."[50] In addition to the positive steps that make subjects' lives more enjoyable, the sovereign ought to avoid making choices that lead to his subjects' misery.[51] Among those choices the sovereign should avoid, Hobbes includes those that enable the prosperity of the wicked.[52]

HOBBES'S ATTEMPT TO PREVENT THE PROSPERITY
OF THE WICKED

In *De Cive* (*On the Citizen*), Hobbes shows himself truly concerned with the ways in which the prosperity of bad men can undermine the political order and diminish life in a commonwealth when the sovereign is responsible for their good fortune. He writes: "It is sometimes good for the safety of the majority that bad men should do badly."[53] Fervently resistant to the discourses that taught persons to distinguish between good kings and tyrants, Hobbes will not allow himself (as, say, Erasmus did) to paint a picture of a tyrant who can only succeed in his malevolent designs with the help of wicked men.[54] And yet, Hobbes fears allowing some men of privilege to remain immune from due punishment.[55]

First of all, the prosperity of the wicked undermines the general belief in an obligation to follow the laws of the state. The problem is not that wickedness is a condition of prosperity (although it might very well be), but rather that prosperity or good fortune tempts the accomplished or merely arrogant persons to think themselves, like the sovereign, above the law. These thoughts and the actions that follow from them beget further bad consequences. They are among the defects and errors in persons' understanding of natural laws, as Hobbes describes it in *Leviathan*, that lead men to violate the laws of a commonwealth (*Lev.*, 28.4).

One of the first "false principles" that qualifies as a defect is that which men derive from having "observed how, in all victories of those who have committed them, and those potent men, breaking through the cobweb laws of their country, the weaker sort, and those that have failed in their enterprises, have been esteemed the only criminals" (28.10). That is, when persons see that potent men are permitted crimes and when they see that it is only the weak and the unsuccessful who are labeled criminals, they come to a false conclusion. They judge that "justice is but a word, that whatsoever a man can get by his own industry, and hazard is his own" (28.10). Witnessing powerful persons acting with impunity begets a poisonous cynicism. The conclusion to be drawn is that "no act in itself can be a crime, but must be made so by the success of them that commit it, and the same fact be virtuous or vicious as fortune pleaseth" (28.10).[56] Sovereign impunity is required, but "potent men" within the state are meant to live within the laws the sovereign enforces and should not, Hobbes cautions, be permitted to break them.

Hobbes's assault on vainglory within the commonwealth, particularly on that of wealthy men, has been marked before. For Leo Strauss or Keith Thomas, his assaults on pride and his quest for a "King of the children of pride" became fodder for a debate over Hobbes's sympathy with either bourgeois or aristocratic values.[57] These assaults also fall easily under the umbrella of Hobbes's general concerns with "human nature." The actions motivated by vainglory tend to exacerbate the dangers of the state of nature by violating the laws of nature, particularly their injunctions against contumely, pride, and arrogance (13.4–7; 15.19; 15.20–22). We can discern more of Hobbes's fear of the prosperous wicked, and expectations of impunity among the great, if descended from high abstractions, be they Hobbes's own laws of nature or grand narratives of class conflict. Hobbes dwells upon and details the particularly troubling effects of vainglorious strivings inside the established commonwealth.

In such a state, where uniform standards of good and evil are determined by the sovereign, the question becomes what to do when the vainglorious or great person expects prosperity or legal immunity. Hobbes warns the vainglorious "that to be neglected and unpreferred by the public favour is not a punishment." He also declares that "benefits which a sovereign bestoweth on a subject for fear of some power and ability he hath to do hurt to the commonwealth are not properly rewards . . . nor graces, because they are extorted by fear" (28.4, 25). Sovereigns who fail to attend to these challenges face danger. Whatever Hobbes's class affiliations, he holds that vainglory based on a "foolish overrating of [one's] own worth" endangers the peace of the commonwealth (27.13). The Mortal God may not be answerable to subjects and may even answer, like God, "from power." Where the privilege of answering from power or good fortune are felt to be bestowed by God himself on "the great" and seen therefore to grant these "great" subjects a similar immunity from the Mortal God's laws, special scrutiny is required.

The vainglory of those whose "wit, riches, blood, or some other natural quality, not depending on the will of those that have the sovereign authority" leads to the presumption "that the punishments ordained by the laws, and extended generally to all subjects, ought not to be inflicted on them with the same rigour they are inflicted on the poor, obscure, and simple men, comprehended under the name of the vulgar" (27.13). Thus, the wealthy hope to escape punishment by "corrupting public justice or obtaining pardon by money or other rewards" (27.14). In a period when so many individuals, including the poor, were granted forms of leniency for their legal transgressions, Hobbes's focus on "the great" and their expectation to escape legal punishment is all the more noteworthy.[58]

Hobbes also observes that men who have "gained a reputation amongst the multitude take courage to violate the laws from the hope of oppressing the power to whom it belongeth to put them in execution" (27.15). Those with an exaggerated false opinion of their wisdom "unsettle the law" with their presumption that "nothing shall be a crime but what their own designs require should be so." The misconstrual leads to the belief that they can outsmart the authorities in criminal acts or reap the benefits of starting a rebellion (27.16). The (1668) Latin *Leviathan*'s equivalent passages concentrate these lessons into a general conclusion on the dangers of allowing the "hope of impunity" to take hold among subjects.[59]

This logic carries over into some of Hobbes's discussions of circumstances that excuse or extenuate crimes and those that aggravate them. The presumption of impunity by force, especially if it flows from "presumption of strength, riches, or friends," must be counted a greater crime than the desire to flee and conceal one's crimes. Such presumption "is a root from whence springeth, at all times and upon all temptations a contempt of all laws" and so ought to be much more harshly punished (27.30). On the other hand, if the sovereign himself is responsible for lax enforcement of his laws, the blame, as we noted in the last chapter, falls partially to him. "Precedent examples of impunity given by the sovereign himself . . . furnishes a man with such a hope and presumption of mercy as encourageth him to offend" (27.32).

In "Of the Office of the Sovereign Representative," Hobbes returns to the question of the administration of justice and how an indulgent maladministration that favors the "great" threatens the peace of the commonwealth. "The safety of the people," writes Hobbes, "requireth . . . from him or them that have the sovereign power, that justice be equally administered to all degrees of people, that is, that as well the rich and mighty as poor and obscure persons may be righted of the injuries done them." This is "so as the great may have no greater hope of impunity when they do violence, dishonour, or any injury to the meaner sort, than when one of these does the like to one of them. For in this consisteth equity, to which, as being a precept of the law of nature, a sovereign is as much subject as any of the meanest of his people" (*Lev.*, 30.15).

That is, when judging or performing the role of arbiter between subjects, the sovereign must not show partiality toward the "great" and against the "meanest."[60] Where there is inequality between subjects, Hobbes writes, it must "proceedeth from the acts of sovereign power." It follows also that when subjects, great or mean, privileged or otherwise, stand before the sovereign "in a court of justice," their inequalities are erased. They have "no more place in the presence of the sovereign . . . than the inequality between kings and their subjects, in the presence of the King of kings" (30.16).

In referring to the inequalities granted between men by sovereigns, Hobbes has in mind the honors given and offices assigned to men. Regarding these and the greatness persons achieve by them, Hobbes writes, "The honour of great persons is to be valued for their beneficence and the aids they give to men of inferior rank, or not at all" (30.16). Hobbes's sovereign is to be valued for the protection he provides, and his beneficence or aid must be of secondary importance.

Nonetheless, Hobbes here seems to have a morally more demanding set of virtues (some of which are traditionally aristocratic) against which to measure the worth of the great. What of pardons? Wrongs done to the commonwealth only may be pardoned "without breach of equity," Hobbes asserts (30.15). However, in a reiteration of Common Law doctrine, "an offense against a private man cannot in equity be pardoned without the consent of him that is injured, or reasonable satisfaction" (30.15). Therefore, it is particularly egregious when great men—especially those made great by the sovereign—injure fellow subjects: "And the violences, oppressions, and injuries they do are not extenuated, but aggravated by the greatness of their persons, because they have least need to commit them. The consequences of this partiality towards the great proceed in this manner" (30.16). This unleashes a cascade of negative consequences. It makes the persons who witness the impunity resentful of the favored individuals but also desirous to "pull down all oppressing and contumelious greatness." Here Hobbes moves from the belief in impunity begotten by impunity for the great to the direct damage done when the great enjoy impunity: their belief in their own impunity grows. They become even contemptuous of the law and authority they ought to obey. Other great men and perhaps even the sovereign himself become to them an "oppressing and contumelious greatness." Such conflicts—either great man versus great man or great man versus sovereign—are the ruin of the commonwealth (cf. 22.31, 33–34).

Hobbes repeats the lesson in the Latin *Leviathan*, wherein breaches against the commonwealth are dubbed "crimes against the sovereign." This text from 1668 lists additional, more democratic, reasons and warnings against allowing the great to harm the common people. The sovereign ought neither to allow the great to oppress the people nor to do so himself on the counsel of the great. The people, he notably declares, are the greatest power of them all, a fact that should be on the minds of "great" individuals who conclude that their greatness is due honor. Deploying a rhetorical inversion of the great's prideful prejudices, Hobbes warns that the people's greatness renders any reproach for someone's humble station both dangerous and inequitable. Even if a sovereign may reasonably castigate a person of ill repute for being "base," the error of castigating the people as a whole ought to be avoided. Hobbes then cites the example of the Beggars' Revolt of 1566 in Holland as a cautionary tale of the dangers of showing "scorn [to] citizens of modest means."[61] This last contribution to Hobbes's civic theodicy is striking. Not only does he declare that the sovereign should prevent the great from insulting the people, but also that the sovereign should refrain from becoming haughty or adopting "an uncivil superiority."[62] When the Mortal God allows the wicked to prosper, Hobbes cautions, he risks losing the faith of his subjects.

HOBBES'S DIFFICULTIES WITH PERMITTED WICKEDNESS: FROM PECUNIARY PUNISHMENT TO DAVID

There are two important moments when Hobbes betrays the difficulty of staying to the narrow path between maintaining sovereign prerogatives and sustaining the subject's faith in the justness of the sovereign's rule. Even as Hobbes boasted of setting a new and more solid foundation for sovereignty, these implicit and explicit tensions reveal his preoccupation with the fragility of a sovereignty that may overindulge subjects with its friendly prerogatives.

The first moment arises in Hobbes's discussion of the commonwealth's "pecuniary punishments." Already an old practice among governments, these were mild as compared with corporal or capital punishment or imprisonment.[63] Some prescribed punishments are so weak, Hobbes observes, that their effect is diametrically opposed to punishment's real purpose. They do not outweigh the benefit of the crime and thereby encourage law breaking (*Lev.*, 28.9). Laws—or any punishment, presumably—that do not exceed the benefits of the criminal act systematically create circumstances wherein the wicked are permitted to prosper.[64] The very instrument that proposes to keep good order within the state becomes a concealed mechanism for the selective immunity of the few from that order.

Hobbes's approach to these flaws in sovereign administration express a certain anxiety. He is blunt in describing the actual purpose of pecuniary punishments, which are "made with design to gather money from such as shall transgress the same." They are "not properly a punishment, but the price of privilege and exemption from the law" (28.18). Therefore, such laws do not "absolutely forbid the fact," that is, the transgression. Only "those that are not able to pay the money" are punished (28.18). These are not, Hobbes determines, good laws. By his criterion for differentiating good and necessary laws, some of the pecuniary laws may seem to qualify as neither. The authorized actions of a sovereign, says Hobbes, are owned by all members of the state, but these laws cannot be "owned by everyone," nor will "no man say it is unjust" (30.20).[65] Yet the problem goes even deeper than the tendency of such laws to encourage the well-resourced to disregard the law.

Hobbes illustrates his concern when he injects a theoretical distinction into his scrutiny of the different forms of pecuniary laws. The laws that exact payments for violations of the laws of either nature or religion are not like the others, he says, because they are not setting a price on the privilege of exemption. They are, instead, real punishments. Were their status as punishments in question, Hobbes would be forced to acknowledge a contradiction of his stricture that disallows exemptions from either natural or religious laws (28.18). A sovereign's leniency in policing the nation's laws against those who would not conform to the state's regulation of religion did not wish, Hobbes recognized, to lend its approval to nonconformity at any price.

Hobbes was not objecting to pecuniary laws that were sufficient deterrents to bad conduct. Some pecuniary laws, however, were written with the mere intent of raising money or, like some bad laws, are mere "traps for money." Especially during Charles I's personal rule, the patent monopolies granted to corporations incentivized the creation of patent-holding companies in established trades that were able to exploit the supervisory roles granted them in their monopolies to destroy other produces or compel them to pay into the corporation. This inspired both royal reversals of some patents but also some particularly impassioned accusations against the monopolists in the Short and Long Parliaments.[66] In these laws is an opening to something more pernicious (*Lev.*, 30.21). What is to stop a sovereign from incorporating pecuniary punishments into his laws so that the well-off pay a large fine while the rest face harsher punishments? What if a class of very damaging yet lucrative crimes committed by the powerful are not truly punished but answered instead with mere pecuniary sanctions that do not annul the benefits of the crimes? The corrupt sovereign's facility with bad law making converts the state into a revenue machine fueled by the transgressions of the guilty.

Hobbes shows an acute awareness that exemptive laws and dictates fail to serve the public good and may cause subjects to lose faith in their Mortal God.[67] Mere money-trap laws, if they substitute for laws that might have prevented pervasive or substantial public harms, stand in tension with the basic justification in Hobbes's philosophy for fleeing the state of nature. Persons contract with others to form a commonwealth to ensure that all are subject to the same law and are protected from one another (14.5). Insofar as a law created by a sovereign with a selective friendly intent and designed to protect persons from harm is converted into a money trap, the protection it would have offered is abjured or at least significantly abated by the sovereign.[68]

The powerful may harm those who will be held to the law because they lack the means to buy their escape. The rather awkward assertion that Hobbes appends—that unlike other laws, the ones that assess fines to keep the laws of nature or religion are indeed true punishments—does not inspire confidence. An exemption for a price, regardless of whether it was called punishment, permitted some where others were forbidden. Moreover, the other laws, located outside the realm of the nature or religion, form a category that stands in tension with Hobbes's notion that civil laws contain the natural laws. Obedience to civil law in and of itself, says Hobbes, is obedience to natural law. Presumably, disobedience carries the same transitive quality (26.8).

The second moment when Hobbes shows a preoccupation with the fragility of the sovereign concerns David. Returning to the asymmetry in Hobbes's use of Job and David, one may observe that Job is perfectly innocent, while David merely professes his innocence. Whereas Job suffers despite his innocence because God may afflict by right of power alone, David, maintaining that he is "godly," complains when he sees the wicked prosper. Yet David, as Hobbes's contemporaries would have known and as Bayle was for a time delighted to illustrate, was a champion sinner.[69]

David operated as a ruthless and rapacious warlord within the kingdom of the Philistines, where he had sought and gained shelter from Saul. Achish, the king of Gath's son, gave David and his six hundred loyalists shelter in a region known as Ziklag. From there they went on raiding parties within the kingdom against the region's subgroups. To save himself from being detected, he left no survivors, then lied about these acts. He told Achish that he had been making invasions against his fellow Jews.[70] David's adultery with Bathsheba, the wife of Uriah, also loomed large. She became pregnant, and this endangered David's status. The unsuspecting Uriah proved unwilling to be with his wife at David's suggestion (David had hoped to reassign responsibility for the pregnancy). Requiring a different solution, David used his commanders to send Uriah to die in the front lines of a battle.[71]

As regards the theodicy problem, David was nearly diametric to Job. Job was innocent and God made him suffer; David was wicked and God made him prosper. In spite of singing the Psalm wherein the fool is denounced, David was himself a fool—and a very successful one. He broke some of his covenants, and he seems to have suffered little as a consequence. In fact, God made him a sovereign, a Mortal God.[72]

Hobbes notes David's murder of Uriah and uses it as an example of an act of iniquity that is not an injury to a subject who authorizes his sovereign (i.e., Uriah) (21.7).[73] Hobbes is anxious to note that David did not go so far as to kill Saul, adhering to God's will that the kings of His people not be killed.[74] Nevertheless, David's record, and what we can (speculatively) call Hobbes's unwillingness to show us the full inversion of Job in David's divine good fortune, are noteworthy.

The omission may be a sign of something Hobbes wishes to repress, because it poses an ongoing problem for his political philosophy: How does a legally immune sovereign, who may answer his subjects with his power rather than with reasons or legal justifications, demand of his subjects that they live by the law? Necessity dictates their submission to an unrivaled and unrestrainable power for the sake of their protection. Nevertheless, within a state founded upon the sovereign's unrivaled and unrestrainable power, it will sometimes be a challenge for subjects to submit to the law rather than follow the sovereign's example. Especially in a system that begins by positing natural human equality, such disconnects would haunt and even threaten to destabilize the civil tranquility Hobbes aimed to achieve. If the sovereign himself decides to indulge his impunity so as to highlight the gap between what he may do or permits some subjects to do what many, or all others, are forbidden from doing, Hobbes appears to believe that there is reason to worry.

In sum, I've argued that among our three thinkers, Hobbes remains the most ambivalent regarding friendly sovereign prerogatives. Over these two chapters I've made the argument that these were always a part of the free range of actions that Hobbes protected among his sovereign's power to make exceptions, and that Schmitt's understanding of "the exception"— a story of hostility and crisis powers—and his claim to find in Hobbes a "decisionist" concept of sovereignty is particularly misleading for the way that it invites us to imagine a very different understanding of the exercise of the law's restraints on subjects in Hobbes's century. Here, I've highlighted the ambivalence by contrasting Hobbes with Leibniz. The latter excuses the prosperity of the wicked as a part of the best of all possible worlds. For Hobbes, it was very unwise to transfer something like that same complacency into a defense of the earthly rule of mortal gods, or to expect the same resignation Leibniz encouraged among those compelled to suffer as the wicked prospered. It jeopardized the sovereign's support among subjects and created inconveniences that even he had a difficult time accepting.

CHAPTER 6

SENECA'S FRIENDLY SOVEREIGN

Seneca is not the only thinker before the emergence of modern states who can inform a more complete understanding of friendly sovereignty, but he is worthy of (and even overdue) our attention for being a particularly apt source in this domain. His style, his talent for *sententiae*, makes it possible to highlight my interests in single phrases. Of the three works considered at length here, Seneca's *De Clementia* is the only one that makes an unqualified case for a friendly sovereign. Hobbes feared the way friendly legal exceptions might alienate subjects. Seneca, by contrast, advocates for the sovereign's use of such exceptions. He declares that this aspect of extralegal power is perfectly aligned with the virtues both required in leaders and beloved by subjects. Citizens who know and recognize their obligations, he asserts, will be appropriately thankful for a sovereign who uses his extraordinary powers in the name of a clement and merciful administration of justice.

My choice of Seneca, however, may occasion two questions. Why, when sovereignty has been so closely connected to the modern state, undertake to explore it in ancient contexts prior to the periods in which modern statehood emerged? Secondly, why, among the ancients, choose to focus on Seneca? Those already convinced of the separability of sovereignty from the modern state form, or merely interested in Seneca's friendly sovereign, may wish to skip the next section.

UNRAVELING SOVEREIGNTY AND THE STATE

The early modern thinkers closely associated with the emergence of a theory of state sovereignty, including Hobbes and Jean Bodin, wrote of "the sovereign" as an office.[1] It was a role, and powers and responsibilities were attached to it. "Sovereign," conceived as an office, was a concept informed by an expectation that occupants of the office should have both powers and responsibilities and might be judged in terms of their exercise of this authority. Hobbes's and Bodin's senses of the office necessarily preceded the modern state form. The capacity to fulfill the powers and responsibilities became critical to what made a state a *state*.

Theirs was also a learned response to a reality that was not tidy. States in their complete form did not emerge suddenly. They did not blossom spontaneously to be either typed or defended by political philosophers *ex post*. The communities they addressed and considered were collections of ambiguous, frequently competing authorities, heterogeneously and often tenuously gathered, if not consolidated. This took place amid a complex blend of confessional, institutional, and territorial conflicts. Hobbes and Bodin defended and contemplated the factors that might foster that consolidation, and what they described, including sovereignty itself, was not *sui generis*. Those who held or claimed to hold sovereign power over the things we call states were themselves contending with competing jurisdictions and the claims of more local or global centers of authority. The modern state's sovereignty might have, with Hobbes's state of nature, imagined spontaneous origins out of nature, but the concept of sovereignty itself was anything but novel.

A vision of a state governed by a sovereign power was in many respects an extension of familiar and even ancient forms, over against their local and jurisdictional instantiations in quest of consolidation. The residue of these older, more particular forms of supremacy struggle with our tidy, analytic visions of power that can claim sovereignty. These older forms achieved uneven degrees of centralization during the sixteenth and early seventeenth centuries, such that even a monarch's "absolute prerogatives," as noted in chapter 4, might not necessarily conform to all that either we or Hobbes might find satisfactory. The "archaic" forms of state sovereignty always lacked this tidiness.

Against the background of this complex jumble, "the sovereign" was, for many, the one meant to impose a just order and to have the last word over a territorial domain. This concept of "sovereignty" has hardened and grown alongside what were increasingly consolidated state forms. The association between the two, especially within the symbolism of the state, has been etched into the collective consciousness. Thus, for a time, when persons wrote of the so-called end of sovereignty, they were referencing the end of states.[2] Although Hobbes himself was not guilty of this conceptual error, sovereignty has for many become inherently tethered to it: the sovereign defended the state, policed its borders, coined money, kept its peace and justice, regulated religion, and demanded these things by right and to the exclusion of rival authorities.

Even Hobbes, who was so anxious to defend and define the sovereign power within the state he describes in his works, would not have been likely to agree with thinkers who simply fuse the concept of sovereignty to the modern state's autonomous rule. He and his contemporaries were aware that before there could be sovereign states and territories, there were sovereigns over other things. God was sovereign over the universe, local and regional lords over their fiefdoms and specific domains. The pope, and in some nations bishops, claimed sovereignty over spiritual affairs. In Hobbes's conception of the state of nature, individuals were sovereign over their untethered and endangered selves. Those who, in the contemporary imagination, helped solidify the automatic connection between sovereignty and state sovereignty did not—indeed they could not—think that they were inventing "sovereignty" itself.

They were instead articulating what they thought sovereignty, this much older concept, *had to mean* in light of the new realities in Europe at the time and as it might attach itself to states' claims to being independent of other forces. If subjects were going to live under a lasting and legitimate authority, sovereignty would have to fulfill certain functions, they argued, and become the last word where the cacophony of competing authorities had grown intolerable. Thus, like Bodin, they borrowed from early concepts of command, domination, authority, and jurisdiction. Bodin announces that he is looking specifically to explore the "marks" of sovereignty, an inherently retrospective and roughly empirical enterprise.

Intellectual historians have linked modernity, including the modernity that informed the political philosophy of the modern state, with spontaneity: a wish to dispense with the past and start afresh. But in Bodin's case, the sovereign's defender does not speak the language of, nor does it aspire to, spontaneity. His work was a quest to discern the underlying order revealed in political and social relations. Hobbes was by nature anxious to announce the originality of his intellectual contributions, and his sovereign state begins conceptually with having imagined away past institutions. He would construct anew, upon a new foundation and a clean slate. When referencing the freshness of his Mortal God, however, even he illustrates a debt to a humanist past wherein imitations of God, including a God that creates, were already a familiar trope for measuring human accomplishment.[3] We take nothing away from Hobbes's jealous preoccupation with guarding the power of his sovereign if we acknowledge that his concept of sovereignty, like all others, had antecedents. In turning to Seneca's *De Clementia*, we consider one of the antecedents that encouraged the powerful to become friendly sovereigns.

SENECA, NERO, AND THE CLEMENT *PRINCEPS*

Generosity and magnanimity were particular topics of concern among Greek and Roman sources who dwelt upon the friendly aspects of sovereign prerogatives. Xenophon, for example, lavishes praise upon Cyrus for his artful use of princely generosity. His discussion of Cyrus's generosity reads as a how-to in building a circle of loyal dependents.[4] It shows Xenophon's keen eye for the means of subordination through generosity, as well as the gap between his perspective and that of more egalitarian philosophies. He writes of Cyrus, for example:

> He used to send such presents around to those also whose services on garrison duty or in attendance upon him or in any other way met with his approval; in this way he let them see that he did not fail to observe their wish to please him.
>
> He used also to honour with presents from his table any one of his servants whom he took occasion to commend; and he had all of his servants' food served from his own table, for he thought that this would implant in them a certain amount of good-will,

just as it does in dogs. And if he wished to have any one of his friends courted by the multitude, to such a one he would send presents from his table. And that device proved effective; for even to this day everybody pays more diligent court to those to whom they see things sent from the royal table; for they think that such persons must be in high favour and in a position to secure for them anything they may want.[5]

Cicero, notably, covers topics of generosity and mercy in *De officiis*, the *Second Philippic* (and somewhat more desperately in his pleas for clemency from Julius Caesar), *Pro Marcello*, *Pro Ligario*, and *Pro Rege Deiotaro*. His early declamation in the Senate trial against Verres is a study in the denunciation of ostentatious corruption of those privileged by position, bribery, as well as the senatorial class's preference for their own.[6] Aristotle discusses magnificence in the *Nicomachean Ethics*.[7]

Needless to say, an inquiry into friendly sovereignty's early emergence in political thought cannot end with Seneca. I have argued, in the introduction, that sovereignty is manifest in far too many forms to offer a definitive picture of all of sovereignty's aspects. This caution applies equally to sovereignty concepts developed before the birth of modern states. I will not attempt, therefore, to argue that the next step of this exploration of friendly sovereignty could have *only* been in the direction of Seneca. I wish merely to show that Seneca is worthy of our attention on this score. Fellow political theorists more accustomed to the consideration of ancients who have received our field's usual attentions will find something instructive in the consideration of his circumstances and the way that he came to be one of the foremost proponents of a friendly sovereign's prerogative.

Seneca's *sententiae* allow me to highlight in a single phrase why I've selected him for this corrective to Schmittian understandings of sovereignty. The ability to kill outside the law is the hallmark of Schmitt's sovereign. It is the *raison d'être* of "the exception." As regards the extralegal power of his sovereign, Seneca took a rather different view. In *De Clementia*, Seneca told Nero that killing outside the law was not the basis upon which a person in his position could distinguish themselves. In this text Seneca asks Nero to consider that this distinction was, however, available to the person who saved the life of the condemned, contrary to law and/or their sentence: "occidere contra legem nemo non potest, seruare nemo praeter me" (Anyone can break the law by taking a life, but only I can do so by saving one).[8] Here, Seneca is instructing Nero to say to himself that killing outside the law is not the unique mark of an emperor. The extralegal capacity for mercy, however, is such a mark.

De Clementia is counted among the most influential of ancient mirrors for a prince, a work of advice built upon a conceit.[9] The words I've quoted were intended to function as if they were Nero's own observations. In this text, Seneca contrives a mirror that speaks to Nero. In taking on the task of writing about clemency, Seneca tells Nero, "I can act as a kind of mirror and give you a picture of yourself as someone who will attain the greatest pleasure of all."[10] Seneca very often uses his words to be, as it were, the speaking image of Nero's ideal self, the ideal sovereign, that Seneca hoped Nero would become. It was a goad, a technique to encourage Nero to answer to, to be, the wise and moral self that Seneca "finds" in the reflection.[11] These observations of Nero's virtuous image were directed back to the living emperor's eyes from the page to guide him in thinking through the responsibility he had taken on and the reputation he should desire to make and sustain.

De Clementia appears to have been completed after Nero's eighteenth birthday, on December 15, AD 55, and before his nineteenth. It therefore falls within the period of Nero's rule classed among the good, "golden" years of his reign, sometimes identified as the quinquennium.[12] In this period, Seneca and his ally, the prefect of the Praetorian guard, Burrus, had maximal influence over the young emperor. Ancient historians such as Tacitus suggest that he and Burrus knew they could only hold Nero's vicious nature at bay for so many years.[13]

ON MERCIFUL READINGS OF SENECA ON MERCY

Scholars who study Seneca's relationship with Nero walk a tightrope. The emperor's infamy, his legendary cruelty—including that which he showed to Seneca—always threatens to overwhelm other observations of Nero's rule. The ancient historians upon whom we rely for so much of our information wrote, like Tacitus, well after the events that brought the tyrant down. If the worst elements of Nero's reign color one's understanding of Seneca's influence on the young emperor, the charity necessary to discover or sympathize with Seneca's good intentions may be lost. The worst elements can also blind one to the high hopes that many Romans shared at the start of Nero's rule. A teleological prejudice might declare that Seneca's efforts were doomed from the start and convict him, as some did, of involving himself with Nero's criminal mother, Agrippina.

On the other hand, Seneca's contemporaries knew that Stoicism, Seneca's philosophy, was intended as a guide to living out one's fate. On his own terms, Seneca might be judged *ex post* as unfortunate. He and Nero were brought together. As a mirror for a prince, *De Clementia* was designed to make the less than perfect young emperor strive to become the more perfect prince that, Seneca declares, the gods had chosen to rule the world. This subtle text need not criticize Nero outwardly to contrast what he was with what he should be. He was already everything he should be, Seneca states. Yet the text also confesses the falsity of this praise through its very form. It makes clear that there would be times when Nero would notice the difference between his best and lesser self. *De Clementia* encourages him to see the difference between the self that does not wish to live up to the virtuous standards and responsibilities of his office and the self he "truly is," that is, the most virtuous prince.

This gap, of course, existed and was yawning. Would a perfect prince require a mirror in which to measure himself against a higher standard? Because there was a gap between what Nero was and what he ought to have been, we have to see *De Clementia* in two lights at once. The prospect of closing this gap—of making Nero the prince he ought to be—bespeaks some of the optimism that Seneca's contemporaries, and perhaps even Seneca himself, felt at the start of his rule. On the other hand, an odor of desperation accompanies some of Seneca's outward optimism and his praise for his master's virtues. Contrary to the uses some political and legal theorists find in it, *De Clementia* is not merely a work that praises mercy in the abstract. It is a political text written for a deeply flawed young emperor by an adviser whose republican hopes for just rule had long since faded.[14] The next chapter will demonstrate that persons reading Seneca's mirror would have turned to it for lessons in how to praise their Caesar. Many would have wanted to praise Nero in conformity with his particular wishes for praise. Such is servitude.[15] *De Clementia* may speak to the hopes of Seneca and Romans generally or indeed to Nero's own hopes for himself as a work in progress, but we cannot ignore the contexts. They suggest that these hopes were unlikely to be achieved. Then, as now, those near to a power they themselves are largely powerless to stop are inclined to dress the office-holder who controls their fate in a costume of virtue. They sometimes hope that the virtuous appearance will penetrate from the garment to the wearer, inducing more praise, even when it is least deserved.

MERCY AND UNEXCEPTIONAL EXTRALEGAL KILLING

Seneca is best known for the death he gladly accepted to escape Nero's reign. Ironically, he made the flattering reflection of Nero's better, virtuous self— the prince as Seneca wished to see him manifest—to remind Nero that only he, as king, could spare a life contrary to law or Rome's juridical institutions. Few knew the truth of this exceptional privilege better than the author of *De Clementia*, written roughly twelve years before the king ordered his suicide. What for us is an inversion of Schmittian sovereign exceptionalism was for Seneca a reflection of circumstances he knew firsthand. Killing outside the law was no longer a matter of distinction in Seneca's courtly surrounds;[16] saving a life, including the legally condemned, had become an established pathway toward winning praise from the highest power.[17]

For the purposes of understanding Seneca's thinking on clemency, he should also be known for his near-death experiences. Before Nero ordered his suicide on June 9, AD 68, the philosopher, poet, and courtly adviser had already experienced at least two imperial death sentences firsthand in prior regimes. The first occurred after his talents as a speaker offended Gaius' (Caligula's) vanity. According to Cassius Dio, Seneca had the temerity to demonstrate his substantial skills as an orator in the Senate on a day when Caligula was in attendance. The emperor believed his own skills in oratory unsurpassed; Seneca's evident talent was an affront, and it probably wounded the emperor's pride. Seneca was said to have escaped execution because one of his admirers convinced the emperor of a falsehood: that Seneca was gravely ill and would die from consumption.[18]

Seneca's second unrealized execution began when he was sentenced to death by the Senate in the year 41. Claudius's imperial palace charged him for adultery with Julia Livilla, an offense he likely did not commit. Julia was one of the siblings born to Germanicus, who included Caligula and Agrippina Nero's mother. Claudius's wife, Messalina, harbored animosity toward Julia, whose good looks were said to make Messalina jealous while threatening to gain her access to the notoriously pliable Claudius. Seneca had a reputation for being charming. It appears he was an opportunistic choice for the schemes of Julia's accusers, and he was caught up in a court intrigue much larger than himself. For her alleged transgression, she was exiled and later ordered to die. She chose death by starvation.[19]

Claudius exercised a more deliberate clemency on Seneca than Caligula, likely owing to Agrippina's intervention. Using the discretion afforded him as emperor, Claudius reversed and revised the Senate's sentence from death to mere exile on Corsica.[20] There Seneca wrote the *Consolation to Polybius* (Polybius was Claudius's freedman). It was a transparent work of praise for Claudius and a plea for the emperor's permission to return to Rome. It did not produce the desired result.

Agrippina's use for Seneca instead precipitated his return in 49. She brought him back to become tutor to her son, Lucius Domitius Ahenobarbus, the future Nero. Agrippina had convinced Claudius to make her son his heir following Messalina's downfall.[21] With this mission accomplished and not wanting to risk reversal, Agrippina poisoned Claudius five years later.[22] Nero became emperor, with Seneca his adviser, speechwriter, and *amici principis* (friend of the prince). Although unofficial, this title gave him extraordinary access to power. It also bound him by duty to attend to the emperor at his palace and in his travels.[23] While in service to Nero, Seneca became immensely wealthy. An accuser, Publius Suillius Rufus, set upon by the enemies he had earned under Claudius, put Seneca's fortune at three hundred million sesterces.[24] His fortune was so great that his detractors questioned his attachment to the austerity normally associated with Stoicism. After the murder of Burrus, Seneca's Praetorian ally in the palace, court rivals whispered in Nero's ear that Seneca's magnificent residence and generosity to citizens were part of the philosopher's design to outshine and diminish Nero's authority.[25]

Seneca wrote *De Clementia* sometime between the end of 55 and 56, not long after Nero became emperor and well before he sentenced Seneca to death.[26] The tract, together with speeches written for the young emperor, was part of a larger effort to link Nero with virtue in the minds of his subjects. Again, it was an attempt as well to cultivate actual virtue in the young man himself. In this rhetorically sophisticated text, Seneca invites Nero to contemplate the unique satisfactions of being sovereign absolute ruler of Rome and indeed the entire world.

In *De Clementia*, mercy is sometimes defined in the abstract as a virtue that everyone should cultivate and from which everyone can benefit: "None of all the virtues suits a human being more, since no virtue is more humane" (1.2.2). Whoever remits deserved punishment *is* clement. It is a virtue many might exercise when they have a right to say that they have been wronged or injured. On the other hand, Seneca makes it quite clear that clemency's greatest and most magnificent exercise is performed by the powerful, none more so than that performed by the most powerful man in the world, the emperor Nero himself: "Yet there is no one in the world that clemency suits more than a king or an emperor" (1.3.3). It is this politicized kingly context that defines clemency in Seneca's account, notes Susan Braund. Clemency here is, first and foremost, the privilege of the *princeps* and a function of his sovereignty over Rome and his insuperable politico-juridical authority.[27] From its very start, the book of special ventriloquism invites Nero to hear the regal better self:

> Have I of all mortals proved good enough and been chosen to act as the gods' representative on earth? I make decisions of life and death for the world. The prosperity and condition of each individual rests in my hands. Fortune announces through my mouth her intended gifts to each human being. Peoples and cities find reasons for delight in my pronouncements. No region on earth flourishes without my will or favour. These myriads of swords now restrained by my peace will be drawn with a nod from me. I have the power to decide which nations shall be annihilated and which relocated, which granted liberty and which deprived of it, which kings should become slaves and whose heads should be crowned with royal glory, which cities shall fall and which cities shall rise. (1.2.1–2)

As Peter Stacey has argued, these passages describe a vision of sovereignty that long outlasted Seneca and Nero.[28] No man can grant greater favors; no man can do worse harms. Seneca undertakes in this work to make the narcissism of Roman imperial sovereignty serve the end of making kingly clemency an ornament that no prince could wish to do without. Although Seneca also demonstrates an interest in the pragmatic advantages of clemency for princes,[29] the work is clearly also designed to make megalomania learn to love itself as a virtuous presence and most of all as a kind-hearted, forgiving father to his children, that is, the Romans.[30] Seneca instructs Nero to prefer this self-love to the coarser vanity of an unstoppable or vengeful beast, flexing its muscles in a different mirror.

Seneca amplified this contrast, emphasizing the difference between the virtues and vices of the petty and the great. For example, he observes that "the harm that brutality in a private context can do is so tiny! But the feroc-ity of emperors is war" (1.5.2). He writes, "Clemency will make any house it enters happy and calm. But in a palace its rarity will make it more amaz-ing." We learn, in the text just prior to our original quote, that princely clemency is *mirabilior*, which could also be translated as "extraordinary," "strange," and "singular" because nothing is more remarkable (*memora-bilis*) than this: "that the person who has an anger that meets no obstacle, who can pass a rather severe sentence that even its victims themselves assent to, whom no one will appeal to or even plead with if he is especially fiercely incensed, should take hold of himself and deploy his power for better and more peaceful ends" (1.5.4). Between the great harms and the great favors, says Seneca, the hostile prerogatives of the king's office are the lower and less dignified of the prince's two exceptional extralegal capacities. Nero should emulate Tarius, a father who caught his son plotting his murder; rather than killing his son, Tarius merely condemned him to a sumptuous exile. He won universal admiration as a result, Seneca says. By contrast, Nero should not follow the example of the knight Tricho, who, like Julius Caesar, was stabbed by the populace in the Forum after flogging his own son to death (1.15.1–2).

Nero of course had greater latitude in killing whom he pleased than Tricho, but return to the phrase quoted earlier that so perfectly inverted the extralegal marks of the Schmittian hostile sovereign. Seneca writes of killing in violation of the law, "Nemo non potest," a double negative. There *isn't anyone* who *can't* do it (i.e., kill outside the law) (1.5.4)![31] Given Mes-salina's, and indeed Agrippina's, track record, how true this must have seemed to Seneca and perhaps to Nero alike. If we flinch at Seneca's "any-one" in this passage (and early modern writers show signs that they did), it is worth remembering that this "anyone" is assumed to reside inside the emperor's palace, where clemency is deemed a higher virtue in light of that household's insuperable lethality.[32]

Seneca's early experiences with the lethality of Roman political intrigues were hardly unique. In Claudius's palace, opportunities were extended to do harms, including murder, with impunity. Imperial killing became more than merely Claudius's affair; it became a power his inti-mates exercised (not least his last wife and likely murderer, Nero's mother, Agrippina).[33] When it came to legal transgressions and all the other extraor-dinary things that make an emperor's capacities and talents shine, killing with impunity was no longer the exclusive mark of the man at the top. Only acts of clemency, the arbitrary sparing rather than taking of life, marked the sovereign leader as distinct. The prince's monologue before his own image continues:

> In this position of enormous power, I have not been driven to unjust punishments by anger or by immature impulse or by the people's recklessness and obstinacy . . . or even by that glory so horrifying but so common in great commanders, and demonstrating power by means of terror. In my case, the sword is hidden— no, sheathed. I am extremely sparing of even the cheapest blood. There is no one, whatever he may lack, who does not win my favour by the fact of his being human. I keep sternness concealed but clemency ready on standby. I guard myself just as if I were going to have to justify myself to those laws which I summoned from their neglect and darkness into light. (1.1.3–4)

The exclusivity of extralegal or unjustified killing having been exhausted, the power to exercise clemency, suggests Seneca, is the exclusive mark of the sovereign.

The monologue ends by reminding the prince just how willful he can be in the application of his mercy. The contrast is the restraint he must exercise in indulging his anger. Earlier in *De Clementia*, he ventriloquizes Nero complaining of how the requirements of rule are a kind of "slavery": "You think it is severe for kings to be deprived of that freedom of speech which the lowest enjoy. 'That amounts to slavery, not sovereignty,' you say. What? Are you not aware that that sovereignty is a noble slavery for you? Your situation is quite different from that of the people who are invisible in the crowd" (1.8.1). Indeed, he is told to hold back his impulses to express his anger or take revenge, for he must guard against being seen as unprincely. His every move is under scrutiny of the world (1.8.1–5). His needed self-restraint on all vice is merely "the slavery experienced by the highest importance—to be unable to become less important" (1. 8.3).

Seneca tells Nero that those constraints are the ones he shares with the gods. By contrast, he gives Nero no cause to complain when it comes to exercising clemency. Indeed, he urges the prince to find a voice for his sovereign swagger in the exercise of clemency: "The fresh age of one person and the extreme age of another moved me. I forgave one man for his high status and another man for his low rank. Whenever I discovered no reason for pity, I showed mercy to myself [*mihi peperci,* or 'spared myself']. If the deathless gods should require a reckoning from me, I am ready today to account for all of humankind" (1.1.4). If we are to understand Seneca's claims on behalf of Nero's sovereign power, the potential accountability hinted at here is a question that must be seen in its specific contexts. Although contemporary advocates of mercy face circumstances quite different than Seneca's, his advice to Nero is still enlisted in the chorus that demands greater clemency and mercy from contemporary leaders in liberal democratic states.

CLEMENCY IN POST-REPUBLICAN CONTEXTS

History has not been kind to Nero, and few make the case that it ought to be. He is remembered, fairly or not, as the cruel emperor who fiddled while Rome burned.[34] His name is synonymous with sadistic and perverse dominance over subjects, courtiers, and members of the Senate. When fully released from the censor of Seneca's better judgment, he could be very inclement, although the historical record suggests that his vicious proclivities were present from the start. In the "golden" *quinquennium*, he nonetheless murdered his stepbrother Britannicus and his mother.[35] Seneca engineered a pathetic, dishonest cover-up story: Agrippina had tried to kill Nero and committed suicide. Roman subjects, already versed in the ways of mass sycophancy, cheered Nero's "lucky escape."[36] Murdering Agrippina is for many the beginning of the end of the five golden years.[37]

Although Suetonius testified to Nero's generosity and mercy as well, his catalog of Nero's transgressions retains its shock value, even in its account of his earlier years. Some nights, Nero dressed as a slave for his own amusement and roamed the city to rob and murder his subjects.[38] He also dressed himself up as a beast and sexually molested those participating in the athletic games he created.[39] Aside from later killing many senators and other family members, he made Christians into human torches in the 60s. This was a part of his reaction to the false rumor that he had been responsible for the fire. He evidently felt it helped to publicize his campaign to blame them for Rome's famous fire.[40]

Pleas for a historian's detachment and circumspection in passing a sweeping judgment on the entirety of Nero's reign, including the first five years, have been made, justifiably, in the name of a better historical understanding. The evidence indicates that there were high hopes at the start of his reign. Romans hoped that he would correct the abuses of the past, including those of Claudius and Caligula, and that he might be the leader who could reunite Rome.[41] Seneca himself worked to foster this climate of hopefulness.

Caution is a sound approach, especially in assessing Seneca, but even sympathetic scholars do not assign him clean hands.[42] How should we assess Seneca's encouragements to exercise friendly sovereign prerogatives? Recent attention on his discussions of clemency as a necessary virtue in "leaders" is not concerned with sovereignty.[43] More often it is seeking to return mercy and clemency to a place of respectability in the present and to correct the predisposition among contemporary liberal legal theorists to pit mercy against justice. Seneca offers a precedent because he is said to have fought a near identical fight against some of his Stoic predecessors.[44]

It is therefore appropriate to ask how and why Seneca attempted to make Nero worthy of the respect and reverence he describes in *De Clementia*. Those looking to revive mercy and clemency today tend to draw upon *De Clementia* as if it were an abstract treatise on mercy, rather than the work of a particular thinker within specific contexts.[45] We ought rather to understand Seneca's defense of clemency as a sovereign virtue, yet this approach requires consideration of Nero, Seneca, and the sovereign ways of prior emperors, their reputations, and their practices. Especially in Augustus's reign, clemency became a celebrated aspect of imperial Roman leadership, although there were already precedents. In 44 BC the Senate, perhaps in spite of aristocratic resentments, commemorated Julius Caesar's clemency by commissioning a temple dedicated to Julius and the goddess of clemency, echoing aspects of Caesar's own popular propaganda.[46] Seneca suggests that his predecessors left room for improvements (1.15–6; 11.1–3). Nero, Seneca says in *De Clementia*, was already their superior on this count, and the text humbly records these perfections to remind the young man of what his grateful subjects knew him already to be.

Does Seneca offer us today a picture of a leader with a dedication to justice *and* mercy, one that might stand as a corrective to those who want to emphasize the tensions between mercy and justice? In the passage from *De Clementia* quoted above, Seneca's ideal Nero declares his willingness to render a reckoning to the gods. How one of Rome's leaders might make such a reckoning could correspond with the transition from republic to rule by *princeps*. In public discourse, the transition did not follow a simple binary between free and unfree. Historians mark the transition through three moments: the republican period; then a middling period, when the Caesars—Rome's dictators—pretended to maintain a republic; the last was Seneca's own. For many, Seneca is the intellectual figurehead of his period, because the philosopher and adviser no longer counted it taboo to recognize the man who governed over Rome a king with absolute powers.[47] The significance is that the pretense of republican rule was no longer operative in *De Clementia*.[48]

With this shift, the idea of what it meant to give an account to the deathless gods, or indeed humankind, also shifted. How Caesar ought to be known, or would be known, as clement was very much a part of that transition. As Melissa Dowling notes, clemency might be praised among military leaders.[49] Having defeated their enemies, they did not give into the temptation to exact unnecessarily cruel revenge. This was a clemency that even republican generals, on behalf of Roman citizens (if they dared defy the factions invested in vengeance), could exercise. As Rome suffered its own civil wars, the chief example of clemency became Julius Caesar. Here clemency turned its face inward. Its enemies were domestic, and its domestic power insuperable. Clemency in this milieu meant the reintegration of former civil war enemies into the fold, even assigning them offices. Clemency was a tool for earning by goodwill the pacification and gratitude of the defeated. This was the clemency that Cicero enjoyed and praised in Julius Caesar in *Pro Marcello* and *Pro Ligario*.[50] Finally, Romans grew accustomed to living under leaders with kinglike powers: clemency was no longer a virtue of the powerful who had experienced warfare against enemies, but that of a kind father, the administrator of his household's justice.[51] Clemency was the virtue of kings, a way to treat subjects already assumed dependent upon his goodwill and his superior sense of justice. To celebrate *clementia* in this period was to acknowledge that superior power of the emperor who had it in his power to exercise it.[52]

Cicero would ultimately celebrate the death of Julius Caesar and condemn him as tyrant. After the defeat of Pompey's forces, Cicero, who had joined Pompey's faction, wrote in praise of Caesar's clemency. He did so, as Chaim Wirszubski observes, because he had no other choice. In speeches from 46 BC, such as the *Pro Marcello*, Cicero "praised Caesar's clemency, fully aware that on it depended the life of everyone, and on it he pinned his hopes for a better future. . . . Cicero realized only too well that there was in fact no law to base a case on, everything depended upon Caesar's will."[53] In *Pro Marcello*, Cicero could make believe that Caesar was looking to a republican future for Rome. Wirszubski's reading takes the transition from Cicero to Seneca to mark the "final collapse" of the idea that Rome's law might be the guardian of freedom. It was no longer the leader's enemies alone who had to count on his clemency: all citizens had to entrust their lives to the clemency of emperor. Clemency was more than the opposite of justice; it was for anyone subject to the emperor's concerns, the highly imperfect substitute for justice according to the city's law.[54] Unlike prior republican forms, it was, Braund notes, a concept of justice that "makes absolutely no mention of civil rights."[55]

In Peter Stacey's reading, Seneca is seen as more than the measure of republican liberty's lost ground. He is an agent of the replacement of republican concepts of liberty. Stacey had argued that Seneca converted Nero's best self into a Stoic ideal. As king, he was placed by the gods above all others on earth. He thus had to live with the heavy responsibility of the duties assigned him by virtue of his perfection. Nero, as prince of Rome, was equated with the Stoic *vir sapiens*, a man of perfect rationality, fit to rule over all others. He was born, and indeed elected by the gods, to assist the public, and in this very limited sense, Rome's new monarchy was also *res publica*, of a cosmic rather than earthly kind.[56] Nero was in fact the new slave, while his wise guidance of his people made them free. He had the burden of being an example to all, a man under constant observation by those who were his rightful subordinates, and was seemingly responsible to laws higher than Rome's own.[57] Fortunately, writes Seneca, there was no question that these virtues were already possessed by Nero. Stacey concludes that Nero had only to be what many Romans acknowledged they needed most.

After years of civil wars, even those Romans who had been in a position to recollect republican liberties had grown, to borrow a phrase from Hobbes, "weary of irregular jostling."[58] Roman conservatism and pride might, as Wirszubski notes, have led many to salute and reverence the memory of the republic, but in the era of *princeps* these memories would have become compatible with professing or practicing loyalty and obedience to their new masters. Romans were, by and large, uninterested in restoring the republic. By this time republicanism was no longer considered a practical politics.[59]

An absolutist ruler could impose peace. He could prevent a return to factionalism and fighting and, it was hoped, conflicts over succession. Republicanism associated kingship with tyranny, including the abuses of the ancient object of republican scorn, the Tarquins. The *princeps* was

therefore in tension with republican ideas of liberty, such as nondomination, or being out from under the threat of a master's arbitrary will.[60]
Neither could the senatorial class expect their body to have final say in matters that concerned the defining affairs of Rome, nor could they form an
effective check upon the concentrated power of the *princeps*.[61] Seneca,
according to Stacey, draws upon Stoicism to redefine liberty in this specific
context. Rome's body politic thus became free on new terms: free of the
corruptions of republican factionalism and chaos and free because it was
ruled by a virtuous prince, indeed the trustee of their well-being, such as
Nero. Romans could now rejoice: they could have all the liberty a rational
man could desire, and none of the destructive factionalism that had accompanied liberty in its prior forms.[62] They were no longer free to destroy themselves. Their freedom meant that they had achieved the cure for what was
tearing them apart.[63] Seneca wrote: "They are driven to this acknowledge-
ment, which people make with the greatest reluctance, by many factors: a
security which is profound, abundant riches, the law elevated above all
injustice, the sight before their eyes of the most joyous form of a state that
has everything it needs to reach the height of liberty—except for the license
to self-destruct."[64] What was then left to Roman citizens was a Stoic notion
of liberty. They could freely submit to necessity, the order provided for them
by their king, with the knowledge that the divine forces of the universe had
dictated this order (*lex naturae*) for them. Freedom was learning to live
within these circumstances and understand that wisdom dictated this
submission to providence. This Stoic freedom was the freedom to liberate
oneself from the irrational and the acceptance that *ratio* governed the universe. In many respects, one may draw a line between this deterministic
view of the universe and the moral complacency of Leibniz, although it
haunted the Hanoverian and he wished to distance himself from it.[65] Liberal theorist Isaiah Berlin makes this Stoic surrender to the rational universe an example of the positive liberty concept he thought dangerous for
those who wished to safeguard liberty; he linked it to withdrawal from the
world, a false liberation.[66]

CONCLUSION

Seneca's clement sovereign stands in almost diametric opposition to
Schmitt's hostile sovereign. Where Seneca, Nero, and their contemporaries concluded that killing outside the law was no longer the exclusive domain

of Rome's sovereign *princeps*, it had exhausted itself as a reliable restraint on those favored by the emperor. Only saving lives outside the law and according to one's will made one sovereign. Moreover, Seneca argued—placing his wishes above the harsh reality of Nero's proclivities—it was the only guarantee of justice that Rome's subjects had. Clemency was a sovereign virtue and prerogative that was celebrated, out of necessity, by those who had to submit to the character and whims of an unchecked political power.

I've asserted that writers who have recently returned to Seneca's defense of monarchical sovereignty miss too much when they treat it as an abstract treatise on clemency. They are correct to note that clemency and justice were not opposites, as some liberal thinkers treat them today.[67] When we more fully immerse Seneca and Nero in their political contexts, however, we see also that the justice the just *princeps* exercises may stand in very strong tension with the ideals of more egalitarian societies, liberal or otherwise. Clemency is a virtue celebrated by those who lack the liberty to demand justice according to laws that issue from the deliberations and representatives of free peoples. We can still value clemency in the abstract: wherever there is grounds for punishment, there may be just and equitable grounds for clemency. It is not wrong in a society given to retributive punishment to seek the virtues and benefits of mercy. Insofar as we find our appetite for clemency growing larger and larger, however, it must occasion us to wonder whether our present conditions are beginning to resemble those unfree societies. They knew clemency was a virtue, unopposed to justice, but it was also because they had few, or no better, means of achieving justice by more egalitarian means.

The next chapter will explore the possible mirrors between the conditions of liberty under Nero and in our societies today by delving further into the role of pretense in Roman political life. Even if we are separated by centuries and many other cultural differences, the command to celebrate a sovereign's virtues may remind us of a growing condition today.

CHAPTER 7

SENECA AND ROME'S NEW MAKE-BELIEVE

Pretense, as noted in the prior chapter, had become an elemental part of Roman imperial practice. Rome lost its republic, and Augustus ruled as a dictator. Augustus nonetheless insisted that he had restored the republic, and Romans repeated and affirmed these false claims. After Augustus, Rome continued to be governed by *de facto* kings, who governed the city as well as an empire that extended itself well beyond Italy to Spain, Greece, Gaul, the south along the North African coast, and the east past modern Turkey to the eastern Mediterranean. Nostalgia for the republic was largely centered in Rome among the elites, whose status was diminished because of the transition.[1]

Seneca facilitated the outward acknowledgment of the reality of governance by kingship and the end of any pretense of a republic. Peter Stacey links Seneca with a replacement program whereby republican concepts of liberty were spurned for concepts built from the ideals of the Stoics. Indifference to a universe that fixes a people or a person's destiny was combined, however uneasily, with the belief that it was best within the rationally governed universe to be governed by the most virtuous.[2] According to Seneca, the Stoic sage was and ought to be king. He cast Nero in this role, holding that his rule was ordained by divine forces. Romans never had it so good, so to speak, and they needed to know and acknowledge that Nero's kingship was as good as it would ever get.

In this chapter, I will describe some of the workings of those early pseudo-republican forms of pretense, and then I will argue that Seneca does not represent an end to the rule of pretense. What some describe as his pragmatism or honesty regarding Rome's political order was not an across-the-board mandate to speak hard truths. Seneca may have undressed old falsehoods, but he spoke new untruths. His frank speech about the fact of Romans' subordination to a king did not in fact push pretense aside. It merely offered pretense a new master.

In Seneca's universe of false praise, Romans would no longer be required to pretend about some things, but they would be required to pretend about others. They would no longer have to pretend that they lived within a republic or that they had a political order structured by a republican constitution. However, they would have to pretend that they were governed by a just and clement king. Melissa Barden Dowling has emphasized that praise for prior emperors' clemency, especially that of Augustus, was proleptic: it was a desperate act. Those who praised his clemency may have done so, in part, to civilize a victorious warrior, hoping to remake the man. Rather than live under the clemency of a conqueror, as defeated barbarians were compelled to do—and then project content about their new good fortune—Romans sought a preferable course through carefully crafted flattery. Before Seneca, Dowling notes, many were prepared to heap praise upon their leader in the hope that he might conform to the gentler formula for reconciliation, healing, and unity after victory in civil war.[3] In Seneca's writing, Nero is at the center of his philosophically appropriated world of make-believe virtue. His project was to make the emperor's sovereign clemency his shining feature.

If we only cast our eyes toward hostile sovereign exceptions, we are likely to miss what Seneca's project has to teach us about extralegal clemency's range of power. Schmitt's hostile sovereign must be acknowledged as sovereign because he is capable of acting like a cruel beast. The warrior has the capacity to step outside the confines of the laws he keeps to engage in acts of extraordinary violence. He is a ravenous wolf who spares his prey when he's so inclined. This merciful sparing of the being within the conquering sovereign's power to kill is the violent exception's immediate correlate.

The friendly sovereign, however, flexes his muscles in more ways than sparing the cornered, and these shows of his power demand a different form of recognition and representation. While subjects are expected to acknowledge the sovereign's virtue, they must acknowledge his virtue in and through its friendly exceptions. This was not the nature of the deference shown to brutish soldiers who withheld their blows. Friendly sovereigns can be extraordinarily kind, or extraordinarily forgiving. Subjects may ask the sovereign for friendly acts and sometimes are made to acknowledge that *only* the sovereign can grant what they ask. Recall that part of state consolidation in England consisted of Tudor attempts to monopolize extralegal mercy. Sovereigns must be (that is, strive to be saluted as) the best, better than ourselves because more powerful, and unchecked by laws and other restrictions that might otherwise restrain those bound to law and custom. Sovereign power marks these better figures as capable of such extraordinarily friendly acts.

PRINCIPATE "REPUBLIC"

How and why did republican pretense become established practice in Rome? Rome entered its principate while refusing to openly recognize the republic that it had lost. The refusal started at the top with Augustus.[4] He insisted that he respected the Senate, which was granting him *de facto* kingship costumed as republican compromise.[5] Rome was still in possession of its republican constitution and its numerous offices and appointments—in name at least—but the Romans, both emperors and Senate, did not wish to fully acknowledge the changes that had in fact taken place. Officially they did not acknowledge the changes, and Augustus and some subsequent emperors, like Tiberius, were intent on keeping up an unconvincing republican pretense.[6]

Rome had deep-rooted motives for hiding its head in the sand in the age of the principate. It had banished the Tarquin kings centuries before (509 BC). Kingship was a form of rule that the republic associated with lesser peoples. Conquered people's kings were made to submit to them. In the age of the principate, then, Roman elites were engaged in saving appearances, as Ronald Syme has noted. This exercise had a particularly poisonous effect on Roman political morale and morality; "compromise" became a cover for dishonesty.[7] In a striking assertion, Paul Veyne compares the emperor's position to that of Stalin. He was a comrade merely in name, a dictator in fact. Emperors so situated were tempted occasionally to purge the Senate, as Stalin purged his party. Veyne states that emperors and dictators did so out of the anxiety wrought by the paradoxes of holding power over *de facto* subordinates whose inequalities were not formally recognized. When the legitimating doctrine could not sustain their actual domination, it opened the door to competition for the sovereign's throne. A potential usurper of the *de facto* throne could begin his campaign by claiming, however insincerely, to restore the republic.[8]

In initiating the principate, Augustus had fundamentally eliminated any meaningful competition for his power.[9] He nonetheless proudly testified in public to his accomplishments, among which he claimed to have rescued the republic: "At the age of nineteen, on my own initiative and at my own expense, I raised an army by means of which I restored liberty to the republic, which had been oppressed by the tyranny of faction."[10] Unless pursuing a conspiracy to unseat the emperor, one dared not contradict Augustus or subsequent emperors on this point from that moment forward.[11]

The people of Rome as well as those in the provinces, many of whom lacked the privileges of republican participation even under the republic, largely accepted the transition to the principate. There had been chaos and mayhem during the empire's many civil wars, and Augustus's victory over his rivals brought peace. Claiming to defend the republic against the threat of Anthony and Cleopatra's co-despotism, Augustus celebrated the peace he had achieved for restoring the law of the republic.[12] Prior to Augustus, bloody conflicts between factions of nobles (the most distinguished part of the senatorial class included families that had at some point possessed a consulship) made competition for control a matter of ongoing dread. For the populations that had to bear the brunt of the fighting, including many among the upper reaches of Roman society, the relief was real.[13] In this context, it was understood that a good Caesar made Roman subjects and soldiers content and grateful—especially inside the city of Rome itself—with games, bread, public works, and by showering the people with largesse and beneficent acts.[14]

Even as the Senate declared him indispensable, Augustus took care not to offend the senators or upper orders. As detailed in the boasts he makes in *Res Gestae*, his testimonial to his accomplishments, it was the Senate that

voted him into a permanent tribunate in 23 BC. This office restored the powers he had given up when he abjured his lock on the consulship in the name
of conformity with the constitution.[15] Later votes in 2 BC to make him *impe-
rium consulare* and then *pater patriae* established a legal though unrepublican more openly extralegal rule built on patriotic solidarity and a growing
acceptance of the emperor as beloved overseer of law, order, and morals.[16]
Formally a private citizen in these later phases of his reign, Augustus ruled
the empire not by law but by his *auctoritas* (authority), as he himself noted.[17]
Res Gestae, displayed on bronze pillars that were erected in front of his mau-
soleum, notes that a golden shield had been created and put on public display in his honor for all he had done for Rome. The shield read: "The senate
and the Roman people gave me this in recognition of my valour, my clemency, my justice, and my piety."[18]

Syme has argued that the emperor's good graces—his beneficent willingness to continue to appoint nobles to offices that proved very lucrative—
also accounts for the stability of the new unrepublican republic:

> After a social revolution the primacy of the *nobiles* was a fraud as
> well as an anachronism—it rested upon support and subsidy by a
> military leader [the prince], the enemy of their class, acquired in
> return for the cession of their power and ambition. Pride and ped-
> igree returned: it masked subservience or futility. The nobles, emer-
> gent from threatened extinction in the revolutionary age, learned
> from adversity no lesson save the belief that poverty was the
> extremest of evils. Hence avarice or rapacity to repair their shat-
> tered fortunes, and the hope that the Princeps would provide:
> Rome owed them a debt for their ancestors. It was paid by the
> Principate, under pretext of public service and distinction in ora-
> tory or law, but more and more for the sole reason of birth.[19]

The principate continued well beyond Augustus and Nero, and the Senate
continued to represent a diminished governing class, which nonetheless
expected from the *princeps* signs of respect for the institution and the nobility. Retaining the support of the people and Rome's armies through norms
of loyalty and the emperor's generosity, the Senate was reduced to the least
essential part of the formula that allowed the *princeps* to hold power. In
Nero's rule they were needed but had long ago given up their preeminence.[20]
Following Augustus's lead, however, the republican constitution continued

to be honored in words. The contradictions gave birth to an elaborate dance wherein the man who in fact controlled all that mattered refused many a high office out of respect for his "equals" among the elite in the Senate while never actually ceding fundamental control.[21] An awkward dance took place in the Senate as well. The senators faced the demoralizing problem of how to bow to the wishes of the emperor while keeping up appearances. They had to act as if the emperor's decisions were the product of their deliberations and free choice. In this scenario, absenteeism became a problem, and emperors began fining senators for nonattendance.[22]

After the assassination of Caligula in AD 41, some in the Senate contemplated restoring the republic but could not find the votes or will to do so. Others in that body preferred the appointment of another *princeps*, yet they discovered once again that the choice was not in fact theirs to make but the army's.[23] When Claudius took Caligula's place, he, like his predecessors, refused honor after honor and first did what he could to erase the memory of the days before his accession, when the constitution was at issue.[24]

Seneca's above mentioned acknowledgment of Rome's kingship—its actual constitution—has been described as sober and honest. "Sober men . . . saw the solid advantages of hereditary succession [i.e., monarchy]," Syme writes. "They could profit from it without inner belief and without ceasing to profess a normal or deceitful devotion to ideas of the 'res publica.'"[25] Likewise, "Seneca's policy was the best available. It derived from recognition of a fact, the monarchy to which they were actually subordinate. With that admitted (and no awkward questions asked), the government proceeded to operate through diplomacy, persuasion, and pretense."[26] Thus, Seneca was writing what the elite were thinking—that Rome was indeed governed by a king—but unwilling to openly articulate. He broke a residual republican taboo with his very use of the term *rex* (king) to describe good rule for Rome and for Nero.

Moreover, in having spoken this truth, Seneca is said to have woken up his fellow elites to the other reality of their dependence. The protection and welfare of the people, especially the members of the senatorial classes, depended not upon the defunct constitution but upon the virtues of the emperor. Seneca warns his contemporaries of the consequences of failing to support their leader:

A disaster like [the dissolution caused by the loss of the emperor] will be the end of the Roman peace and will demolish the prosperity of our mighty people. This people will be free of that danger precisely as long as it understands how to submit to the reins. If it ever breaks them or does not allow them to be replaced once they have been shaken off by some disaster, this unified fabric of the greatest empire will fragment into many particles, and the end of this city's obedience will be the end of her domination. For that reason it is no wonder that emperors and kings and whatever other name the guardians of the public order have are cherished even beyond the degree of our private relationships.[27]

It was therefore all the more important that someone—Seneca himself!—teach Nero to hold himself to the standards of virtue. Since constitutional limits on the emperor's power were make-believe, there is reason to paint Seneca as a practical political philosopher.[28] According to Miriam T. Griffin, Seneca draws upon Greek works on kingship and the virtuous king and deliberately draws the *princeps* into their rubric in order to recommend a course for Rome in keeping with its new reality:

> The practice of applying to the Princeps virtues prominent in Hellenistic treatises on kingship was already long established. Seneca meant to apply the fundamental doctrine as well: everything turned not on constitutional forms and legal limitations, but on the character of the ruler. The power of Caesar was absolute; it was how he exercised that power that made the difference between good government and bad. It was the task of the Princeps' advisers to develop virtue in him; it was the duty of his subjects to remain peaceful and obedient as long as he looked out for their welfare.[29]

Because clemency—or at least its neighboring traits, pity and mercy—is not associated with prior Stoic thinkers, Seneca is seen as something of an innovator in the history of Stoicism. In fact, Stoics like Cato held to the opposite view, as Seneca himself noted. Cato ruled out clemency as an invitation to vice and decay among authorities. Greek Stoics Chrysippus and Diogenes Laertius simply took a hard line against leniency as contrary to upright justice.[30]

Above all, however, clemency was a king's virtue and therefore in fundamental conflict with any understanding of virtue that might inform republican perspectives. Clemency was the kind of virtue republicans might and did refuse to accept when offered by a conquering king or tyrant.[31] More than rejecting clemency as a policy for the republic, Cato refused Julius Caesar's offers of mercy. As a republican, it was "more hateful than death."[32] Cassius and Brutus might have fought for Pompey, ridiculously figured as a defender of the republic to suit Augustus's needs during the principate, but when Caesar welcomed them back instead of killing them, they were not obliged to thank him any more than we owe a thief thanks for not killing us after he has robbed us of what is ours.[33] Seneca's message to expect and wish for Nero's clemency was situated in a different milieu. The hierarchy of prince and subject, or indeed of prince and senatorial classes, was an open fact to be acknowledged.

Thus, in spite of the opinions of earlier Stoics who rejected clemency, Seneca presses on. This necessitates certain mental gymnastics. As a Stoic virtue, Seneca argues, its opposite could not be another virtue, notably severity. Severity was a virtue because it ensured that those due punishment actually received it. Severity in applying the law gave justice its full due. Clemency was not justice's opposite but its ally. Its opposite, said Seneca, was therefore something else. It was the very un-Stoic surrender to emotion. For those who could punish, and did so too harshly, clemency's opposite was the passions that reveled in the cruelty of punishment. Conversely, for those who would not give justice its due and did so out of not reason but unjustified passion, their flaw was pity toward the punished. The clement authority did not give in to either cruelty or pity. The properly clement authority, said Seneca, did not withhold punishments out of a desire to indulge their pity for the suffering experienced by the guilty, but in conformity with higher, rational, imperatives. Although he will use the example of Alexander the Great's exploits in war in *De Clementia* to condemn cruelty in general, in his more philosophical moments in *De Clementia* Seneca writes of clemency's opposite as specifically attached to circumstances where punishment is, in fact, due. This cruelty is not the will to punish those who deserve it, but to take punishment of the guilty to excess. Clemency, or at least an important aspect of clemency, chooses the gentler options.

Was Seneca a speaker of hard truths to his contemporaries? One may concede that *De Clementia* acknowledges the fact of the emperor's monarchical power. Given the flattery required to advise his prince, and the circumstances historians of his realism reveal, one may question Seneca's reputation for speaking sober truths. The measured frankness of an adviser to an absolutist king aside, the frankness of Seneca and his contemporaries needs further consideration. In the context of a wider public already interested in the virtues of the *princeps* and in his clemency in particular, the most significant understanding of Seneca's philosophical mirror for Nero may not be its frank acknowledgment of a republic no longer operative.[34] Rather, it is better understood as a concession: there may have been no choice but to love the *princeps* for his clemency.

SENECA AND NERO

De Clementia as we know it is incomplete. We can only speculate about what its entirety might have intended. The text that survives is, as discussed in the last chapter, a mirror for an exceptionally vain prince, one who would enter himself into musical and athletic competitions knowing that he would always win.[35] Despite Nero's deficiencies—or because of them—Seneca assisted him by putting forth in *De Clementia* a very attractive image of the young emperor as a savior for Rome.[36] There would have been nothing unusual in celebrating the new emperor as relief from the abuses of past rulers.[37] Yet Seneca attempts in *De Clementia* to appeal to the emperor's vanity in order to lure and convert the actual Nero into a more attractive and virtuous version of himself. A careful combination of praise and admonition, it is a psychologically adept piece of pedagogy.[38]

The last chapter demonstrates how *De Clementia* encourages Nero to control, or "guard," himself as if he were subject to law. It was never going to be an objective easily met. First of all, Nero was not, as *princeps*, subject to law. He was a source of law, and there was no effective means of enforcing law against him, as there had been no effective means of enforcing it against his earlier counterparts.[39] Second, Seneca had in Nero an unstable, self-indulgent, and dangerous narcissist who had become emperor at age seventeen in AD 54. How to convince such a person that he ought to bring himself under control?

Tacitus, in the *Annals* (AD 109), and Suetonius (b. AD 69) retrospectively assert that Seneca knew from the beginning that Nero would be anything but easy. According to Tacitus, Seneca in his dying moments said, "Who is not familiar with Nero's brutality? Nothing remains after murdered mother and brother but to add the slaughter of teacher and guide to the heap!"[40] Early in their relationship, Seneca decided that the young man's least praiseworthy inclinations would have to be at least partially indulged so as to prevent the disastrous consequences of more complete surrenders to vice.[41] As Cassius Dio, a third major source on this period, records, it was not ultimately a winning strategy for Seneca.[42]

Clemency may have been a new Stoic virtue—as such it would have to be considered its own reward—but Seneca makes clear that he is willing to attach instrumental reasons for being a clement emperor.[43] It is pleasurable, said Seneca, to be an emperor who is recognized, loved, and protected by his people because he exhibits this virtue. As the people's indispensable guide, he will be like those kings whose subjects "protect his sleep with nightly watches . . . defend his flanks with a surrounding barrier." All this and more will be his due out of their unanimous love.[44] Even when goading Nero not to emulate beasts or women, who, says Seneca, rage with undignified anger, he blends the lesson with the allure and respect and reverence due exalted princes.[45]

The power to spare lives makes the emperor like the gods, elevated above his subjects and worthy of the highest admiration. Like the gods, the emperor must tolerate insults and injustices with the equanimity that attends unassailable rank:

> Greatness of spirit adorns greatness of standing. . . . It is characteristic of greatness of spirit to be calm and peaceful and to look down from a height upon injustices and insults. . . . Savage implacable anger does not suit a king, because he does not maintain much superiority over the person with whom he levels himself by getting angry. But if he grants life and status to people who have risked losing them and who deserve to lose them, then his action is one exclusive to the man who wields power. . . . To save life is the prerogative of exalted rank. It should never win more admiration than when it has the luck to equal the powers of the gods, by whose kindness we all, good along with bad, are brought into the light. So an emperor should adopt for himself the spirit of the gods. . . . Let him take pleasure in the existence of some of them and some of them let him simply put up with.[46]

Why should we think that Nero didn't count on having it all? Or that this passionate and unkingly young man did not expect to be both unkingly, unmerciful, and cruel *and* possessed of the sovereign power to enjoy a publicly professed reputation for being clement, wise, kind, and tolerant? To address this question in Nero's contexts, I'll first discuss the high hopes that were part of the propaganda campaign around his accession. A potential challenge to my negative view of Nero's early years is the fact that on a comparative basis, and if we look at Nero's so called "golden years," there is evidence that he truly wished to earn his reputation for clemency.

Better than Claudius

Seneca's purpose in *De Clementia* was not exhausted by the attempt to shame a princeling brat into good behavior. The other purpose was propaganda. In this and other works from this early period in Nero's rule, Seneca aimed to raise the hopes of Roman subjects and script the praise they ought to use for the new absolutist ruler. Like most propaganda, the hope was that the people's praise should conform to the official self-image Seneca was crafting. That image would have been the product of *De Clementia* but also of the speeches he prepared for the young emperor.[47] Their new ruler was a hero who rescued Rome from the abuses of his predecessor, Claudius.

If current emperors were golden and guiltless, dead emperors typically lost some of their immunity from criticism. Upon transition, a new emperor was often anxious to show that he would avoid the horrendous mistakes and missteps of the emperor just before, especially if there were grumbles beneath the *de rigueur* admiration for a change of power. Nero followed custom and deified Claudius by decree. Though Seneca wrote the speech that accompanied the decree deifying Claudius, most of his efforts pull in a very different direction.[48] Nero would be the one who rescued Rome from Claudius's disgraceful ways. Guided publicly by Seneca, Nero would usher in a new era.

A key text in Seneca's effort was *Apocolocyntosis* (*The Pumpkinification of Claudius*), the satire written in 54, shortly after Claudius's death and at the start of Nero's rule.[49] *Apocolocyntosis* is counted a Menippean masterpiece.[50] It is not, however, the product of Seneca's highest ethical impulses. Claudius ended his rule, as Nero eventually did, despised by many of his subjects. The satire plays upon some of the sources of that hatred, which in fact speak to the extralegal status of the sovereign *princeps*.

What incited such contempt for Claudius? Since Augustus, the administration of justice for the Roman elite had centered on the emperors. Augustus took it upon himself to judge cases and became known not merely for possessing this very public power but equally for his tireless dedication to the cases he judged. This practice politicized Roman justice by appropriating to his own jurisdiction any cases involving senators or the upper orders of society. In keeping with the republican pretense of this era, the separate justice Augustus afforded senators appeared to signal their distinction when in fact it marked their subordination.[51] Claudius too frequently acted as judge, but his approach earned him ridicule.[52] He was attempting to correct for the irresponsibility of Tiberius and Gaius (Caligula), who had not been diligent in their administration of justice, and the effort put him at a disadvantage. To make good on his intention, Claudius was compelled to handle a large backlog of untried cases, the volume of which diminished the quality of his justice. He settled some cases unceremoniously in his private apartments; some he settled with summary justice. The proceedings were not noted for their dignity; *Tacitus* records the great fees extracted by the corrupt court advocates close to Claudius.[53]

Seneca draws upon this sordid history of sovereign legal supremacy in the *Apocolocyntosis*, putting Claudius himself on trial by the gods in heaven. He is ejected, deemed unworthy of his deified status, and tried again in the underworld. A funeral chorus sings his praises mockingly: "No other could more quickly master his briefs, after hearing only one side of the case, and often neither."[54] In heaven, Seneca's deified Augustus recollects his murdered decedents (including Julia Livilla) and angrily demands, "Tell me, deified Claudius, why did you convict any of these men and women, whom you killed, before you could examine the case, before you could hear the evidence? Where is this the customary practice? It is not so in heaven."[55] He is also formally charged with the judicial murder of 35 senators and 321 knights, or members of the equestrian class. Claudius's defense is cut off before it is completed, and he is ultimately sentenced to be a clerk in a courtroom from hell.[56]

Nero appears to have delivered on his promise of a more just and clement rule for a period of time.[57] Against the background of Claudius's mismanagement of justice, these may have indeed appeared golden years.[58] After deifying Claudius, Nero entered the Senate and, as Tacitus records it: "He laid out the pattern of the coming principate, deviating especially from what recently roused resentment. *I will not be every trial's judge: with accusers and defendants sequestered in one house the power of the few runs riot. Nothing in my household is venal or bribery-permeable. Home and state are separate* [discretum domum et rem publicam]."[59] Nero began with an ostentatious act of clemency: he brought back Plautius Lateranus, who had been exiled under Claudius on charges of committing adultery with Messalina, the emperor's wife prior to Agrippina. Nero delivered speeches on clemency to the Senate to coincide.[60]

Clemency was demonstrated in other ways as well. Vengeance against potential enemies from the prior regime was not the rule at the start. For example, Sullius Rufus, a notorious accuser who assisted Claudius and Messalina in their judicial murders, was not prosecuted until he openly attacked Seneca.[61] Other changes were ascribed to the influence of Seneca and Burrus as well. For these Nero wins some measure of praise, even from the skeptical.[62]

Public Instruction, Display, and the Benevolent Prince

De Clementia is read as a work of public instruction for the emperor and therein also a work of reassurances and sometimes warnings for the senators, citizens, and subjects looking on.[63] It advocates punishing persons when the law calls for it, but it reminds Nero never to be angry or arrogant in the administration of justice, especially when administering justice for those who affront the emperor personally.[64] Reaching well beyond a narrowly tailored concept of clemency, it is, especially in book 1, a meditation on duties and practices of kingship and the king's relationship with his subjects. Clement virtue dictates acts of generosity and goodwill and the emperor's dislike of cruelty; it forbids the temptations of vengeance.[65] Even angry words should be avoided: they might open the door to unjust harms by vicious men anxious for the emperor's favor. Security comes not from the fear inspired by cruelty but from being loved by one's subjects.[66] As public lessons for Nero in good governance, they were more than mere lessons, and not merely for the emperor's ears: they were the propaganda of a regime that would have its subjects know and affirm its new credo.

Seneca promises a happy marriage of prince and people. A kinder, gentler emperor follows the example of the gods who are so forgiving of emperors. Why rain down nerve-racking thunder, asks Seneca, when your clemency might make the skies clear and cloudless?[67] Indeed, Nero ought to look upon the subjects he treats with clemency as extensions of himself. This regard will keep him from ruling with hostility and brutality.[68] If he learns to govern in the right spirit, he can, and of course will, avoid the unhappy fate of tyrants, who enter into a vicious cycle, Seneca asserts, unlike their better counterparts, "kings." (Seneca notably does *not* differentiate kings from tyrants, good from evil princes, based on the power and authorities they claim. It is merely the use or abuse of those capacities that is the basis for

Seneca's distinction.[69]) Tyrants engage in cruel acts to make their subjects fear them, which fosters the subjects' hatred in return. The tyrant registers the hatred, and it raises his fears of his own people. The tyrant then commits more cruel acts out of desperation.[70] "This, you see, is perhaps the very worst aspect of cruelty—that you have to persist with it. No way back to better things is open. Crimes have to be safeguarded with more crimes. And is there anything more unhappy than a person who finds evil inescapable?"[71] In one of the great ancient anti-Neronian works, *Octavia* (named for a wife Nero murdered), the character of Nero is made to refuse this lesson to Seneca's face:[72]

> SENECA: Praise lies in doing what one should, not what one can.
> NERO: The mob tramples on a supine ruler.
> SENECA: But overthrows a hated one.
> NERO: Steel is the emperor's protection.[73]

The play and the historical record indicate that Nero did not maintain such control over himself, if he ever had it in the first place.[74] Important for understanding the exercise of friendly sovereignty is that for Seneca, Nero, and his predecessors, sovereignty was to be known and asserted by more than arbitrary cruelty and violence.

Nero was on occasion neither cruel nor clement but recklessly generous, apparently driven by a desire to make spectacular gestures. His clemency and other friendly sovereign acts demanded an audience. In AD 48, a year in which there were persistent public complaints against tax farmers, he one day decided to make a gift to "the human race": he would eliminate every one of these "indirect" (i.e., farmed) taxes. He had to be persuaded to give up this plan.[75] Despite strong opposition in Rome, Nero's love of things Greek was so strong that he gave his generous impulses full rein on a monumental scale: he liberated the entirety of Achaea (the central northern-coast region of the Peloponnese that includes Patras Πάτρα) from direct rule and tribute obligations. He would later rob Greek temples of their treasure, but his generous acts tempered the severity of the injury.[76]

Suetonius, reflecting on Nero's good qualities, would write that he would never deprive himself of the opportunity for

> acts of generosity and mercy, or even for displaying his affability.
> The more oppressive sources of revenue he either abolished or

moderated. . . . He distributed four hundred sesterces to each man of the people, and granted to the most distinguished of the senators who were without means an annual salary, to some as much as five hundred thousand sesterces; and to the praetorian cohorts he gave a monthly allowance of grain free of cost. When he was asked according to custom to sign the warrant for the execution of a man who had been condemned to death, he said: "How I wish I had never learned to write!"[77]

Nero even orchestrated public acts of clemency in his legal prosecution of a senator in AD 62.[78]

As Veyne has argued, Nero's desire to express an unsurpassable generosity mingled with the narcissistic temptations built into the office of the *princeps* as established by Augustus.[79] That is, to the people inside and outside Rome who lived under Nero's rule, his greatest gift was his very being. He gave public and semipublic performances, easily recognizable to us as narcissistic acts, but not merely narcissistic, Veyne argues. The plebs had monarchical yearnings that they were long accustomed to having satisfied. Nero offered himself as a gift, but he was also received as such by the people.[80]

When Nero gave in this way, perhaps revealing his own insecurities, he tried to ensure that the adulation he received was delivered as he saw fit.[81] Suetonius notes that he organized squads trained in the "Alexandrian method of applause." The squads consisted of a handful of knights (compensated in gold pieces) and over five thousand plebian youths who attended his performances.[82] For those who had to endure the inevitable inconveniences of his generosity, there could be rich compensations. Suetonius's account of music and athletic competitions isn't just an entertaining embarrassment; it's instructive. The customary rules regarding the frequency of Olympic competitions were to be broken when Nero traveled in Greece. The prescribed intervals between Olympic competitions, the Olympiad, had been so regular that it was for Greeks an early measure of time. It was thought to be determined by the gods themselves and previously made the object of specific treaties, affording safe travel for athletes between hostile kingdoms in Greece.[83] Under Nero, the games would begin—and sometimes begin again!—when *he* arrived. They also included innovative competitive forms deemed best by him, notably a musical competition. Nero's own performances could be exceptionally long:

No one was allowed to leave the theatre during his recitals, however pressing the reason, and the gates were kept barred. We read
of women in the audience giving birth, and of men being so bored
with the music and the applause that they furtively dropped down
from the wall at the rear, or shammed dead and were carried away
for burial. . . .

On several occasions he took part in the chariot racing, and at
Olympia drove a ten-horse team, a novelty for which he had cen-
sured King Mithridates in one of his own poems. He lost his balance, fell from the chariot . . . though he . . . retired before the finish,
the judges nevertheless awarded him the prize. On the eve of his
departure, he presented the whole province with its freedom and
conferred Roman citizenship as well as large cash rewards on the
judges. It was during the Isthmian Games at Corinth that he stood
in the middle of the stadium and personally announced these
benefits.[84]

Power and legal impunity thus extended in these many friendly directions
during the principate. The king's power to be clement, or generous, was his
unstoppable way of exhibiting a big heart. It was equally how sovereignty was
known: both how it *wished* to be known—how it demanded recognition—
and how content, resigned subjects, accustomed even to their dependence,
would justify their requests and wishes. Generous acts were customary and
expected in this and later ages.[85] During his picnics for the people, Claudius
would "cut loose," Suetonius notes, showering the crowds with largesse, using
the exposed left hand, plebian style, and cracking jokes. At one such event,
four brothers pleaded for the release of their father, a chariot driver in the
gladiator show. Claudius released him, preaching as he did so the value of
big families: "It can win favour and protection even for a gladiator."[86]

In AD 60, Nero created Neronia, his Roman incarnation of the Olym-
pics. Not the first to stage athletic competitions in his own honor, he may
have been emulating Augustus, who initiated the Secular games.[87] In the same
statement (erected on pillars) where Augustus claims to restore the liberty of
the republic, he marks the recognition for clemency upon the shield created
to honor him. The pillars and shield also make clear that grateful "republic's"
unending thanks for his monumental generosity toward soldiers and citizens. It is largely a catalog of payments to plebs, state coffers, buildings built,
games provided, and so forth.[88]

Suetonius paints quite a negative picture of Claudius. The value placed on clemency and generosity are manifest in his contempt. Nero's predecessor is never more bumbling in Suetonius's account than when he publicly mismanages these aspects of his rule or displays imperial rage. Friendly sovereigns of irresolute temper invited trouble. Suetonius recorded, for example, that those who attended Claudius's court proceedings sometimes called the emperor back after he declared a case closed. Sometimes attendees tugged on his clothing to "impose upon his good nature" and then ran after him.[89] Gladiators who had participated in one of his grand spectacles—the celebration of a major public work, the draining of Fucine Lake—thought to do the same. Not unlike his predecessors, Claudius staged a mock sea battle upon the lake, for which a triton was even built. It was to rise up from the water and blow a conch to signal the beginning of the battle. The gladiators, however, thought they had secured a last-minute reprieve from being required to risk their lives for the people's entertainment:

> Before allowing the water to escape from the Fucine Lake, he arranged to have a sham fight on it; but when the gladiators shouted: "Hail, Caesar, we salute you, we who are about to die!" He answered sarcastically: "Or not, as the case may be." They took him up on this and refused to fight, insisting that his words amounted to a pardon. Claudius grew so angry that he was on the point of sending troops to massacre them all, or burning them in their ships; however, he changed his mind, jumped from his throne and, hobbling ridiculously down to the lakeside, threatened and coaxed the gladiators into battle.[90]

Generosity, forgiveness, clemency, and kindness were all ways for Rome's princes to express their power. The negative example of Claudius may best illustrate the power of friendly sovereignty by the disdain it registers for insufficiently princely expressions. This class of attitudes and behaviors was a key aspect of sovereign authority. Moreover, maintaining decorum in matters of friendly sovereign prerogatives was no less important than exercising the destructive and violent capacities of his office. If Nero wanted it all—that is, both the latitude to indulge his worst vices and the privilege to receive public praise for such a high virtue as clemency—his ambition would not have made him unusual among imperial palace rulers.

CONCLUSION

If Rome no longer was required to pretend that it was a republic, then a new form of pretense was required of them. They were indeed governed by a king. He was clement and just: he upheld the laws, was fair and dispassionate, and was indeed *the* source of justice for Romans. Under Seneca's guidance, one can spot a period of relative improvements when measured against the failures of Claudius's quavering sovereign control over "justice," but this was neither permanent nor a fundamental goal for Nero. Nero sought praise, and many of his people sought to benefit from praising him. All the better for the advantaged to praise him, as did Seneca, for his generosity and clemency.

There is no doubt that Seneca is asking in *De Clementia* that Nero and his subjects think of him as a king and see him reflected in the text's portrayal of a clement and benevolent monarch. But who was the true audience for Nero's reflection in this image? Interpreters of *De Clementia* have sometimes assumed that the burden of recognition is entirely upon Nero. Departing from the purely Stoic notion that the sage is the only truly free man, Seneca allows his ventriloquized Nero to complain of the "slavery" of living in the public eye and of always having to be virtuous, whereas ordinary men—those who lack the godlike authority of the *princeps*—are free to indulge their vices in private and with fewer consequences. If being emperor is a noble slavery, then Seneca clearly encourages Nero to take up the chains. It is a constraint he should proudly share with the gods, those who cannot escape their importance.[91]

I would like to suggest, however, that placing the burden of self-recognition on Nero is only half the answer to this question. Whatever Nero's obligation to reflect the virtuous self Seneca describes in *De Clementia*, the obligation pales in comparison to the obligation—or, better, threat—it places on the subjects who gaze along with him. Even if they don't agree with Seneca that Nero is, as the philosopher has drawn him, the very best ruler, they had best pretend they do. Among the pretenders, some may have done so out of opportunism, others merely out of fear.[92] It is in the character of servitude that motives commingle and blur among the subordinated.

In Seneca's play *Thyestes*, likely belonging to a period after the philosopher retreated from Nero's service in the late 60s, King Atreus responds to a servant with a statement that represents an expectation held by absolutist sovereigns:[93]

> ASSISTANT: You have no fear of hostile talk among the people?
> ATREUS: This is the greatest value of kingship: that the people are compelled to praise as well as endure their master's actions.[94]

Atreus's assistant will persist in reminding this cruelest of kings a lesson Seneca himself attempted to teach in *De Clementia*: if the prince counts on the fear of the people to compel praise, they will fear him and be his enemies. He would do better to seek sincere praise by actually doing what is good and honest. In a near perfect inversion of Seneca's observations on the unique powers of the clement king to save lives, Atreus observes: "Sincere praise often comes even to a lowly man; false praise comes only to the mighty. They [the people] must want what they do not want!"[95] Who wants what they do not want? A subject, or a king, who is divided against themselves. Nero's best self wins the struggle with himself when he endures the noble slavery of virtuous kingship. For Atreus, on the other hand, the satisfaction resides in false praise alone and is a sign of power. Subjects who do not want his rule must yield false praise. Reflecting hopes that Seneca might have thought naïve, the assistant observes that if the king wants what is honorable, "everyone will want the same." Atreus has an answer:

> ATREUS: Where a sovereign is permitted only what is honorable, he rules on sufferance.
> ASSISTANT: Where there is no shame, no concern for the law, no righteousness, goodness, loyalty, rule is unstable.
> ATREUS: Righteousness, goodness, loyalty are private values: kings should go where they please.[96]

During the principate, T. E. J. Wiedemann notes, politics had indeed become a matter of privacy for the emperor.[97] It was Seneca's hope that when Nero looked into this mirror privately, he would say to himself, "I guard myself just as if I were going to have to justify myself to those laws which I summoned from their neglect and darkness into the light."[98] The "as if" is taken quite seriously by Seneca's interpreters. When they point to the compromise that Seneca appears to be imposing upon his allegedly sincere but unrealistic republican colleagues, it is often with reference to this passage. A magistrate who has to hold himself to the law of the constitution is one thing, they argue, but that period was long past. Rome, Seneca tells them, would have to settle and hope for an emperor or king who merely acts "as if" he was accountable to the laws. Indeed, if the laws apply at all, it is because the king "summoned at his command"—or at least didn't interfere with—standing laws, practices, and the regular guidance of Rome's jurists. In order for Rome to be governed by virtues, they would first have to become the active private and internalized values of the king himself.

On the other hand, if these virtues were not internalized—if they were merely a part of Nero's costume—then matters are much worse. For the most part, they were. Both Seneca and Nero knew that the obligation to be "as if" accountable to the law bespoke a tacit obligation that became all the more pressing the more Nero transgressed. That obligation did not rest with the king, but rather in the servile Roman subjects. That is to say, when Nero's propagandist wrote that the emperor would act "as if" accountable, the hardest truth was that when—the truly unaccountable—Nero didn't behave well, his subjects would still be forced to declare their reckless and transgressive sovereign a virtuous man, a virtual god among them. They were obliged to pretend that Nero was the good king he wasn't. This was an "as if" pretense that would not have been an entirely novel experience for subjects of a nonrepublic who were required to speak of their condition "as if" they were a republic. Historians who track republican pretense in Rome may mark Seneca's innovation in acknowledging kingship, but they do not attribute the innovation to a popular shift from the make-believe republic to the make-believe virtuous king. The reigning investment in republican hypocrisy outlasted Nero and Seneca by many years.[99] Perhaps Romans didn't notice or appreciate the difference. False praise of any kind was, as Seneca's Atreus knew, the mark of sovereign domination. If neither yielded the justice they promised, why trouble oneself to learn a new script?

Seneca might ultimately leave one with a great distaste for pleas for a merciful sovereign. It is not because mercy or clemency should always be unwelcome. Those who today ask for a greater place for mercy might also have occasion to show us that a greater measure of mercy will make an improvement, especially if they can convince us that we live in a fundamentally just society. On the other hand, such pleas might be a sign of a less fortunate condition. Understanding mercy in the context of Roman imperial sovereignty gives us today cause to reflect on the pathetic condition of the many communities who feel they have no choice but to plead for greater quantities of mercy or clemency.

Unless we decide to join Seneca in celebrating our philosopher-kings, we should keep in mind that those who are most inclined to ask the powerful for mercy—indeed those most likely to praise Caesar for his mercy, generosity, and other friendly exercises of his sovereignty—are not fortunate. It may be that they, like Nero's applause squads, celebrate a false sovereign virtue because they are content with pervasive servitude. They live within an order so far outside a law-bound justice that their praise of clemency betrays a deeper and lasting loss, rather than gain, for their societies.

Sovereignty that is known for being generous and forgiving may be the sign of numerous conditions. Not all the possibilities signal a loss of dignity or the unavailability of justice. A people that enjoys the widespread application of a justice they can endorse might reflect and decide that their legitimately placed authorities have become too severe. Here clemency might be welcome. It is, however, a sign of misfortune when one must substitute Seneca's sovereign clemency for such a justice. Still worse, as Seneca himself knew from personal experience, is to be compelled to praise the sovereign's clemency and other friendly virtues in the knowledge that the virtues one begs for and praises are almost entirely fictional.

CONCLUSION

In reviewing Jules Michelet, Thomas Hobbes, Seneca, and some of their contemporaries on the friendly aspects of sovereignty, my purpose has been to restore a missing piece of the sovereignty puzzle. When we think of sovereignty as a concept, and how sovereign power exerts itself, I hope I have reminded readers that the capacity for extraordinary violence and extralegal hostilities is not sovereignty's only mark. Extraordinary grace, favor, and forgiveness have been, and remain, significant parts of the sovereign's repertoire. I hope I have helped restore these aspects to our theoretical consciousness. The political climate of the last four years, during the writing of this book, has offered numerous practical reminders of the friendly sovereign's power.

The hostile sovereign powers that Carl Schmitt associated with "the exception" nevertheless predominate in how sovereignty is known today, and such power has long been linked to sovereignty. Schmitt gives his readers the impression that he had recovered a concept of sovereignty that was resident in the seventeenth century and perhaps most at home inside Thomas Hobbes's so-called decisionist concept. However, not all aspects of Schmitt's decisive hostile sovereign reach as far back in time as he would have us believe. As I've shown, there were no seventeenth-century decisionists. Hobbes and many of his contemporaries and predecessors had a fuller view of sovereignty's many aspects, and Schmitt's hostile sovereign should not be allowed to eclipse the friendly prerogatives inherent in their ideas of sovereign office. Contrary to Schmitt, even some liberals of the nineteenth century, including Michelet, knew sovereignty's aspects better than he did.

I have also shown where contemporary advocates for mercy and clemency have underestimated the downside of political worlds in which mercy is ascendant. This is not to join with those who posit that mercy and justice are antithetical.[1] Rather, it is a plea for a more fully contextualized and politicized understanding of the historical circumstances in which mercy—and especially the sovereign exercise of mercy—is revered. Efforts to link mercy with the fulfillment of justice must be understood in their full, often deeply inegalitarian contexts. As a palliative to liberal severity in the administration of justice, we might wish for a deeper appreciation for mercy as a virtue that counterbalances the excesses and cruelties in the administration of justice or in criminal law. Nonetheless, we should not wish for a return to the historical contexts that have been most conducive to the desperate desire for a merciful sovereign. We might even count ourselves fortunate that we have lived with concepts of justice, however deficient, that offer us more attractive options than throwing ourselves upon the mercy of persons deemed our betters.

Of the three thinkers examined in this book, Seneca was the most in favor of a friendly, clement sovereign. While Seneca has much wisdom to offer, anyone who appreciates egalitarianism ought to decline his help in finding the sunnier, clement side of despotism. Seneca deserves wider study, but I, for one, will not be saddened if he should be left off the reading list of any of our modern-day "leadership seminars." At the very least, any such assignment ought to be paired with King Atreus in Seneca's *Thyestes*.

Even absolutists have expressed their doubts about the sovereign's extraordinary power of generosity and forgiveness. Hobbes, for example, recognizes that freewheeling acts of mercy or liberality are likely to cause trouble for a sovereign. Witnessing the impunity of favorites or indeed the extraordinary favor conferred upon the most favored is likely to make subjects lose faith in their mortal god. As noted, Hobbes could not have been the decisionist Schmitt declares him to be. Indeed, he found legal exceptions suspect, not least those friendly exceptions that benefited the few at the expense of the whole. His contemporaries agreed: sovereign power is meant to defend the state, if necessary, by lethal and even legally extraordinary measures. The question Hobbes's contemporaries debated was less whether those in possession of sovereignty ought to have these powers, but whether the kings who claimed sovereignty were using them in service to the state's defense. They were suspected by those who resisted and revolted of deploying their extraordinary powers, both friendly and hostile, in service to forces, factions, and friends at court whom many of the governed counted as enemies.

Michelet happily challenged the faith that sustained loyalty to clement monarchs. He hoped to displace it entirely with a new faith, a revolutionary political theology. The distribution of unmerited grace in both monarchy and Christianity was anathema to him and his new faith. As a nineteenth-century liberal, Michelet's understanding of sovereignty (both hostile and friendly) occupies a place in intellectual history that Schmitt's framework works to erase. Michelet's own hostility to all that might undermine the unity of his France was real. It fueled a chauvinism that could rival the hostility that Schmitt believed essential to politics and sovereignty. Michelet was never more aggressive than when chiding the sovereign French people for being too welcoming, too friendly, toward those he considered the enemies of his France, the Revolution, and human progress.

Because sovereign power tends to exert itself in a thousand directions, all studies of sovereignty take on an open-ended quality. The study of sovereignty's friendly aspects can be no exception to this rule. I hope the three views of the risks and advantages of friendly sovereign power presented here will help set the stage for further inquiries. Although I touched on Charles I's and James II's relations with Catholic subjects, I have not attempted a systematic study of the very interesting phenomenon of sovereigns who cultivate threatened minority populations (either from within their own territories or by recruiting them from outside) or the benefits sought on both sides of these relationships. Neither have I attempted to describe here a Foucaultian microphysics of friendly sovereign persons, but I suspect that the world of flattery, submission, and special permissions in universities, corporate bureaucracies, or indeed within online social networks is another fertile field for the growth of millions of friendly sovereigns, each negotiating power relations by granting or withholding favor or forgiveness.

In light of the open-ended field of possible inquiries, I would like to conclude by offering a coda of resonant examples of friendly sovereignty. It can begin with a brief return to Seneca. As we noted, clemency had not been classed among the traditional Stoic virtues before Seneca made his argument on their behalf. In fact, Stoicism was associated with a cool, detached severity in the enforcement of laws, especially in republican contexts. Cato the Younger, the Stoic hero, embodied this severity.[2] Although he lauds Cato the Younger, Seneca resists this strand of Stoic thought.[3] Arguing that clemency is indeed a virtue, he is thought an innovator among Stoics and Romans.[4] He is engaged in more than a philosophical gambit, however, when he tells Nero that his reflection (in the mirror-text *De Clementia*) shows a man already possessed of clemency and other virtues. When he tells the young emperor that the ideal king was, like himself, matched to the image of the Stoic ideal, that he was the embodiment of *vir sapiens* (the Stoic sage), Seneca is engaged in both a personal and a political venture.

The universe had delivered the circumstances whereby Seneca was adviser and *amici principi* (semiofficial friend) of the emperor. It is not hard to imagine that Seneca was resolved, as a Stoic, to be and do his best. "What is the duty of the good man? To offer himself to fate."[5] Cultivating virtues in the person whom the fates had placed at the top the world might have appeared the best way forward to Seneca, hoping that a young emperor already showing signs of indulging the whims of his worst passions might learn self-control.[6] The one trait, mercy, that occasionally showed itself in Nero's unruly personality might provide the opening wedge in coaching him into a more admirable and steady life. It proved, of course, to be a false hope.

NERO'S FATE

Nero's early moments looked to some like they were the beginning of a fated golden age. Despite his promotion of this myth, it is hard to believe that Seneca himself believed it, unless Seneca imagined that he himself was to be the source of Nero's luster. Ancient historians were likely mindful of the gap between reality and the false promises of providence when they wrote of Nero's demise. In their accounts, Nero is made to show himself neither an ideal human being nor an ideal king. Stoics like Seneca knew that few people were either, but Nero's reported departures from perfection were outstanding. After putting up with nearly fourteen years of his rule, Suetonius writes that "the world . . . cast him off" and includes reports of a frantic and undignified exit.[7] According to this account, after the revolt by pro-praetor (former magistrate) Vindex in Gaul, Nero conducted himself so as to demonstrate his indifference. Falling somewhat short of the Stoic resolve, his first expression of indifference took him immediately to a gymnasium where he could devote his attention to an enjoyable athletic contest.[8]

After news of Spain's revolt under Galba (governor and Rome's next emperor), Nero deviated yet further from even the flawed calm he had hoped to put on display.[9] He is said to have fainted and become mute and insensible for a long duration. A great temper tantrum followed, which included banging his forehead and ripping his clothes. He would cry out that all was over now. The thirty-one-year-old's nurse could not console him. Other emperors, she noted, had suffered similar evils. He insisted that his problems were unparalleled. Following this meltdown, Suetonius writes, he was steadfast in one regard: he publicly and ostentatiously maintained his habitual lazy and lavish lifestyle. When good news came from the provinces, he staged feasts and composed and performed songs, complete with bawdy gestures and lyrics, mocking his enemies.[10]

His early response also included several abhorrent plans that Suetonius describes as characteristically Neronian in their cruelty, among them "to depose and assassinate the commanders of the armies and the governors of the provinces, on the ground that they were all united in a conspiracy against him; to massacre all the exiles, or all men of Gallic birth in the city to prevent them from assisting the rebellions of their countrymen inside the capital. He likewise contemplated turning over the Gallic provinces to his armies to ravage. Others involved poisoning the entire Senate at banquets, setting fire to the city but first letting the wild beasts loose, that it might be harder for people to protect themselves" (43).[11] The urgent need to take the field in his defense made these plans impossible. It was, Suetonius asserts, these practicalities, rather than moral qualms, that deterred him. Nero abruptly put himself in the place of Rome's two consuls, ending their terms prematurely. It is said that, while speaking of his plans, Nero declared upon arrival in Gaul that "he would go before the soldiers unarmed and do nothing but weep; and having thus led the rebels to change their purpose, he would next day rejoice among his rejoicing subjects and sing paeans of victory, which he ought at that very moment to be composing" (43). His first plans for the military campaign were to make sure there would be wagons to carry his concubines and theatrical instruments. The concubines were given masculine haircuts and Amazonian axes in preparation for Nero's wartime performance.

To pay for his defense, he attempted to impose massive and exacting taxes. They were resisted. Refusals were also said to be accompanied by a demand that he draw the money instead from the many rewards he had paid to the informers he had used to terrorize his subjects (44). He was reviled and mocked by the people in this last period. As he prepared to meet the fleet he had prepared for his flight from the palace in Rome, one of his guards—having refused Nero's requests to accompany him—asked him (quoting Vergil's *Aeneid* 12.646) if it were such a dreadful thing to die. Nero contemplated going as a supplicant to his enemies. He fantasized about appearing to the people dressed in black and begging their pardon for his offenses. Maybe, he is said to have thought, they would at least allow him to be the prefect of Egypt. Suetonius writes, "Afterwards a speech composed for this purpose was found in his writing desk; but it is thought that he did not dare to deliver it for fear of being torn to pieces before he could reach the Forum" (46).

His own death was by suicide with the assistance of a servant. This occurred after several earlier initial attempts wherein he lost the will but could not find the help he desired. At one point in that process he is said to have cried, "Have I neither friend nor foe?" (47). Moved again to take his own life rather than face the much more painful death planned for him by the revolt, Nero died uttering a falsehood—whether his own or another's is indifferent. A cavalry officer sent to capture him attempted to stanch the wound in his neck. Suetonius asserts that the officer, ordered to take him alive, was pretending to rescue the emperor by attending the wound. As if the soldiers sent to apprehend him were actually attempting to save him out of loyalty, Nero's last words were "Too late!" and "This is fidelity" (49).

CHOOSING THE FRIENDLY SOVEREIGN

According to Peter Stacey, Seneca did more than associate kingship with the Stoic sage. *De Clementia* was his attempt to convince Romans that choosing to subjugate themselves to a virtuous ruler was in fact a better liberty than the republican ideal. That older definition of liberty had taught Romans that monarchy was a government fit for slaves rather than free men, raising the broader comparative question.[12] Although many sovereigns, both hostile and friendly by reputation, declared that they were chosen by higher powers to rule, consent theory declared that the protective sovereign is the reasoned choice of individuals at risk in Hobbes's "state of nature." Who then among the would-be governed chooses the friendly sovereign?

Among the three thinkers considered in this book, Seneca is the sole advocate of a friendly sovereign. As with most Stoic considerations, the question of choice is conditioned by an acceptance that events, including those that determine who governs, are not chosen by human beings but by providence. Stacey has argued that Seneca drew upon his Stoic background to make a principality more palatable; that is, Romans might learn to adjust their definition of liberty. Again, this did not mean that Stoicism was doctrinally attached to any one form of government. Before, during, and after Seneca, one could find Stoics working both with and against monarchical forms, each resolved to live out their fate according to their understanding of traditional Roman morality. Each would assume the responsibilities they deemed appropriate to their assigned station, be it as slave, citizen, senator, or emperor—that is, when their Stoicism didn't compel them toward a complete withdrawal from public and political life.[13]

In other moments, Seneca sounds less like a Stoic and more pragmatic in recommending clemency to his sovereign. In these moments, he advocates for the monarchical form out of a desire for domestic tranquility, a peace to be achieved in no other way for a fractious people than by imposition of overwhelming force. On this view, an overpowering *princeps* was not a principled choice but a necessity. In the case of Rome, it was declared a necessity by both the will of a war-weary people and the Roman armies; their desires, rather than the republican nostalgia of the senatorial class, determined the shift of political events.[14] Their wish to prevent a return to civil war may recall Hobbes's philosophy. We could say that the Romans chose an overpowering monarchical form of government because they grew "at last weary of irregular jostling and hewing one another, and desire with all their hearts to conform themselves into one firm and lasting edifice."[15] But this desire for safety and an end to civic strife is a plea first and foremost for a powerful prince, not necessarily a virtuous one. Virtue was a secondary consideration after his capacity to marshal the forces necessary to impose and keep the peace.

Insofar as we might challenge Seneca's justification for clement princely government as a lesson in the Stoic resolve to live with the fate the higher powers assign to us, the clement sovereign is not so much a choice as an *ex post* rationalization. Whereas Hobbes's sovereign derives his power by consent, few among the governed properly choose Seneca's clement sovereign.

He is foisted upon them. What they choose to do is make the best of the rule that has already been imposed on them by praising, often insincerely, the virtues they most hope he will actually possess. Seneca's is an unconvincing fable of liberation, but, as Stacey has also noted, it eventually becomes a powerful ideology for telling others that God has chosen their monarchs for them by bestowing on all-powerful leaders the lofty virtues for which their loyal subjects know them.[16]

If many have no choice, this does not mean that others don't affirm their satisfactions with a friendly sovereign. This choice is often made in periods of fractiousness and competition between the governed, and not with an eye toward desperate necessities in times of war. It is not motivated by circumstances that Seneca describes for Roman subjects: to embrace fate and accept the new regime and its superior justice. It is instead the choice of persons who in most cases already live subordinate to an authority they did not choose. They nonetheless "choose" a friendly sovereign in that they wish themselves to be the chosen, or the "elect," of their governing deity. They ingratiate themselves with their sovereign in hopes of seeing the benefits they offer, or bestow, on the sovereign returned many-fold. That choice is driven by a wish for more personal advantages than the public good.[17]

Turning from Seneca's fantasies of selflessly devoted sage-kings and their grateful subjects to the hard realities of Hobbes's or Michelet's monarchs, we see a world of craven subjects and manipulative masters. On one side, the sovereign dangles and sometimes delivers preferences and privileges; on the other, the subjects offer insincere praise and selfish, not selfless, loyalty. Such subjects are not yet weary of the jostling with one another to achieve the favor of the sovereign. Michelet complains that the monarchical sovereign over this regime governs for his elect, not the whole. For the elect, the greatest fear is not death but disfavor. The greatest hope for the excluded is not equality—not even the ugly equality of vulnerability under Hobbes—but a reversal of fortunes. They would rather supplant the members of the present elect to gain the favor they know they deserve. If they would create a new sovereign, it would not be to change the form of government but merely to supplant the present sovereign with one who governed for themselves, self-described as truly deserving, hitherto deprived of grace.

Those who seek a friendly sovereign are therefore often in competition, but they lack the intensity of appetite in those who seek Schmitt's hostile sovereign. They know whom they wish to see favored and disfavored, though the system does not insist upon unity. The victorious part does not take the place of the whole like Emmanuel-Joseph Sieyès's Third Estate, Marx's proletariat, or the warrior despot or absolutist who himself must represent the state. Those for whom the sovereign does not govern must remain to both service the needs of the chosen and to allow the chosen to enjoy the pleasures of being the object of jealousy. There must be subordinates, so that the elect can display their benevolence by elevating individuals as needed or desired from the ranks of the damned. Therefore, the friendly sovereign's exceptions are not designed to found or refound a unified state in most cases but are the product of a divided, factionalized society that seeks neither unity nor commonality or equality. The friendly sovereign and his sought-after exceptions are in most cases the promise of a triumph over domestic rivals or of one faction or class over another. Although mercy may be a virtue independent of the political system, not all political systems that place a high value on mercy are virtuous.

The friendly sovereign's faithful, if they continue to enjoy his favor, do not subscribe to a common faith with members of the wider community. They cling to their distinctions. They are acutely aware of their status as favored or disfavored, and they very quickly live and compete in a system in which degrees of favor or disfavor measure the differences that make a difference among their fellow subjects. Alexis de Tocqueville noted that he and Michelet lived in a century that slowly undermined the distinctions that sustained the feudal nobility by the consolidation of power, first under absolutism and then under the centralization of eighteenth-century revolutionaries.[18] By the nineteenth century, through Napoleon, the Restoration, and then the July Monarchy under Louis Philippe, the competition for favor as well as the effort to displace another stratum's king begat contexts in which the quest for a friendly sovereign of one's own became particularly intense. The disgust and disaffection the less favored harbored for the regime is apparent in contemporary cartoonist Honoré Daumier's caricature of Louis Philippe as Gargantua in *La Caricature*.

Hobbes and many of his contemporaries understood the quest for favor quite well. When they were not seeking it themselves, they dismissed the rebels of the civil war as merely frustrated favor seekers. Hobbes was torn between protecting his sovereign's prerogatives, including the friendly ones, and cautioning the sovereign against extralegal favors such as monopolies, patents, and suspensions of the law. He knew the exercise of such friendly prerogatives would draw the ire of the majority and lead the sovereign to suffer defections.

BEASTS AND THE FRIENDLY SOVEREIGN

In response to Cato the Elder's likening of kings to predatory beasts, Hobbes famously asserted that men were both like wolves and like gods to one another.[19] Hobbes's absolute sovereign is, on some accounts, the inhuman being that permits human beings to live their lives by pacifying their treachery and factiousness with the threat of his superior power. He thereby makes and protects the order within, granting a peace whose benefits humans enjoy, but only at the price of permanent vulnerability to a wolfish protector's savage extralegal capacities. In John Locke's philosophy, such a sovereign was likened to the master over his animals rather than a justifiable political power: he keeps order among the creatures and stops them from harming one another, not out of regard for their common good or any legal limits. As an absolutist monarch, his subjects exist only for his pleasure or advantage.[20]

If the extraordinary powers and cunning necessary to the hostile sovereign's role elicit beastly comparisons, is there a corresponding comparison for the friendly sovereign? There is. The friendly sovereigns—both those who exercise extraordinary generosity and those who are extraordinarily merciful—are not made over into beasts, however. The subjects are instead assigned the role. Seneca, I noted, was not alone among ancient political thinkers in considering the friendly aspects of sovereignty. Xenophon commended Cyrus's generosity as a means of securing his subjects' loyalty. He compared the beneficiaries of Cyrus's largesse to dogs gathered at the dinner table and struggling to be near their master.[21] The first in line for scraps is highest and first in the master's affections. In Michelet's France, Daumier inverted Xenophon's tableau. In his cartoon of February 9, 1831, in *La Caricature*, he invites his audience to picture Louis Philippe's loyalists as beasts on all fours, anxious to gobble up the goodies surrounding the throne. The caption reads: "Very humble, very obedient, very submissive, and most of all, very voracious subjects."[22]

The merciful side of the friendly sovereign's repertoire has lent itself to animal tales. Both Seneca and the historian Cassius Dio (AD 150–235) make reference to a moment, possibly mythical, when the supremely powerful Augustus learned from his wife, Livia, how and why he should be merciful with those who conspired against him.[23] The news of the conspiracy by Cinna, grandson of his former rival, Pompey the Great, pains the emperor. He had spared him as an innocent born into the enemy camp and had preferred him above others for office.[24] In Dio's account, Augustus complains at length that he must not only fight off Rome's enemies but also live in constant fear of his domestic friends.[25] Livia counsels clemency, and the result is said to be quite successful. Cinna learns that he is discovered in his plot and is brought before Augustus, who speaks to him in person. In spite of his disappointment, he forgives Cinna and appoints him to a term as consul. Cinna then remains ever loyal to the man who might have lawfully executed him. Though the subsequent evidence in his own history belies the assertion, Dio writes that that Cinna's was the last plot ever hatched against Augustus.[26]

Livia's conversation with Augustus is turned into a lengthy meditation on the practical political advantages of being merciful and gentle with subjects. After a career that brought him, by bloodshed, into a princely position over the republic, Augustus needs a new and timely change of method, she argues. It is especially important to change his method to dissuade his subjects from thinking that he did these bloody deeds willingly. As part of her analysis of the advantages of clemency, Livia notes: "Hence it is that a man will more readily submit to the most terrible hardships—and gladly, too—if he has been persuaded, than if compulsion has been put upon him. And so true it is that, in following both these courses, man is subject to a compelling law of nature, that even among the irrational animals, which have no intelligence, many of the strongest and fiercest are tamed by petting and subdued by allurements, while many even of the most cowardly and weak are aroused to fury by acts of cruelty which excite terror in them."[27] In his analysis of the conversation, Eric Adler observes that Livia's arguments for clemency resonate with others that Dio makes elsewhere in his corpus. In putting these words into Livia's mouth, however, he adds another political dynamic. Livia's reasons for using clemency are purely instrumental, and she is equally willing to recommend that Augustus reserve his deadly force for subjects who pose a real threat to his rule. Her outlook is one of pessimism, not generosity. The vast majority of subjects are likely to wish to do wrong in the pursuit of power for themselves. In her view, clemency is required, if for no other reason than that few subjects would survive if severity were used against all who deserved it. For subjects who pose a true threat, owing either to the prince's real vulnerability or to the subject's incorrigible aggression, Livia does not hesitate to recommend lethal solutions. In short, as Adler suggests, one and the same Machiavel can recommend both bloody reprisals and clemency—a point underscored by Dio's later mention that Livia herself was suspected in Augustus's death, paving the way for her son, Tiberius, to take the throne.[28]

AUGUSTUS'S CLEMENCY

Seneca's account of Augustus's pardon of Cinna is repeated in Montaigne's *Essays*, then augmented and put to use in 1639 by Pierre Corneille in *Cinna, ou la Clémence d'Auguste*.[29] Corneille was celebrated both during and after his lifetime. Michelet and his romantic contemporaries lauded and appropriated Corneille as a creative genius who had thrown off the fetters of religious tradition and monarchical authority through willful individual self-assertion.[30] Corneille's contribution is more mixed in Michelet's account than in that of others for whom the heroism defined itself against the power of the state, especially Cardinal Richelieu.[31] By applications of immense force, Richelieu was building absolutist structures for Louis XIII, putting down rebellions and Protestant navel and political strongholds, like La Rochelle in 1628, or the greater tax revolts of Corneille's own Rouen. His repressions were followed by selective, triumphant acts of mercy.[32]

Because of Richelieu's reputation, Michelet describes the French as having received *Cinna* as satire against the minister with whom he quarreled.[33] Katherine Ibbett has suggested that "to oppose Corneille and Richelieu is to oppose French integrity to Italian duplicity." The traditional "curricular Corneille" is a man of *générosité*, of the aristocratic ethos of self-sacrifice.[34] Corneille stands for duty, for virtuous gestures performed without selfish, instrumental calculations.[35] Against this pure French virtue stands Richelieu, a man of Italian (Machiavellian) vice. Ibbett and others have located Corneille's *Cinna* in a world looking to overcome its Machiavels.[36] In Corneille they see a writer of characters who must grapple with Machiavelli's—and, for that matter, Livia's—argument that the appearance of virtue is sometimes a necessary strategy for those who would remain in power.

In Corneille's dramatization, Augustus's enemies profess a desire to avenge their fallen family members and regain the republic. Augustus himself thinks that he is confronted with a binary choice: either fight his opponents to the death (convinced though he may be that he deserves their hatred) or give up the principate, saddened and dismayed by a world where, as Cinna demonstrates, he cannot even trust his friends. Although he resists at first, Augustus ultimately heeds Livia's advice:

> Try how pardon works on Cinna, and
> Turn his confusion into punishment;
> Seek now to follow the most useful course.
> His death can anger an excited town:
> Mercifulness can heighten your prestige,
> And those your rigour would antagonize
> Perhaps by your indulgence will be touched.[37]

One could argue that Corneille was a more faithful student of Machiavelli than some of his admirers would admit. Others have argued that the strategic characteristics of Corneille's Augustus amount to a sophisticated undressing of absolutist monarchy's lawless power.[38]

I do not seek to choose between these perspectives on Corneille or claim a definitive reading of *Cinna*. I am interested in what the moral murkiness in Corneille's staging of princely authority can help us understand about choosing or consenting to friendly sovereignty. The governed, as I noted earlier, generally do not choose a friendly sovereign in the same way that consent theorists like Hobbes imagine the choosing of a sovereign upon exiting the state of nature. Those who possess sovereign power and exercise its friendly prerogatives know, however, that many subjects will nonetheless yield a harvest of gratitude. As harsh as Richelieu was to those who stood in the way of the consolidation of state power, he cultivated an image of himself and Louis XIII as forgiving and generous counterparts to the ancient Roman emperors.[39]

In the same period that he was contemplating how the fear of a violent death might lead individuals to lay down their defenses and submit to a common power, Corneille was drawing from Seneca's account of the clement Augustus to imagine another miraculous conversion. He adds a fictional character, Emilia, whose father, like Cinna's, was killed by Augustus; but unlike Cinna, the grandson of Pompey, Emilia is the daughter of C. Toranius,

Augustus's tutor.⁴⁰ Augustus is nonetheless fond of Emilia and considers her as a daughter. The love is not reciprocal. Of all the conspirators plotting to kill Augustus in the name of the republic and to avenge a slain father, Emilia is the least flexible in her dedication to Augustus's demise. After Cinna is apprehended, she comes voluntarily to make herself a victim of Augustus's justice. She declares that if she cannot kill her adopted father, then she could at least excite others to avenge her and Cinna.

After Augustus learns that Emilia is looking to avenge her father's death and after Emilia, Cinna, and the other conspirator, Maximus, declare their wish to suffer death at his hand—that they might die as good Romans in opposition to a tyrant—Corneille's Augustus finally declares his mercy:

> I'm master of myself as of the world;
> I am. I wish to be. O days to come,
> Preserve for ever my last victory!
> I triumph over the righteous wrath
> That ever can be handed down to you.
> Cinna, let us be friends. This *I* entreat.⁴¹

Incapable of ending the treachery of those who seek vengeance against him for his bloody rise to power, Corneille's Augustus, like Seneca's, secures his future with a sovereign act of clemency. The act affects all the conspirators; it is not unlike a counterpart to the sobering conversion Hobbes imagines in those who submit to a force that threatens them with violent death.⁴² Emilia is the first to speak after Augustus pardons Cinna, gives him the object of his desire (i.e., Emilia, in marriage), and tells the conspirators, "By my example, learn to curb your wrath."⁴³

> I yield, Sir, to this generosity.
> Its crystal radiance gives me back my sight.
> What appeared justified is now a crime,
> And—what death's terror had no power to do—
> I feel in me burgeon repentance's flower,
> And my heart's prompting gives assent to it.
> Heaven has decided your supremacy,
> And I, my lord, am the best proof 'tis so.
> I dare give this decisive evidence:
> Heaven changes me; then it can change the State.⁴⁴

The play outwardly affirms Augustus's complete mastery over himself and the world. Cinna and Corneille's Emilia affirm their fidelity and subordination to the one who decides to escape the dictates of his past severity and pardon the unpardonable. When Charles II was invited back to the throne that his father lost in the English Civil War when he was executed, he was welcomed back to London as Augustus.[45] Upon his return from exile, he declared an Act of Indemnity and Oblivion.[46] Not long thereafter, those who sided with and sacrificed for his father's cause declared themselves unwilling to share Charles II's forgiveness of their former foes. Hobbes was among them, as evidenced by his Restoration-era complaints against Presbyterians. Along with the king, prewar tensions returned later in the century. When sovereign grace or force is distributed arbitrarily, sovereignty itself is often at risk of discovering that its mastery is an illusion.

NOTES

INTRODUCTION

1. Augustine, *City of God* 1.1–8, esp. 7–8; 1.13, n8, n22; 2.2.

2. Schmitt makes these claims across a number of texts, the most prominent of which is *Political Theology*. Schmitt's views on sovereignty will be presented in greater detail in the course of my argument.

3. Weber, "Politics as a Vocation," 77–78, 81–83.

4. Schmitt, *Political Theology*, 5, 13.

5. Schmitt, *Concept of the Political*, 25–27.

6. Ibid., 29–31, 33–35.

7. Ibid., 35; Schmitt, *Political Theology*, 5–15. For a discussion of intensity in Schmitt's thought on politics and political conflict, see Shapiro, *Carl Schmitt*.

8. Where the power to make law, like Rousseau's Legislator, and the capacity characteristic of commissarial dictators to act outside the law in times of crises come together there begins a transition into "sovereign dictatorship," and this mobilizes a constituent power, or *le pouvoir constitu-ent*. Schmitt, *Dictatorship*, 109–31. For a treatment of this creative power in Schmitt's thought, see Kalyvas, *Democracy*.

9. Schmitt, *Concept of the Political*, 31.

10. One of the more powerful and near continuous criticisms of Schmitt has been that his understanding of a people's unity, in spite of his insistence against German legal positivists of the difference between legality and legitimacy, is rarely more than fleeting affinity for hostility itself. In this, therefore, he resembles the liberals and romantics that he so often denounces. For examples of such criticisms, see Kracauer, "Revolt of the Middle Classes"; Strauss, "Notes on Carl Schmitt"; Meier, *Lesson of Carl Schmitt*; Derrida, *Politics of Friendship*; Kennedy, *Constitutional Failure*.

11. Morrill, "Religious Context"; Morrill, "Attack on the Church of England."

12. For some reflections on this contribution and its reach, see Strong, *Politics Without Vision*, 219–62; McCormick, "Fear, Technology, and the State"; Meier, *Carl Schmitt and Leo Strauss*. This is by no means a comprehensive list.

13. A notable example of Schmitt's influence, mediated via Giorgio Agamben, can be found in Danner, "After September 11"; Agamben, *State of Exception*. For scholarly discussion of Schmitt's potential influence over persons and sovereign exceptions made during this period, see Scheuerman, "Carl Schmitt"; Scheuerman, "Emergencies."

14. Agamben, *State of Exception*; Agamben, *Homo Sacer*.

15. "Sovereign power is fundamentally premised on the capacity and the will to decide on life and death, the capacity to visit excessive violence on those declared enemies or on undesirables." Hansen and Steppuat, "Sovereignty Revisited," 296, 301. Working toward a new place for sovereignty concepts in anthropology, Hansen and Steppuat exemplify Agamben's influence over understandings of sovereignty with striking, unqualified clarity and force. Among political theorists, Agamben's reception has been mixed. See, in particular, Norris, *Politics, Metaphysics, and Death*; Passavant, "Contradictory State." Arguments in this book can only indirectly address Agamben-inspired views of sovereignty. I start at the source, as it were, of this focus, and Agamben's flow from a partial appropriation of Schmitt, critically supplemented by Walter Benjamin's critique of him (emphasizing that "the exception" becomes the rule within modern states). An extension of friendly sovereignty to what Agamben identifies as zones of exclusion would ask: Do not bare lives also experience local friendly extralegal sovereigns? What is the status of mercy of grace in these contexts? Did these informal sovereigns,

private colonial trading companies, or functionaries of the late modern state's governmental institutions strengthen their grip only through the use of extraordinary and unregulated violence? Or, as among early modern sovereigns, also through their own—and in many cases sanctioned by the state sovereign's—extraordinary forms of favor or forgiveness? Judith Butler's discussion of the indefinite detainees in Guantanamo proposes a thesis adjacent to Agamben's: she finds a reanimated, anachronistic sovereignty that is not quite itself: as in conceptions of old absolutists, it and its functionaries are not checked by the separations of powers. They return to the supposed full discretion of old, but this time via the deployment of the apparatuses of governmentality described by Foucault. The functionaries who man these institutions like the Guantanamo prison are "petty sovereigns." They are not fully under control of the executive, thereby removing them from a form of accountability, and so they exercise an unconditional capacity to act in detaining and harming those in the legal no-man's-lands like Guantanamo. This new old sovereign can only be resurrected in the context of (indefinite) emergency rule and claims its overarching right to unconditional discretion to preserve the nation in the face of a threat. Butler, *Precarious Life*, esp. 65.

16. In a prominent edited collection introducing Schmitt to many, we learn that Schmitt "picks up where Hobbes leaves off," connecting the war of all against all in the state of nature to the factional conflict in Weimar, and that Schmitt modernizes the seventeenth-century absolutists like Hobbes and Bodin. Hirst, "Carl Schmitt's Decisionism," 9, 12–13. Reinhart Koselleck's reading of Hobbes is strongly influenced by Schmitt. Koselleck, *Critique and Crisis*, 23–40; Pankakoski, "Conflict, Context, Concreteness." A subtle reading of Hobbes's place in Schmitt's career is Thomsen, "Carl Schmitt." I am not the first Hobbes scholar to distance Hobbes from Schmitt. See Habermas, "Horrors of Autonomy"; Sorell, "Schmitt, Hobbes"; Holmes, "Does Hobbes Have a

Concept"; Slomp, *Carl Schmitt*; Schröder, "Carl Schmitt's Appropriation."

17. Schmitt, *Leviathan*.

18. On the Roman presence and pressures from within the royal household, specifically those cultivated by the Catholic queen Henrietta Marie, see Hibbard, *Charles I*. Not every sovereign, person, creed, or faction accused of "popery" in the seventeenth century was Catholic. Hotter Protestants accused Laudians of popery, and James I had long associated Presbyterian and Puritan challenges to royal authority with "popery" in that they, and the Roman Catholic Church, had attempted to undermine royal prerogatives and authority. Nonetheless, anti-Catholicism and anti-popery were often tethered. On the complexity of anti-popery (which was by no means identical to mere anti-Catholicism), see Harris, "Anti-Catholicism and Anti-Popery"; Lake, "Anti-Popery." On the centrality of Laud's offenses in the eyes of those who chose to take sides against Charles I, see Morrill, "Religious Contexts," "Attack on the Church," and "Charles I." Morrill's emphasis on the religious rather than constitutional reasons for rebellion have spurred some, including Sommerville, *Royalists and Patriots*, to reassert the salience of constitutional motives.

19. House of Commons, "Grand Remonstrance," 207.

20. Ibid., 219. This included the specific services of the Secretary of State, Sir Francis Windebank, "a powerful agent for speeding all their desires."

21. Ibid., 208–9. British failures against Spain at Cádiz (in 1625) are also said to have been so badly botched "as if it had rather been intended to make us weary of war than to prosper in it."

22. Ibid., 212–13.

23. Ibid., 212–14.

24. K. Sharpe, *Personal Rule*; Burgess, *Absolute Monarchy*; Kishlansky, *Monarchy Transformed*; Kishlansky, "Tyranny Denied." In referencing the Remonstrance's grievances, we need not credit most or even all to establish our central point: that sovereignty was at stake in the crown's extralegal

capacities to favor, pardon, or show leniency (or use dispensing powers; see chapter 5) to those whom many of his subjects detested. This holds regardless of the merits of their complaints.

25. Miller, *Mortal Gods*, 228–33.

26. *New York Times*, "President and His Power." Scandalous presidential pardons have attracted the most attention, for example: George W. Bush's pardon of Caspar Weinberger, Bill Clinton's pardon of Mark Rich, and of course Gerald Ford's pardon of Richard Nixon. Thanks in part to the campaigns for greater mercy, following a wave of severe legislation that distributed unjustly heavy sentences on small offenders, large-scale commutations had for at least a moment transformed from last-minute disgraces to publicly celebrated steps in the direction of a more just society. Cf. Sarat, *Mercy on Trial*; Shear, "Obama's 78 Pardons"; *New York Times*, "At Long Last, a Measure of Justice." Thanks to Donald Trump's more personal approach to pardons, the pardon scandal in its older forms has returned: Schmidt and Vogel, "Prospect of Pardons."

27. Schmidt et al., "Trump's Lawyer Raised Prospect"; Sullivan, "What We've Learned"; Karni, "President Trump Grants Pardon"; Baker, Haberman, and LaFraniere, "Trump Commutes Sentence"; Haberman and Schmidt, "Trump Pardons"; Haberman and Schmidt, "Trump Gives Clemency"; Savage, "Trump Pardons Michael Flynn."

28. Landler, "Trump to Invite Putin"; Yourish and Griggs, "8 U.S. Intelligence Groups"; Mueller, *Report*; Jurecic, "What's New in the Unredacted Mueller Report?"

29. Davis and Haberman, "Trump Pardons Joe Arpaio"; Philipps, "Trump's Pardons for Servicemen."

30. Ackerman, *Decline and Fall*, 1–14. For Ackerman, this is a significant reversal of his prior optimism regarding the presidency and its role in constitutional renewal, as he acknowledges.

31. The capacity to interfere on an arbitrary basis over the choices I am in a position to make defines a relationship of domination in Philip Pettit's first formulation or republican liberty, but interference,

as he defines it, "cannot take the form of a bribe or reward; when I interfere I make things worse for you, not better." Pettit, *Republicanism*, 52; Sparling, "Political Corruption."

CHAPTER 1

1. Although there are many attempts to define or redefine sovereignty in international law or international relations that largely abjure historical inquiry in favor of received claims regarding "archaic" notions of sovereignty—often as a prelude to introducing what now must be introduced on the presumption that prior notions of sovereignty could not possibly have contemplated today's "global" conditions—the counter-thrust to demand historical inquiry into what earlier thinkers were actually attempting in their claim to, and about, sovereignty has been growing. It has already grown to the point where the question for some is not necessarily whether to historicize but how. We can see a sign of this in three distinct pleas for historicization in a recent volume from 2010: Skinner, "Sovereign State"; Baranger, "Apparition of Sovereignty"; Koskenniemi, "Conclusion." For one of the most thoroughgoing late nineteenth century to mid-twentieth century treatments of sovereignty in international law, see Koskenniemi, *Gentle Civilizer*. This marks a significant shift toward the concrete exploration of sovereignty claims and may be contrasted with the genealogical approach within the history of ideas in international relations. Cf. the deconstructive, and professed Nietzschean, approach taken in Bartelson, *Genealogy of Sovereignty*. For Bartelson, the greatest difficulty in the grasping of sovereignty is ultimately not a matter of knowing particulars but is "connected to the possibility of knowledge in general" (14). What perhaps all authors will agree upon is that discussions of sovereignty inevitably lead toward contentions regarding the learned disciplines that make a claim to speak on the subject, and that the topic sets a kind of recursive trap from which escape is hardly a given.

2. Sovereignty, one scholar concludes after case studies on the legal assertions of recent states, "is neither a historical nor a sociological fact but part of a political vocabulary whose point is not to register aspects of the world but to achieve them: to preserve a status quo, to support or oppose particular contestants." Koskenniemi, "Conclusion," 232.

3. Mill, "On Liberty," 48.

4. For a partially Arendtian-inspired polemic against sovereign individuality in political theory, see Krause, *Freedom Beyond Sovereignty*.

5. Bodin, *Six Bookes*, 84.

6. Condren, *Argument and Authority*, 15–29. Bodin and those who shared his definition of sovereignty sought to define the office, to identify those who lived up to or fell short of its responsibilities. We can see a debate about duty without, to put it crudely, making Kantians of them before their time. Strictly speaking, it was not persons, but, as Condren suggests, *personae* that were a function of the office and office talk, and within this preconceptual framework, there was a great deal of flexibility, fragility, and contingency, as well as embodied visions of officeholders and their duties. It was this very flexibility—the tendency to use casuistry to justify interested acts in the name of these duties after the fact—that begot Kant's rejection. Ibid., 346–47. Recent scholarship connecting Bodin with a trust suggests another more historically sensitive perspective. D. Lee, "'Office Is a Thing Borrowed.'"

7. Stacey, "Sovereign Person"; Condren, *Argument and Authority*, 15, 19–20; Plato, *Republic* 343a–345e.

8. Bodin, *Six Bookes*, 36, 511.

9. On Schmittian misreadings of Bodin, see Keohane, "Bodin on Sovereignty."

10. Baranger, "Apparition of Sovereignty."

11. Bodin, *Six Bookes*, 1, 101.

12. Ibid., 1.

13. Ibid., 1–2.

14. Figgis, *Divine Right of Kings*, 1–16.

15. For conflicting historical views on labeling kings "absolutists," compare Sommerville, "Absolutism and Royalism"; Burgess, *Absolute Monarchy*.

16. Hobbes, *Leviathan* 14.4–5. References to *Leviathan* (abbreviated *Lev.*) are generally to the chapter and section number in the Curley edition.

17. Bodin, *Six Bookes*, 72, 92, 104.

18. Ibid., 86.

19. Sommerville, "Absolutism and Royalism."

20. He's noted, for example, that resistance and limitation are distinct. Burgess, *Absolute Monarchy*, 19.

21. For a contemplation on sovereignty as a locus of the anxious, see Brown, *Walled States*.

22. Hobbes, *Lev.*, chap. 29.

23. Locke, *Two Treatises*, 398–428.

24. Ibid., 186–87, 191, 197–98, 238–39.

25. Maritain, *Man and the State*, 28–53.

26. Ibid., 44–49.

27. Arendt, "What Is Freedom?," esp. 163.

28. "Freedom needed, in addition to mere liberation, the company of other men who were in the same state, and it needed a common public space to meet them—a politically organized world, in other words, into which each of the free men could insert himself by word and deed" (ibid., 148). See also ibid., 154.

29. Plato and Aristotle, in Arendt's *The Human Condition*, stand accused of fleeing the frailty and unpredictability of action. The recasting of human relations into ruling and being ruled, and ultimately into a division between those who know and do not act, and those who act and do not know, is laid at their feet. This then sets us down a long path upon which making rather than acting, craftsmanship rather than witnessed performance becomes our controlling conception, and this is also deeply implicated in the appeal of sovereignty and the abandonment of true freedom. Here again in this text, Stoicism's mistaken, and withdrawn, conception of freedom (a freedom unmolested by the fact of human plurality) is said to take hold. Arendt, *The Human Condition*, 220–36.

30. "Christian will-power was discovered as an organ of self-liberation and immediately found wanting. It is as though the I-will immediately paralyzed the I-can, as though the moment men *willed* freedom, they lost

their capacity to *be free*. In the deadly conflict with worldly desires and intentions from which will-power was supposed to liberate the self, the most willing seemed able to achieve was oppression." Arendt, "What Is Freedom," 162.

31. For Arendt, freedom was among ancients largely uncontaminated with the divided self she decries. This is a self that divorces the "I will" from the "I can." Where will, living now in a condition where the two are divorced, as distinct from a capacity for action, can pursue freedom outside the realm of human intercourse. It is not that ancients were always capable of what they willed. Quite the contrary, sometimes necessity thwarted their capacities to act, and this they found agonizing. Importantly for Arendt, the will that was so thwarted understood itself as unfree and did not measure its freedom in terms of a mere, unworldly, "free-will." Ibid., 159–61.

32. For an interesting discussion of her unusual views of the American founding— she asserts that the American Constitution was the first to propose a polity without sovereignty—as a failed, if inspiring, route toward a defense of secularism against political theology, see Moyn, "Hannah Arendt."

33. For an earlier Marxist disassociation between freedom and sovereignty that likewise condemns Rousseau and the absolutists, see Veblen, *Absentee Owner-ship*, 21–39.

34. Rousseau, *On the Social Contract*, 1.6–7. References are to book and chapter number.

35. Ibid., 2.4.

36. Ibid., 1.8.

37. Ibid., 3.1, 10–11.

38. Ibid., 3.13.

39. Paine, "Rights of Man," 338.

40. Kant, "To Perpetual Peace," 72.

41. Ibid., app. I, II. A left-liberal German legal theorist of the Weimar era, Hermann Heller, would see in Kant's declaration against a right of ethical resistance—and with the subsequent growth of administrative states wherein formal legal certainty became paramount—an opening for might

to make right. Order for its own sake left the state bereft of its obligation to seek ethical legitimation. See Heller, "Essence and Structure." Among North American scholars of Weimar jurisprudence, especially those interested in finding a space between Hans Kelsen's positivism and Carl Schmitt's anti-positivism, there is a lament that Carl Schmitt's confrontation with the liberal Kelsen critic Heller is not better known— although recently Heller's work has been revived as a part of the critique of authoritarian liberalism, and the question has become how, among some critics of austerity imposed upon nations from without their borders, to best put Heller to use. See Dyzenhaus, *Legality and Legitimacy*; Dyzenhaus, "Gorgon Head of Power"; Dyzenhaus, "Kelsen, Heller and Schmitt"; Scheuerman, "Hermann Heller." Michelet, another liberal who wished that enlightenment predecessors had not abandoned popular sentiments for rational analysis, is no precursor to Weimar liberals such as Heller. They would disagree on the use of religion in uniting nations. They do, however, occupy a common blind spot: that within the Schmittian framework adopted today. It fosters a proclivity to obscure the view of liberalism's past, such that those liberals who had reservations about rationalist excesses tend to find themselves in a logically excluded middle—an exclusion that erases too much history in its quest for a past to affirm the centrality of present existential choices.

42. Hegel, *Hegel's Philosophy of Right*, secs. 257–59, 278.

43. Ibid., secs. 273–78.

44. Weber, *Economy and Society*, 600–601.

45. Hegel, *Hegel's Philosophy of Right*, secs. 182–87.

46. Ibid., sec. 257.

47. Ibid., sec. 279.

48. Ibid., secs. 264–66.

49. Ibid., sec. 279. For an argument that suggests that Hobbes's concept of authorization of his sovereign (if not necessarily a monarch) in *Leviathan* performed this same work centuries earlier against defenders of the people's sovereignty, in this case,

especially against Henry Parker, see Skinner, "Hobbes and the Purely Artificial Person."

50. James, *Pragmatism*, 58–73.

51. Laski, *Studies*, 1–25.

52. Ibid., 12.

53. Ibid., 14.

54. Schmitt, *Political Theology*.

55. Ibid., 18–19.

56. The most relevant target, although Schmitt paints with a broader brush, is Hans Kelsen: see Kelsen, "Legal Formalism." He begins by describing the Pure Theory of Law as follows: "The Pure Theory of Law is nothing other than a *theory of positive law* and pretends to be nothing else. It refuses to respond to the question of the correct law, without judging the dignity of this question. It wants to discover only what *is* in the law; not what *ought* to be." The extreme polarizing framework that Kelsen adopts almost begs for the Schmittian rejoinder and makes reliance on "sociological fact" as much an absolute choice as Kelsen's refusal to consider the question of what law ought to be for a given people. This polarization, as others have noted, does not represent the full spectrum of Weimar jurisprudence or indeed neo-Kantian thinking. See, for example, Dyzenhaus, "Gorgon Head of Power."

57. Schmitt, *Constitutional Theory*, 62–66, 154–55.

58. Schmitt, *Political Theology*, 5.

59. Ibid., 7, 16–25; Krabbe, *Modern Idea*. In *Das Problem der Souveränität und die Theorie des Völkerrechts: Beitrag zu einer reinen Rechtslehre* of 1920, Kelsen had argued for using the neo-Kantian model of a universal legal order above the partial legal orders of individual states as a way of conceptualizing international law's theory.

60. Hobbes, *Lev.*, 17.13.

61. Derrida, "Force of Law."

62. Derrida, *Politics of Friendship*.

63. Derrida, *Rogues*.

64. Agamben, *Homo Sacer*.

65. Kalmo and Skinner, "Introduction."

CHAPTER 2

1. Schmitt drew the unfavorable contrast between Weimar's liberal constitutional aspects, "which attempt to repress the question of sovereignty by a division and mutual control of competencies," and the restored Bourbons who used, as we'll review below, article 14 of the 1814 Charter: "it would grant exceptional powers [as the 1814 Charter], which made the monarch sovereign." Schmitt, *Political Theology*, 11. He neglects to note the consequence of this decision: the 1830 Revolution that removed the Bourbons.

2. It is instructive to contrast Schmitt with Marx on Guizot. Although he tends to ignore Guizot's assault on sovereignty, Schmitt emphasizes his characteristically liberal admiration for Parliamentary, representative government. As Marx could testify, this by no means disqualified Guizot as a practitioner of political, and class, antagonism. Marx could convict Guizot of occasional bad history, especially when trying to convict his fellow Frenchmen of having mistakenly staged a revolution against him, but he would never have dreamed of accusing the man who ejected him from France of lacking the will or intellectual disposition for class conflict. Marx, "Review of Guizot's Book"; Marx, "Manifesto of the Communist Party," 473; Marx, "Speeches on Poland," 103; Marx, "June Revolution," 131. The same might be said of the entire triumphant bourgeoisie in the eyes of Lorenz von Stein, whom Schmitt sometimes admired and sometimes shunned. Even with his occasional praise of Lorenz von Stein (e.g., Schmitt, *Constitutional Theory*, 61–62; Schmitt, *Concept of the Political*, 24, 47, 70; Schmitt, *Political Theology*, 60), Stein's understanding of how liberals in nineteenth-century France used constitutionalism, explicitly, as a tool for class dominance is difficult to accommodate in Schmitt's framework. See Stein, *History*. On Schmitt's view of Guizot, see also Larmore, *Morals of Modernity*, 184–86.

3. Michelet began, writes Paul Viallaneix, with an "instinctual socialism" that did not lead to sympathies with some of Babeuf's ideals and the thought of Fourier, Saint-Simon, or Proudhon. Viallaneix, *La Voie Royale*, 40, 395–406. Against Blanc and

Buchez, Michelet rejected the Christianization (and specifically Catholicization) of the Revolution. Sacrifice and redemption were also themes in their apology for the Terror. Kipper, *Jules Michelet*, 147–48; Buchez and Roux, *Histoire Parlementaire*, 1:1–2. Buchez is explicit in linking revolutionary fraternity with what he describes as the spark of social energy that made it essentially one with the invisible historical force, the moral devotion, that had been initiated by Christ. Cf. Michelet, *The People*, 150n. See also LeFort, "Edgar Quinet." Louis Blanc spoke of the difference between Robespierre and his liberal opponents from among the revolutionaries as the difference between the followers of Voltaire and Montesquieu, on the one hand, and Rousseau on the other: a contrast between proponents for individual liberties against those who prioritized the advantage of all. Blanc, *History of the French Revolution*, 567–68.

4. On Babeufism, see Michelet, *The People*, 68. On the Terror, see below.

5. On who was, and was not, injured or arrested on the streets, see Pinkney, *French Revolution of 1830*, 98, 252–74.

6. Gildea, *Past in French History*; Furet, *Revolutionary France*; Mellon, *Political Uses of History*.

7. The urge to correct historians who celebrated the past, especially the histories that sustained ultraconservative narratives regarding the proper course for the present, began with the historians who preceded Michelet. Conservative liberal constitutionalists deployed it against Burke and de Maistre. Liberty, Germaine de Staël argued, was an ancient thing struggling to assert itself against the counterforce of domination. De Staël, *Considerations*, 24–25, 25n10, 27–28; see also 542–48. Her followers, including Guizot and Thierry, added Bonald and Chateaubriand to the list. Mellon, *Political Uses of History*, 5–11, 58–62. Michelet adapted a similar framework, but then recast the liberty lauded by the monarchical conservatives. Their notions would also be superseded. On still earlier antecedents, see Viallaneix, *La Voie Royale*, 172–78.

8. Necker's niece De Staël had familial stakes in this debate. On burial, resurrection, and messianism in this era, see Gildea, *Past in French History*, 89–90.

9. For an American parallel, see Twain, *Life on the Mississippi*, 465–70, on the malign influence of Sir Walter Scott and his satires of chivalric romantic nostalgia through Tom Sawyer's dangerous fantasies and *A Connecticut Yankee in King Arthur's Court*. Cf, however, Crossley, *French Historians*, 48–49, on Scott among French romantics.

10. Furet, *Revolutionary France*, 273–75, 280–84, 294–306.

11. See, for example, Michelet's condemnation of Volney, whom Thomas Jefferson had befriended and surreptitiously translated. Volney taught "that history is *a science of dead facts.*" Michelet, *The People*, 152. Crossley, *French Historians*, 187–88.

12. De Tocqueville, *Old Regime*, 1:99–101.

13. LeFort, "Permanence."

14. Michelet and Quinet, *Jesuits*, 3. Michelet was not alone in targeting Jesuits; even those much less antagonistic than he could single them out. On the contentiousness of Catholic education and a survey of rival positions on the question, see Collingham, *July Monarchy*, 303–17.

15. Anderson, "Constitutional Charter of 1814," art. 5–6.

16. Ibid., cf. art. 5–7. M. Price, *Perilous Crown*, 186; Rosanvallon, *La monarchie impossible*.

17. M. Price, *Perilous Crown*, 117–19.

18. In February 1831, the Ultras (the ultraconservative faction, returned and exiled French nobles who were least willing to compromise with political and religious realities in France after 1789) attempted to have a ceremony at Saint-Germain-l'Auxerrois in remembrance of their assassinated hero, the Duc de Berry. In response an anticlerical mob rose up, anxious to punish the Church that had aided the Ultras. They sacked the church while the National Guard stood by passively. Days later the archbishop's palace was pillaged. Crosses were torn off most churches in Paris, and in provincial France, immense crosses

that had been erected in the Restoration's efforts at resuborinating the nation to spiritual authority were the object of "iconoclastic rage." Furet, *Revolutionary France*, 332.

19. Newspaper culture informs many historians' understanding of the period. While many Catholic newspapers, a distinct set of papers from the merely Legitimist press, mourned the loss of the Bourbons, and did so on both sides of the Gallic Church divide, there were some newspapers that saluted the sovereignty of the people and saluted the Orleans monarchy. It should also be noted that for some Catholics of this age, the separation of church and state was welcome. For the range of Catholic press opinion, see Dougherty, "French Catholic Press"; Collingham, *July Monarchy*, 303–17.

20. Eames, *Budget of Letters*, 269, letter dated July 28.

21. Michelet and Quinet, *Jesuits*, 3, 9.

22. Ibid., 2.

23. Ibid.; Michelet, *Priests, Women, and Families*; Michelet, *Love*. For three critical perspectives on Michelet's understanding of gender roles, see Moreau, "Revolting Women"; Mitzman, *Michelet, Historian*; Vinken, "Wounds of Love." This last places his views on gender in the context of his battles with the Church.

24. Barthes, *Michelet*.

25. Schmitt, *Political Theology*, 62–65. Schmitt's polarizing lens largely erases the memory of the French Revolution's many far-from-atheistic opponents of the Church. All must be seen in the terms put by his ultraconservative hero Cortes: "Christ or Barabbas?" This is the moment where Pilate accedes to the wishes of the crowd (or the Jews, on the anti-Semitic reading) to grant a Passover pardon. They choose the insurrectionary Barabbas rather than Jesus. It is one of the opportunities Schmitt had to reference the sovereign prerogative to pardon that he forgoes.

26. Cassirer, *Question of Rousseau*, 73–75.

27. Rousseau, *Letter to Beaumont*, 22.

28. Damrosch, *Jean-Jacques Rousseau*.

29. Rousseau, *On the Social Contract*, 1.1. Notions of decline animate much of the

First Discourse, but in the *Second* we learn, for example, that man, like the domesticated animals, becomes weaker and less capable than those that remain in nature. Rousseau, *Origin and Foundations of Inequality*, 51. Unlike the fixed animals, our free choice tracks a trajectory toward imbecility. Ibid., 53. Only the civilized complain of their life and think of committing suicide. Ibid., 60.

30. Rousseau, *Origin and Foundations of Inequality*, 77.

31. "Man, seek the author of evil no longer. It is in yourself. No evil exists other than that which you do or suffer, and both come to you from yourself." Rousseau, *Emile* [Savoyard Vicar], 282; see also 287. To his accuser after the publication of *Emile*, the Bishop Beaumont: "The cause of evil, according to you, is corrupted nature, and this corruption itself is an evil whose cause had to be sought. Man was created good. We both agree on that, I believe. But you say he is wicked because he was wicked. And I show how he was wicked." Rousseau, *Letter to Beaumont*, 31.

32. "I found it in our social order which—at every point contrary to nature, which nothing destroys—tyrannizes over nature constantly and constantly makes nature demand its rights. . . . By itself it explained all the vices of men and all the ills of society. . . . It was not necessary to assume that man is wicked by his nature, when it is possible to indicate the origin and progression of his wickedness." Rousseau, *Letter to Beaumont*, 52.

33. For a psychological reading of Michelet that traces his various conceptions of nature to the shifting state of his relationships to his mother, wives, and love interests, see Mitzman, *Michelet, Historian*. Michelet's naturalist works drew their political philosophy from nature. For an argument for the persistence of nature, see Kaplan, *Michelet's Poetic Vision*. In his history of the French Revolution (1847), Michelet could speak of France as the mother to whom its citizens return, and this as a return to a natural, primitive sociability. Although he evokes Rousseau (who emphasizes the independent solitude

of the natural man), he clearly also departs from him in this instance. Michelet, *Historical View*, 390–93. For a view of Michelet as anarchist, see White, *Metahistory*, 135–62. For an interpretation of Michelet as having reversed his position on nature—linked to regrets he himself felt after experiencing guilt in relation to his own family, see Mitzman, "Michelet and Social Romanticism."

34. Rousseau, *Emile*, 282–84.

35. Michelet, "Introduction to World History," 25. In 1827 he published a translation of Vico, *Principes de la Philosophie de l'Histoire*. On Vico and Michelet, see Rubini, "Vician 'Renaissance'"; Mali, "Jules Michelet."

36. Michelet and Quinet, *Jesuits*, 60–71.

37. "This carnal, material principle, which introduces justice and injustice into the blood, and transmits them, with the tide of life, from one generation to another, violently contradicts the spiritual notion of Justice which is implanted in the depths of the human soul. No; Justice is not a fluid, to be transmitted with generation. Will alone is just or unjust; the heart alone feels itself responsible. Justice is entirely in the soul; the body has nothing to do with it." Michelet, *Historical View*, 18 (English excerpts from *Histoire de la Révolution française* are from Cocks's translation, titled *Historical View of the French Revolution*). Cf. Rousseau, *Letter to Beaumont*, 29: "Is it conceivable that God creates so many innocent and pure souls purposely to join them to guilty bodies, to make them contract moral corruption thereby, and to condemn them all to hell?" Michelet, unlike Rousseau, does not, however, treat the notion of grace won again by baptism and then subsequently lost by bodily temptation. Rousseau also doesn't plant justice, so much as innocence, in human souls.

38. "This false liability for the actions of others disappear from the world. The unjust transmission of good, perpetuated by the rights of the nobility; the unjust transmission of evil, by original sin, or the civil brand of being descended from sinners, are effaced by the Revolution." Michelet, *Historical View*, 7–8.

39. This is not to say that the urge to be the Church's reformer was not felt by Michelet. Viallaneix, *La Voie Royale*, 388.

40. Barthes, *Michelet*, 211.

41. Rousseau, *Letter to Beaumont*, 48.

42. Bolingbroke hoped to rally the competing factions, Whig and Tory, against Walpole, whom he accused of buying members of Parliament with the promise of ill-gotten gains in the speculative markets. Implicitly comparing his corrupted contemporaries to the significant, but less troublesome, moral and political failings of the Restoration, he wrote: "They might have sold their birth-right for porridge, which was their own. They might have been bubbled by the foolish, bullied by the fearful, and insulted by those whom they despised. They would have deserved to be slaves, and they might have been treated as such. When free people crouch, like camels, to be loaded, the next at hand, no matter who, mounts them, and they soon feel the whip, and the spur of their tyrant; for a tyrant, whether prince or minister, resembles the devil in many respects, particularly in this. He is often both the tempter and the tormentor. He makes the criminal, and he punishes the crime." Bolingbroke, *Dissertation Upon Parties*, 56 [Letter, VII]. Harrington quoted Machiavelli on enriching men with "lands, castles, and treasure" in order that a free polity might be converted into a monarchy (Machiavelli, *Discourses on Livy*, 1.55, cited in translation in James Harrington, *The Commonwealth of Oceana*, ed. J. G. A. Pocock [Cambridge: Cambridge University Press, 1992], 15). See Machiavelli, *Discourses*, 247; Machiavelli, *The Prince*, 62–68. Algernon Sidney connected the fall from equality with the temptations of honors, preferment, and luxury. Sidney, *Discourses Concerning Government*, 184–85.

43. As previously noted, the capacity to interfere on an arbitrary basis over the choices I am in position to make defines a relationship of domination in Philip Pettit's original formulation, but interference, as he defines it, "cannot take the form of a bribe or reward; when I interfere I make things

worse for you, not better." Pettit, *Republicanism*, 52; Sparling, "Political Corruption."

44. MacLean, *Democracy in Chains*. In spite of the work's somewhat sensational subtitle, this is a work of legitimate historical research on the origins of public-choice economics.

45. The assault, however, sometimes sought heroic personalist leaders as a force to supplant the suspected elite with a new leader. Bonapartism became a force in midcentury France when popular outrage with the elites controlling the political parties in France's legislative bodies was mobilized in favor of an emperor who professed his (often false) fidelity to popular sovereignty. Gildea, *Past in French History*, 62–78. Michelet was consistently against Bonaparte and Bonapartists, and it was under Napoleon III that he permanently lost his academic and archival appointments. Cf. Marx, "Eighteenth Brumaire," sec. 7.

46. On the eve of the 1830 Revolution, this is what the ultraconservative journal *Drapeau blanc* demanded of the university professors who had been critical of the Bourbons as the Polignac administration announced its restrictions on the press's freedoms. Pinkney, *French Revolution of 1830*, 58.

47. Collingham, *July Monarchy*, 135. As Collingham also notes, Voltaire was preferred by more conservative defenders of the revolution. Michelet, champion of a petty-bourgeois liberalism, celebrates both.

48. Rousseau, *Discourse on the Sciences and the Arts*, 6.

49. Rousseau, *Origin and Foundations of Inequality*, 88–89.

50. Ibid., 68–69, 77–79.

51. Ibid., 31–39; Rousseau, *On the Social Contract*, 182, 215–16, 226; 4.4–6.

52. Rousseau, *On the Social Contract*, 164.

53. Ibid., 1.7.

54. This is not to suggest that Rousseau was immune to vicious acts of generosity, as I show below, but also to degrading expressions of dependency. See, for example, his plea to Margaret Cavendish, October 20,

1766. Rousseau, *Reveries of the Solitary Walker*, 173–75.

55. She was sometimes mistakenly identified as a marquise. For a compact account of his complicated relationship with d'Épinay (and her circle) in which issues of generosity and, from his host's point of view, ingratitude were an issue, see Damrosch, *Jean-Jacques Rousseau*, 256–83.

56. Rousseau, *Oeuvres complètes*, 1:1092–93, cited in Starobinski, *Largesse*, 161.

57. Ibid.

58. Starobinski, *Largesse*, 8–31.

59. Cf. Suetonius (1914), Titus, 7–9.

60. Starobinski, *Largesse*, 25–26, 29. See Jacques Stella, The *Liberality of Titus* (Allegory of the Liberality of Louis XIII and Cardinal Richelieu), ca. 1637–38, Fogg Museum, Harvard University, http://www.harvardartmuseums.org/art/227880.

61. Plutarch, *Cato the Younger* 66.2; 69.1–70.1, 5–6; 71.1–2.

62. Starobinski, *Largesse*, 14–15.

63. Rousseau may have had other motives for public displays of generosity toward children. A defensive impulse may have been active in his case to demonstrate to the public—that had learned of the fate of his own, orphaned, children—that he, in fact, loved them. Rousseau, *Reveries of the Solitary Walker*, 79–83.

64. Starobinski, *Largesse*, 8–31; Bloch, *Royal Touch*.

65. Michelet, *Historical View*, 36–38.

66. When Michelet escaped poverty, he sometimes took the opportunity to be charitable, but as Paul Viallaneix notes, the society that would make charity its solution to poverty and unemployment was no solution for Michelet, who tended toward an instinctual, if ultimately futureless, socialism. Viallaneix, *La Voie Royale*, 37–40.

67. Michelet, *Historical View*, 23.

68. That project was interrupted to write his history of the revolution as events approached a crisis during the waning days of the July Monarchy. Ibid., 24.

69. Furet, *Revolutionary France*, 269–75. The czar had been pushing for the Bernadotte line, then newly installed and

still the monarchs of Sweden. Germaine de Staël, Benjamin Constant's lover and who had connections to Guizot, held that the czar had in fact been hoping to accommodate France's democratic norms. She also expressed great admiration for Bernadotte. De Staël, *Considerations*, 553–57, but cf. 554n.

70. Anderson, "Constitutional Charter of 1814," article 9; Furet, *Revolutionary France*, 271.

71. Anderson, "Constitutional Charter of 1814." Equality before the law regardless of title (art. 1), Freedom of religion and the press, although with qualifications (art. 5–8) were elements of this constitution, as was the availability of offices open on the basis of merit (art. 3). M. Price, *Perilous Crown*, 56–57.

72. Duguit and Monnier, *Constitutions*, LXXIII–IV.

73. This could be an issue for all French liberals, including those predecessors much to Michelet's right. See, for example, De Staël, *Considerations*, 569–74.

74. Anderson, "Constitutional Charter of 1814," 457–58.

75. Edward Bird, The Arrival of King Louis XVIII of France in Calais in 1814, Burton Constable Hall, https://artuk.org /discover/artworks/the-arrival-of-king -louis-xviii-of-france-in-calais-in-1814 -77478 (accessed July 8, 2017).

76. Louis XVIII's conclusion notably declared the charter enacted in "the nineteenth year of his reign" when it was in fact the first. It was almost as if the revolution, the Thermidor Republic, and Bonaparte had never existed. His desire to blot out that past was also made explicit in the preamble. Anderson, "Constitutional Charter of 1814," 464, 458.

77. During this "romantic piece of bad theatre" wherein in the Church and the aristocracy applauded their own regained supremacy, Charles was also anointed with holy oil, received the ring, the scepter, the hand of justice, and the crown. Furet, *Revolutionary France*, 301. On the "bad theatre," see Walton, "'Quelque Peu Théâtral.'"

78. Furet, *Revolutionary France*, 301; Bloch, *Royal Touch*, 226–28.

79. Walton, "'Quelque Peu Théâtral.'"

80. Furet, *Revolutionary France*, 329–30; M. Price, *Perilous Crown*, 190–91. Casting Louis Philippe as France's William III was a way to promote and guide the eventual outcome of the 1830 Revolution. We see this especially in the writings of Adolphe Thiers in *National*, for example on February 12, 1830: "A dynasty did not know how to reign over a newly constituted society, and another family that knew better was chosen . . . the family closest to the deposed prince." Cited in Pinkney, *French Revolution of 1830*, 53.

81. Michelet, "Introduction to World History," 58.

82. For a discussion of the regime's difficulties with those to its left, see Furet, *Revolutionary France*, 340–77; M. Price, *Perilous Crown*. Liberals in England also sometimes fell out of love with the July Monarchy. Curiously, John Stuart Mill, who had been an enthusiast for the revolution, came to lament that the Doctrinaires (whose leader, Guizot, held the reins for many years in regimes of Louis-Philippe) had not been able to win concessions prior to the July Revolution during the restored Bourbon reign. Varouxaks, "French Radicalism." Although few in France then identified with "republicanism," the opposition grew in both intensity and into many fragmented factions, some liberal, others more terrorist. Collingham, *July Monarchy*, 132–42.

83. See Daumier, *Gargantua*, 1831, Fine Arts Museums of San Francisco, 1993.48.1, http://library.artstor.org/#/asset/AMICO _SAN_FRANCISCO_103859585.

84. Unattributed, *Cidevant Grand Couvert de Gargantua*, ca. 1791, Musée Carnavalet, Histoire de Paris, G.26137; unattributed, *Le Gargantua du Siècle ou l'Oracle*.

85. De Tocqueville, *Recollections (Souvenirs)*, 5.

86. Fortescue, "Morality and Monarchy." Pilbeam, *Republicanism*, 140–54. As Pilbeam

notes, the banquet goers, while critical of the government and to its left were not, in the main, a vehicle for working-class expression. One reason the banquet campaign was such a threat to the regime was the ability of banquet makers to attract notables.

87. Between 1830 and April 1847, there were eighteen failed attempts at electoral reform. The push to increase the size of the electorate was among these. Fortescue, "Morality and Monarchy," 87, 89.

88. Ibid., 87–88.

89. Ibid., 90–91. The accuser was a member of the Chamber of Deputies, Émile de Giradin, founder of the popular newspaper *La Presse*, who made the accusation in the edition of that paper on May 12, 1847.

90. The *Red Book* was not only printed in multiple editions in France in 1790, but sympathizers with the Revolution printed it, complete with red ink, in Great Britain. See *Livre Rouge, or Red Book*.

91. Nineteenth-century ultraconservatism regarding the order they wished to "restore" can mislead us if we assume that the French Church was simply a pillar of the *ancien régime*. It was their wish, of course, to utilize the Church and its followers in rebuilding what the estates had lost. In fact, the Gallican Church upheld a tradition of French sovereignty over its own Church and in resistance to the pope's authority over decisions it considered within its own ambit. For a time, the revolution actually improved the position of some clergy as it now negotiated with the new, popular sovereign, and it enjoyed support among some clergy. With the issuance of the *assignats*, however, the land-purchasing bourgeoisie and peasants found themselves literally invested in the revolution and in conflict with the Church. (Cf. Michelet, *Historical View*, 348.) It was Michelet's great frustration that revolutionaries, most notably Robespierre, had sympathy with the Church rather than attempting to make the revolution a religion unto itself to compete with the Catholic Church. See Furet, *Revolutionary France*, 78–85. Furet is at pains to point out that the revolutionaries of 1790 did not themselves know or realize the antagonism that they were to ultimately create between the Catholic Church and their revolution. Indeed, Michelet's frustration with the absent radical intents regarding the alteration of state religion in the deliberations of May–July 1790 that produced the Civil Constitution of the Clergy is evidence, for Furet, of the exhaustion of their revolutionary intentions on this front. Writing in full bitterness after his voluntary exile from Napoleon III's France, Michelet wrote: "Nullifying an arbitrary religion which favored the elect should have implied the *affirmation of a religion of equal justice for all*: nullifying the possession of property through privilege should have implied the *affirmation of property without privilege, available to all.*" Michelet, *History of the French Revolution*, 7:14. The title of this chapter was "Revolution Was Worthless Without a Religious Revolution." Or in 1847: "Nothing was more fatal to the Revolution than to be self-ignorant in a religious point of view,—not to know that it had a religion in itself." Michelet, *Historical View*, 366.

92. Furet, *Revolutionary France*, 81.

93. Michelet, *Historical View*, 341. "The Passion of Louis XVI" was distributed, according to Michelet, on February 18 of 1790, a "libel" to declare the Assembly antithetical to the people, royalty, and religion. Ibid., 346.

94. "To this legend [i.e., The Passion of Louis XVI] the Assembly was able to oppose another, of equal interest, which was that Louis XVI, who, on the 4th of February, had sworn fidelity to the constitution, still kept a permanent agent with his brother, amid the mortal enemies of the constitution; that Turin, Treves, and Paris, were like the same court, kept and paid by the king." Ibid., 347.

95. Retaining their privileges, they no longer served essential roles in local and national governance and their authority wilted in kind. De Tocqueville, *Old Regime*, 1:93–99.

96. His claim is to have unearthed a submerged democratic mode of governance

akin to that which he found in America. According to de Tocqueville, it was hidden all along in the old parishes of all nations' medieval period. De Tocqueville, 2:129. De Tocqueville's *Democracy in America,* of course, bespoke earlier aspirations for a democratic fate that was declared a future for France, rather than a recovery of something past.

97. Michelet, *Historical View*, bk. 3, chaps. 10–12.

98. Ibid., 60; *Livre rouge.* For an English translation of the eighth edition, with commentary and complete with red print, see *Livre Rouge, or Red Book.*

99. Jailors, Michelet says, told lies about friends and family on the outside to the imprisoned. Their wives had died, or possibly remarried. The friends they asked for were the ones who betrayed them. Michelet, *Historical View*, 64.

100. For a discussion of how philosophical debate regarding the general will was shaped not only by skepticism as to the possibility of the people discovering that will, but subsequent debate regarding the *sens commun* issuing from the Scottish Enlightenment at the time Michelet was formulating his thoughts, see Viallaneix, *La Voie Royale*, 165–72.

CHAPTER 3

1. Michelet, "Introduction to World History."

2. Michelet, *The People*, 147. The contrast with Schmitt's view on the papacy is instructive. He would have opposed any concept of an impersonal pope. For him, unlike Michelet (for whom laws might be a reason with force to overwhelm an enemy), such a papacy would, necessarily, be a part of the modern era's materialistic incapacity for representation. Schmitt, *Roman Catholicism*, 14, 18–20.

3. "Two evils, the greatest that can afflict a people, fell upon France at once [in the nineteenth century]. Her own tradition slipped away from her, she forgot herself. And, every day more uncertain, paler, and more fleeting, the doubtful image of Right

[Droit] flitted before her eyes." Michelet, *Historical View*, 3–4. Here Michelet decries the worship of force, especially that of Napoleon, and in this he shares Guizot's view that might cannot be allowed to usurp the place of right. See also Michelet, *The People*, 148, 154, 158. France had lapsed in her pedagogical responsibilities, most especially in knowing her own history. Tellingly, and in spite of our association of Michelet with French chauvinism, he celebrated Haiti's revolution (contra Napoleon) and assigned Louverture the role of the world's new pedagogue. Michelet, *Oeuvres complètes*, 21.588–89.

4. Michelet, "Preface of 1869," 149–51. Michelet criticizes Augustine Thierry (1795–1856) in particular. Thierry had also supported the Revolution of 1830 and was a proponent of lowering the focus from the elites toward the social and archival evidence of the daily lives of peoples. The nobility had described themselves as descending from the race of Franks. Thierry pit one class's racial pride against another. He was the champion of the race they had declared to conquer, the Gauls. The triumph of the Third Estate was, he declared, the victory of the Gauls over the Franks, whose history had been allowed to eclipse that of its conquered race. Thierry, *Formation*. The Revolution of 1830 was to have been the Gauls' final triumph over their class enemy. He likewise wrote of England in terms of the conflict between Norman and Saxon races and identified himself as favoring liberty's struggle over despotism, thus Saxons over Normans and Gauls over Franks. Collingham, *July Monarchy*, 259–60; Mellon, *Political Uses of History*, 9–12. To criticize other historians for having accepted races within a deterministic framework was not, however, to reject the concept of race itself. Racial identities were an element of fatality that had to be dialectically overcome, and so it is wrong to say that the idea or concept of race is obliterated in Michelet's thought. See Rétat, "Jules Michelet." Readers of Foucault's Lectures at the Collège de France will recognize Thierry's race wars and

Foucault's salute to his and Guizot's (and occasionally Michelet's) turn towards a new locus of forces in their histories. Foucault, *"Society Must Be Defended."* In the struggle from this lectern against sovereignty, Michelet does not join Foucault and Guizot, even as his method insists upon a history without heroes and power relations that emerge out of extra-juridical sources amongst populations.

5. See Michelet, "Preface of 1869," 150:

Contrary to those who purse this racial element and exaggerate its influence in modern times, I drew from history itself an enormous, and too little noticed, moral fact. It is the powerful labor of oneself on oneself, whereby France, by her own progress, transforms all her rough elements. From the Roman municipal element, from the Germanic tribes, from the Celtic clan,—which are annulled, have disappeared—we have produce in the course of time completely different results, even contrary, to a great extent, to everything which preceded them. Life exerts upon itself an action of self-gestation, which, from preexisting materials, creates absolutely new things.

In other contexts, Michelet tells the upper classes of France that they are degenerating and that to revitalize themselves the men must marry women of the lower classes. He speaks of this as grounds for seeing the utility of race mixing. Michelet, *The People*, 127–30; see also 159–60.

6. Referring to a national education in which Frenchmen know themselves as the leading light of the world, he writes: "The day when this people, returning to themselves, will open their eyes and consider themselves, they will understand that the first institution that can make them live and last, is to give to all . . . this harmonious education." Michelet, *The People*, 149; see also 157.

7. Even in his popular work he singles out Buchez, whose works enjoyed popularity, for this flaw: ibid., 150–51n.

8. Michelet, *Historical View*, 6.

9. In later parts of the history, he would, for example, describe the subordination of previously independent leaders of the revolution. Danton, for example, becomes little more than the tool of Robespierre, able to save himself from the Terror by striking at his master's enemies. Michelet, *History of the French Revolution*, 7:61–72.

10. Michelet, *The People*, 154n. The Committee on Public Safety's domination of the Assembly yielded Robespierre's "monarchy," and it too exercised clemency to bolster its grip on power. Michelet, *History of the French Revolution*, 7:75–79.

11. Michelet, *History of the French Revolution*, 7:61–91, esp. 61, 65, 71, 75, 77–78, 88. These books were published in 1853, after the embittering experience of the fall of the second republic and his departure from his posts at the Collège de France and the National Archives.

12. The theme continues as he notes further that "our fathers," by which he means the revolutionaries and philosophers of the eighteenth century, "found despotism in heaven and on earth, and they instituted law. They found individual man disarmed, bare, unprotected, confounded, lost in a system of apparent unity, which was no better than common death. . . . The religious dogma of the day held him bound for the penalty of a transgression which he had not committed; this eminently carnal dogma supposed that injustice is transmitted with our blood from father to son." Michelet, *Historical View*, 7.

13. Michelet, *The People*, esp. part 3.

14. Michelet, *Historical View*, 7n; Michelet, *The People*, 157.

15. Furet, *Revolutionary France*, 374–75.

16. Michelet, *Historical View*, 18.

17. Michelet, *History of the French Revolution*, 7:14–15.

18. De Tocqueville, *Old Regime*, 1:99–101.

19. Stark, *Sociology of Religion*, 1:151–73.

20. Viallaneix, "Jules Michelet."

21. Michelet, *Historical View*, 403–4.

22. Describing the reconstituted France as "natural" marks a shift, or at least a tension, in Michelet's relation to nature. Although always at war with "fatality," Michelet was not always consistent in identifying his friends and foes in this fight.

Early in his career, nature was allied with fatality. Later, nature is permitted to join his side. Cf. his 1830s "Introduction to World History."

23. Thus, when the people-God expresses its will, it does the miraculous. Here again a contrast with Schmitt: for Schmitt, the miraculous is the opposite of the general. In Michelet the miraculous, the spontaneous creation, issues *only* from the rare moment of full generality, out of fundamental commonness. Whereas Schmitt makes the mechanical application of law the picture of generality, the rule, Michelet locates a generality that is prior to law and legislative or even constitutional law. Cf. Michelet, *Historical View*, 383; Schmitt, *Political Theology*, 36.

24. Whitman has been shown to have "borrowed" from Michelet, but the larger question for scholars has been how his thought on human unity may have influenced the American. The passage quoted above is not thought of as specifically influential, although concepts of democratic communion do speak to resonances between the two. See Geffen, "Walt Whitman and Jules Michelet"; Allen, "Walt Whitman and Jules Michelet."

25. Cf. Schmitt, *Dictatorship*, 106.

26. Ibid., 127–47. In his one, brief mention of Michelet in Schmitt, *Political Romanticism*, 10, he likely repeats the view of the early twentieth-century French radical Right, then resentful of the renewed attention on the centenary of Michelet's birth. On likely reasons for his sympathies with the French radical right, particularly Charles Maurras's attack upon romanticism, see Balakrishnan, *Enemy*, 11–13, 16, 24–25, but see also 55–57. Schmitt's brief description of Michelet—the French pro-Revolutionary, anti–Middle Ages *ying* to the Gothic celebration of the latter's *yang*—is, in the least, quite compatible with Maurras's attack upon the historian. It is noteworthy that France had, in fact, romantics that were also conservative (Maurras undertakes to convert Chateaubriand into a cause of France's "religious anarchy," a thinker indebted to the revolution who merely takes on mere appearance of its fervent

opponent). Maurras's wish was to obliterate Michelet from the French curriculum. What he had written in his history of France, Maurras had said, was not, in fact, the history of France or its people, but only the pomp of its plebeians. Maurras, *Trois idées politiques*, 6, 11, 23, 26. See also Kipper, *Jules Michelet*, 224–25.

27. Cf. LeFort, "Permanence," 217. For LeFort, Michelet's empty place is not sufficiently empty.

28. In the original, Michelet wrote: "O mes ennemis, disais-tu, il n'y a plu d'ennemis!" Michelet, *Histoire de la Révolution française*, 31–32. Montaigne, *Complete Essays*, 140 ("Of Friendship"). Montaigne guides readers to think of the ways that things we might call friendship fall away from the ideal form—a theme taken up, augmented, and made political in Derrida, *Politics of Friendship*. Michelet is not, perhaps like Schmitt, in search of perfect enmity, but is here recasting post-revolutionary France's conflicts with other nations, the Church, and its past as premature in its expectation of peace with a world not yet converted to its own, new, ideals.

29. Michelet, *History of the French Revolution*, 7:61–92. Compare this, for example, with the contention with the religious left theism of Lamartine, who assigns atheism and hypocrisy to autocrats including the Bourbons and Napoleon but also assigns the Terror to the atheistic, materialist side of the revolution. Lamartine, *Atheism Among the People*.

30. "What mighty power alters the nature of things and determines the black is white and the priest is republican? Sort our friends with the utmost severity, but go gentle with the enemy! Doesn't this vague and arbitrary system remind you of something? . . . Yes, of what the old system called 'Grace.'" Michelet, *History of the French Revolution*, 7:70–71. When grace for enemies became too dangerous a thing for Robespierre to maintain and expand, after Desmoulins had so elevated the cause and called for a Committee on Clemency to free the many already imprisoned, Robespierre

abandoned his friends for those more severe Hébertists. Ibid., 7:87–89, 97. For Michelet this was not a sign that Robespierre was not a practitioner of the system of "Grace," merely that his unreal reputation for constancy and incorruptibility had been challenged.

31. Furet, *Revolutionary France*, 103; Sieyès, "What Is the Third Estate?"

32. Gossman, "Jules Michelet," 594. As victims of the Church and as preservers of knowledge during the Dark Ages, however, the Jews of the Middle Ages and Renaissance are recuperated for an audience assumed to be anti-Semitic in Michelet, *Histoire de France*, vol. 10, 11–32.

33. Gossman, "Jules Michelet," 594.

34. Michelet, *The People*, 75.

35. Schmitt, "Age of Neutralizations."

36. Having been the direct antagonists of the ultramontane such as Schmitt celebrates—the followers of Bonald, for example—Michelet (and even Guizot's) liberalism stands in no need of a reminder of the question of what may or may not meet the test of supplying legitimacy to a state or regime. Schmitt's fallacy, like that of his nineteenth-century conservative counterparts, is to assume that merely raising the question of legitimacy's grounds in debate equates to a political victory, as if all liberals were locked within the abstract rationalism that Michelet abjures. Neither liberals nor their enemies could claim such a victory.

37. Michelet, *Historical View*, 8–9.

38. Ibid., 9.

39. The Anglophile strain among the French of course predated Michelet's age. It famously included Montesquieu and Voltaire, and it emerged again during the July Monarchy. Price, *Perilous Crown*, 17–18.

40. Michelet, *The People*, 25, 73n.

41. Michelet, *France Before Europe*, vi–viii, xix, 32–33, 65–71, 81–93. Michelet's continuing fears of technology in this work are expressed in the context of grand battles between Europe and its barbarian enemies. The millions of subordinate Russians under the czar form one vast "steam engine" (90). Cf. Schmitt, "Age of Neutralizations";

McCormick, *Carl Schmitt's Critique*, 83–117. There were, however, differences. Whereas France was advanced because it had mixed its races, Germany would never reach this state of advancement because it was incapable of reconciling its regional peoples. Jules Michelet, *France Before Europe*, 98.

42. For Schmitt, Guizot stands largely as a defender of parliamentary government. Schmitt, *Crisis of Parliamentary Democracy*, 2, 4, 7, 23, 35–36, 51. He is also put to use in Schmitt's assault upon positivism for excluding sociological factors in matters of legitimacy. Schmitt, *Guardian of the Constitution*, 105. For a criticism that touches on Schmitt's assertions regarding Guizot, see Larmore, *Morals of Modernity*, 184–86. Schmitt nonetheless ignores the Frenchman's war, as historian rather than a minister, on sovereignty, preferring to target Benjamin Constant. Guizot, *History*, 61. Cf. Schmitt, "Age of Neutralizations"; Schmitt, *Concept of the Political*, 74–75.

43. It is at least possible that this blind spot conformed with the wishes of Charles Maurras, whose radical right thinking Schmitt admired. Maurras had witnessed the great influence of Michelet and had wished to see that influence obliterated from French education. Maurras, *Trois idées politiques*. See also note 26 of this chapter.

44. Not only Leo Strauss but the Weimar (and later American) critic Siegfried Kracauer made this point, each in their own way. See Strauss, "Notes on Carl Schmitt." The point is further developed in Meier, *Carl Schmitt and Leo Strauss*; Meier, *Lesson of Carl Schmitt*. Before Strauss had introduced this point, however, it had been made in a more brusque, and in many ways prescient, way about both Schmitt and his followers among those writing in *Die Tat* in 1931 in Kracauer, "Revolt of the Middle Classes." For a linkage between Schmitt and the industrial elites of Germany, see Cristi, *Carl Schmitt*. Schmitt's blindness toward his own commonalities with liberalism, including the political romanticism he condemns, is also a theme developed in parts of McCormick, *Carl Schmitt's Critique*.

45. In intellectual history the thesis is generally supported in the essays one finds, for example, in Dyzenhaus, "Gorgon Head of Power." See also Caldwell and Scheuerman, "Introduction." Schmitt's contextual connections to the liberal milieu of the Weimar era have been marked: Caldwell, *Popular Sovereignty*, 42–62. So, too, parallels to Weber's liberalism and nationalism: Mommsen, *Max Weber*, 382–89; Mayer, *Max Weber*, 78. So, too, his connection to the affinities between his thought and the convergence of industrial capitalism and autocratic regimes: Cristi, *Carl Schmitt*; Maus, "1933 'Break.'" This need not make Schmitt a liberal *thinker*, but a critic of liberalism still tethered strongly to its historical development. It is therefore noteworthy that the criticism of liberalism's critics, "the orphans of lost illusions," have in some cases come to see that a wide variety of anti-liberalisms today correspond to the false hope of finding singular liberal doctrines, rather than seeing liberalism whole, which was not a doctrine but a culture, built upon political philosophies that often failed to take account of the societies that liberal political revolutions helped to displace. Rosanvallon, "Market," 159.

46. See the discussion of the Italian elite's difficulties in attempting a bottom-up liberalism, and how they fell into a commonly traveled path of top-down interventions in order to bring the people to the social order they would not take up voluntarily, in Bellamy, *Liberalism and Modern Society*.

47. Caldwell and Scheuerman, "Introduction"; Mommsen, *Max Weber*.

48. The growing reception for the program to revive a prior, social theory of equality—one that precedes a liberal theory of justice, or notions of mere equal opportunity for individuals, in the works of Pierre Rosanvallon suggests that the struggles of nineteenth-century France are a particularly fruitful comparative vantage point for discovering contemporary liberalism's blind spots. Rosanvallon, *Democracy Past and Future*.

49. Caldwell, *Popular Sovereignty*, 42–62.

50. Strauss, "Notes on Carl Schmitt."

51. Mommsen, *Max Weber*, 381–89, 404–5, 410, 448–50. For an earlier, less thoroughly researched wartime comparative perspective that resonates with Mommsen's connections—in spite of the distance Mommsen put between himself and this scholar of French political thought—see Mayer, *Max Weber*.

CHAPTER 4

1. For a discussion of the connections between political unrest and the distribution of non-exceptional patronage within a vision of a corrupted, hierarchical body politic in the years leading up to the civil war, see Linda Levy Peck's discussion of the resentment brought through the sale of titles and the monopolization of patronage relationships through favorites in Peck, *Court Patronage*, 185–221.

2. Hobbes, *Lev.*, 29.1. I advance a more fully developed view of Hobbes's ambitions in Miller, *Mortal Gods*.

3. Ibid., 21.21 (Review and Conclusions).

4. As the artificial person who represents subjects, the subjects *own* their representative's words and actions. Ibid., 16.4.

5. "If there had not first been an opinion received of the greatest part of *England,* that these powers [of the sovereign that should have remained whole] were divided between the King, and the Lords, and the House of Commons, the people had never been divided and fallen into this civil war, first between those that disagreed in politics, and after between the dissenters about the liberty of religion" (ibid., 18.16). The need for united authority will be forgotten in peacetime, "except the vulgar be better taught than they have hitherto been" (ibid.). See also the Latin *Leviathan*, ibid., note 9.

6. Hobbes, *Lev.*, esp. 46.35 R&C: 8; see also 24.6, 8; 28.10.

7. Burgess, *Absolute Monarchy*, 210–11.

8. Bodin, *Six Bookes*, 171ff (bk. 1, 10, pp. 236ff in 1583 French).

9. Kesselring, *Mercy and Authority*.

10. Ever since Douglas Hay's sparkling, but contested, analysis of mercy as exercised in eighteenth-century English courts ("Property, Authority and the Criminal Law," from 1975), some core questions have been pressing for those who study the history of crime, prosecution, the courts, and the political and social orders alongside them: Who, or what, has had the benefit of dispensing mercy, who exercised this power, and to what effect? These contested questions (raised and refined by one of Hay's critics, Peter King; see "Decision-Makers") have helped animate inquiries into periods both before and after the eighteenth century, including Kesselring's. See also Herrup, *Common Peace*; J. Sharpe, *Crime in Early Modern England*. This chapter does not add or subtract from the impressive empirical work that has been mounted to speak to these questions, but it does begin downstream from the more widely accepted view that issued from these contentions: that mercy contrary to law's proscribed punishments, as a species of the generosity that persons or groups can deliver or withhold, has indeed been a mechanism for domination. It is sometimes achieved, other times sought, and protected by those who seek control, including persons, factions, classes, and sovereigns. (Hobbes, as we will see below, feared its effects when a sovereign put it to use with regard to "the great.") Moreover, for those who maintained those systems, the mercy so exercised was a part of a larger conception of justice and criminality in a community that was very far removed from legal formalism. For Hay, after 1688 it was not the diminished king, but the anxious and clever pre-industrial rural ruling classes that had defeated him in the Glorious Revolution that secured this benefit. This explains why, argues Hay, they were unwilling to accept the centralized police bureaucracy and rationalizing legal reforms designed to augment the certitude of prosecution and punishment over the deterrent/exemplar effects sought from spectacular punishments in law infrequently administered. The reformers risked re-enabling a monarchy whose institutional power they had defeated. Nonetheless, they required an ideology of reverence for the property rights that would suit their tenuous position as they faced a potentially unruly multitude now subordinate to their will. Arguments from humanity, rationality, and efficiency made by legal reformers did not, he maintained, resonate with them. They were best served with the status quo: severe punishments dictated in law that were only occasionally followed in the administration of the so-called bloody code. The pervasive uses of mercy and pardon were precisely what they needed, if carefully administered, to keep the lower orders in check. To translate Hay's assertions into the terms of this chapter, he argued that the ruling class had, through their preferred means of adjudicating crime and the ceremonies of assizes, created a political theology for the law that had taken the place of a weakened and de-legitimated Church. It crafted an obedient population that could internalize the rules that kept them in check by teaching them that justice was not for the ruling class, but for all. Hay's assertions were contested in Langbein, "Albion's Fatal Flaws," by those who insisted that the law was indeed serving the poor. A more nuanced picture allows that the poor were served by the law, and that the ideology of the dominant orders may have, in fact, actually responded to its own independent concepts of justice and criminality, as well as growing dissatisfactions with the cruelty of capital punishments for minor property offenses—even as it resisted the thinking that would have introduced a centralized police force into the nineteenth century. It did so in ways that did not make the law merely the tool of a particular class, or political and social hierarchies of one region or another, but which nonetheless reflected the fears, especially in and around London, of a mass moral deterioration among the poor. Beattie, *Crime and the Courts*, 619–37; King, "Decision-Makers."

11. James I, *Declaration*.

12. Donne, *Pseudo-Martyr*; Raspa, "John Donne on Royal Mercy."

13. For recent histories that nicely illustrate this aspect of the tensions, see Harris, *Restoration*, esp. 62–63, 176, 232, 255, 327–28; Harris, *Revolution*, 182–236. James II's "popish" plans, and what others have read as attempts at toleration for his co-religionists, take on a more sinister tone in the recent, controversial Pincus, *1688: The First Modern Revolution*.

14. See also Hobbes, *Lev.*, 22.5:

The Sovereign, in every Commonwealth, is the absolute Representative of all the Subjects; and therefore no other, can be Representative of any part of them, but so far forth, as he shall give leave; *And to give leave to a Body Politique of Subjects, to have an absolute Representative to all intents and purposes, were to abandon the Government of so much of the Commonwealth* [emphasis mine], and to divide the Dominion, contrary to their Peace and Defence, which the Sovereign cannot be understood to doe, by any Grant, that does not plainly, and directly discharge them of their subjection. For consequences of words, are not the signes of his will, when other consequences are signes of the contrary; but rather signes of errour, and misreckoning; to which all mankind is too prone.

15. Braddick, *God's Fury, England's Fire*; Harris, *Restoration*; Harris, *Revolution*.

16. Hoekstra, "Hobbes and the Foole."

17. As tempting as it may be to assume that impunity from punishment follows a simple linear pathway, increasing as the station of the alleged offender climbs, the historical record reveals any number of other variables (and as well see much more leniency and nonprosecution than we might expect), including the question of who made the charges, the ability of the defendant to find creditable witnesses to his character, as well as economic and urban and rural variables. For a textured look at these issues beginning with the Restoration, see Beattie, *Crime and the Courts*.

18. "A punishment is an evil inflicted by public authority on him that hath done or

omitted that which is judged by the same authority to be a transgression of the law, to the end that the will of men may thereby the better be disposed to obedience." *Lev.*, 28.1.

19. Birdsall, "Non Obstante."

20. The Latin *Leviathan* augments the argument of granting impunity to the great: "Will not he who offers impunity to the murderer of my father or son be called in some way a murderer also?" Taking note of what he incorrectly paints as popular revolts in Holland, the so-called Beggars, Hobbes turns the tables. The multitude assembled are greater than the individual great men that an unwise sovereign indulges with impunity: "Why are not the common people to be honored, because they are many and much more powerful?" Hobbes, *Lev.*, 227–28n9OL.

21. Monopolies are an ongoing object of suspicion among Britain's elite in Peck, *Court Patronage*.

22. Hill, *Century of Revolution*, 30–31.

23. Ibid., 31. One of the more infamous, if not comic, cases of resented monopoly favoritism was that of the so-called Popish Soap. A number of Catholic aristocrats connected with the Earl of Portland had formed a company to buy the patent for a superior soap formula and to secure the right to prevent the sale of soaps not certified by themselves to be "sweet and pure." The arrangement also promised to yield his majesty's government 4 pounds for every ton. Gardiner notes, based on their reported plan of production, that the plan would promise the Crown 20,000 pounds a year. A subsequent royal proclamation forbid the use of any oil other than olive or rapeseed. This further undermined rival English soap makers; they had been using imported fish oils. Conflicts between soap makers and those looking to profit and share in the revenues (Hobbes's pleurisy of the artificial man) reached a fever pitch. It included a Star Chamber trial against traditional English soap makers. They were charged with soiling the reputation of the new soap and of manufacturing contraband soap. (The godly preferred it.) An inquiry was conducted with public side-by-side

washtub tests of lathering and "sweetness." Testimonials from aristocratic household-ers in favor of the new soaps were likewise gathered. The affair involved figures no less important than Archbishop Laud, and after Portland's death, an angry and frustrated Lord Francis Cottington, Commissioner of the Treasury. Gardiner, *Personal Govern-ment of Charles I*, 165–72.

24. K. Sharpe, *Personal Rule*, 120–24; 257–62; 707.

25. For an extensive and detailed discussion of how Tudor sovereigns negotiated these arrangements, see Kesselring, *Mercy and Authority*, 2, 3: "The Tudor monarchs used pardons to exact deference from subjects of all social ranks: nobles and commoners alike sued for mercy. They displayed mercy to petty offenders facing fines and to felons fearing death, to rebellious subjects and to those newly subjugated. They did so partly to bolster perceptions of their legitimacy and to foster habits of obedience, but also to ease the extension of their power. In these respects, mercy became a tool of state formation."

26. See ibid., 136–43, for a detailed discussion of the various performances of sovereign mercy, including those that make clear the hierarchy between noblemen who may themselves be compelled to ask mercy of the monarch either on their own behalf or on behalf of others.

27. Ibid., 3.

28. From the point of view of Hay, "Property, Authority," pardons and mercy may have been, as it were, the weapons of a weak eighteenth-century ruling class: one which would administer just enough terror by capital punishments and floggings to keep the lower orders in place, but never with a perfect obligation to follow severe punishments proscribed by law so as not to spur wider resistance. In light of this perspective, and with the benefit of subsequent research, we might improve our understanding of what it meant for Hobbes to make pardon a law of nature. Not only were pardons pervasive; we must also note that prosecutions for crimes were conducted (or in most cases not con-ducted) by the victims at their own expense. Beattie, *Crime and the Courts*, 35–73. We should consider how pardoning (or, at least, nonprosecution) may have corresponded to the everyday experience not only of sovereigns but also of individual subjects who suffered injuries at the hands of others. Hay's "new legal history" is, as Kesselring notes, no longer new, and while a Marxist preoccupation with class domination is now less in focus, the question of the necessity of pardons and mercy is not. Kesselring, *Mercy and Authority*, 4–8.

29. Kesselring, *Mercy and Authority*, 16.

30. Ibid., 57–60.

31. In the original German: "Souverän ist, wer über den Ausnahmezustand entscheidet," and in the French translation by J.-L. Schlegel, "Est souverain celui qui décide de la situation exceptionnelle." Cited in Tuchscherer, "Le décisionnisme de Carl Schmitt," 26.

32. Ibid., 5. See note 31 for the original German and the 1988 French translation.

33. Schmitt, *Political Theology*, 33.

34. There are many discussions of Schmitt's relation to Weber; McCormick, *Carl Schmitt's Critique*, has informed my view. Views ranging from broad-brush condemnations of German ideology to increasingly detailed points of connection and disconnection include Mayer, *Max Weber*, 78; Mommsen, *Max Weber*, esp. 448–53; Colliot-Thélène, "Carl Schmitt Versus Max Weber"; Kalyvas, *Democracy*; Magalhães, "Contingent Affinity."

35. "Europeans always have wandered from a conflictual to a neutral domain, and always the newly won neutral domain has become immediately another arena of struggle, once again necessitating the search for a new neutral domain." Schmitt, "Age of Neutralizations," 90.

36. With characteristic ambiguity, Schmitt also suggests toward the end of the essay that that which the prior generation of sociologists had called soullessness among those with the spirit of technicity was not true soullessness, or merely mechanistic. It

was "still spirit" but "perhaps an evil and demonic spirit," as well as an "activistic metaphysics—the belief in unlimited power and domination of man over nature, even our human nature." Ibid., 94. A more persistent opposition in this essay is the opposition to technicity as a solution that satisfies the wish to escape controversy and moral and political choice.

37. "The living camera—a Rolleiflex or Rolleicord is far more than a soulless instrument built from little wheels and polished glass. In the amateur's hands, it becomes alive as if by magic. The Rollei is speedy and swift . . . success alone decides. . . . The Rolleiflex amateur is definitively safeguarded against doubt and uncertainty. Did I really make an exposure: This question can no longer arise." Franke & Heidecke, *Success Alone Decides.* The pamphlet, in English, includes photos of happy female soldiers and military hardware.

38. Schmitt makes this assertion in the context of an assertion that "all significant concepts of the modern theory of the state are secularized theological concepts." Schmitt, *Political Theology*, 36. It is, therefore, a rival (deist) political theology, he claims, that banishes miracles.

39. Schmitt condemned the legal formalism and an overwhelming trend toward ever-heightened claims of objectivity, and especially the (Weberian) link between legality and legitimacy. He targets Hans Kelsen as a part of this, of whom he writes, for example: "The objectivity that he claimed for himself amounted to no more than avoiding everything personalistic and tracing the legal order back to the impersonal validity of an impersonal norm." Ibid., 29.

40. Strauss, "Notes on Carl Schmitt"; Strauss, *Political Philosophy of Hobbes.* Strauss was certainly interested in showing his teacher that he had worshipped the wrong idol. There is a strong tendency to fight one anachronism with another here by converting Hobbes into the bourgeois theorists looking to obliterate the aristocratic martial virtue in favor of mere survival.

41. Schmitt, *Political Theology*, 33; Schmitt, *Crisis of Parliamentary Democracy*, 43; Schmitt, *Dictatorship*, 16.

42. Schmitt, *Political Theology*, 33. Schmitt, *Dictatorship*, 16–17: "The state cannot do any wrong, because any regulation can only become law if the state makes it the content of an official command, and not because it corresponds to any ideal understanding of justice. *'Auctoritas, non veritas facit legem'* (Hobbes, *Lev.*, chap. 26). The law is not a norm of justice but a command." In his critique of parliamentary democracy, Hobbes is at war with the progenitors of the *Rechtsstaat*; see Schmitt, *Crisis of Parliamentary Democracy*, 42–44. This last births another strained, anachronistic, contest. Hobbes's insistence upon the difference between counsel and command (and that law is the latter) is converted into another illusory contest Hobbes didn't have between his sovereign's laws and the yet unborn defenders of an enlightened civil law jurisprudence sent back in time to suffer defeat in the seventeenth century.

43. Schmitt, *Political Theology*, 33.

44. "The difficulty consisteth in the evidence of the authority derived from him [the sovereign], the removing whereof dependeth on the knowledge of public registers, public counsels, public ministers, and public seals, by which all laws are sufficiently verified: *verified I say, not authorized; for the verification is but the testimony and record, not the authority of law,* which consisteth in the command of the sovereign only." Hobbes, *Lev.*, 26.16 (italics mine). This is an opposition between command and the record of the law, not between command and counsel, or between command and abstract ideal.

45. Ibid.

46. Schmitt might have quoted the passage in the earlier, original English, but one suspects it would not have served his purposes. I have quoted it in full in note 44 of this chapter.

47. Burgess, *Absolute Monarchy*, 159.

48. Goldie, "Ancient Constitution."

49. Schmitt, *Political Theology*, 34.

CHAPTER 5

1. Hegel, *Philosophy of History*, 15–16.

2. "God gives not Kings the stile of *Gods* in vaine, / For on his Throne his Scepter doe they swey: / And as their subjects ought them to obey, / So Kings should feare and serve their God again." James I, *Basilicon Doron*, The Argument, 1.

3. Hobbes, *On the Citizen*, 15.18; Hobbes, *Lev.*, 45.13. On this score, Hobbes did not struggle to fully disentangle the duties of slaves from those of civil subjects to the sovereigns they were required to worship. Cf. Skinner, *Hobbes and Republican Liberty*, 124–77.

4. Hobbes, *Lev.*, 18.18, 3, 6.

5. Ibid., 31.6. Hobbes, *On the Citizen*, 15.6.

6. Leibniz, *Essais de Théodicée*, 1710; I shall reference Leibniz, *Theodicy*. "Theodicy" is a composite: θεός God + δίκη justice, or "Justice of God." Strictly speaking, theodicy concerned the distribution of punishments and rewards in the afterlife as well.

7. God's justice was a point of contention between Hobbes and Bishop Bramhall. The distinction between special and operative will and other distinctions Bramhall introduced to spare God from being the immediate cause of a given man's choice to do evil, Hobbes argued, are nonsense. Hobbes and Bramhall, *Liberty, Necessity, and Chance*, esp. 132–33, 138–47.

8. For Bramhall, Job was a sinner, contra Hobbes. Nonetheless, his afflictions were not punishments but "probationary chastisements to make trial of his graces." Importantly, his afflictions do not come merely from God's omnipotence. Ibid., 133–34, 145.

9. "Wherefore, as by one man sin entered into the world, and death by sin; and so death passed upon all men, for that all have sinned." Romans 5:12.

10. He expresses doubts of a different kind regarding original sin in *Lev.*, 27.1. Here he counts it too severe to think that our first thoughts are sinful.

11. Ibid., 12.30; 20.16; 42.62; 33.20, p. 258; 35.8–9; 40.11.

12. God's triple word includes "the dictates of *natural reason*, by *revelation*, and by the *voice* of some man, to whom by the operation of miracles he procureth credit with the rest." Ibid., 31.3.

13. Ibid., 31.5; Hobbes, *On the Citizen*, 1.14.

14. Human sovereigns might suffer the "natural punishments" that are the consequences of his ill-considered actions (ibid., 31.40). For another reading of Hobbes that stresses the moral, if not structural, limits on Hobbes's sovereign, see May, *Limiting Leviathan*. As with Dyzenhaus, there are parallels with Lon Fuller's theories on the morality of law (for example, against justifying punishment via retroactive laws). May's reading makes the somewhat contentious claim that the *Dialogue Between a Philosopher and Student of the Common Laws* can be read as if it were a completed expression of the philosopher's thought. Cf. Cromartie, "Textual Introduction."

15. Cf. Hobbes, *Dialogue of Common Law*, 124. For a reading of Hobbes on punishment that stresses this forward-looking aspect of Hobbes's view of punishment and mercy to the exclusion of any other factors, see Tuckness and Parrish, *Decline of Mercy*, 151–57.

16. Another reading that pulls Hobbes away from the Austinian positivism on this and other scores is Ristroph, "Sovereignty and Subversion."

17. There is little to stop these harms, because Hobbes's sovereign never forfeits his original right as an individual to everything in the state of nature (and indeed is augmented in his power after the commonwealth is instituted). See *Lev.*, 28.2. In addition, those who would create means of stopping these harms undermine the state's stability. Hobbes, *On the Citizen*, 7.4, 6.6–12.

18. The passage addresses the question of whether the sovereign is subject to civil law. One might object that civil law is not natural law. But if natural law could be enforced from within the state by subjects against their sovereign, would not the very same objections apply?

19. Psalms 73:1–3; *Lev.*, 31.6. The 1651 editions of *Leviathan*, p. 188, include marginal notes that misidentify these passages as Psalms 72, an error sometimes repeated in modern editions.

20. Cf. Hobbes, "Answer," 293–94.

21. Psalms 73:12–13.

22. Cf. Epicurus, *Extant Remains*, 83–85 [Menoeceus Sections 123–24].

23. Psalms 3:7.

24. For a comparison of the isolated Leibniz (who rejected both natural equality and who preferred Aristotelian hierarchy to social contract theory) with both Hobbes and Locke, see Jolley, "Leibniz on Hobbes."

25. In his infinite power, God could have made thousands of worlds, but He *chose* to make this one. By the principle of sufficient reason, there *is* a reason to account for it. Because He is perfect, He could not have chosen anything better. There could be no better world than this one. The evils we must endure on earth, including the political ones, are a part of a plan which, reason dictates, must be best. Leibniz, *Philosophical Essays*, 94–101.

26. The fear of an earthly sovereign is not in same category as fear of God. Rule by consent bolsters Hobbes's earthly sovereign, whereas the legitimacy of submission to God is dictated by the weakness of man; there is "no kicking against the pricks." Hobbes, *On the Citizen*, 15.7.

27. "There are diverse persons who speak much of piety, of devotion, of religion . . . who prove to be by no means versed in the divine perfection. . . . People have pleaded the irresistible power of God when it is a question rather of presenting his supreme goodness; and they have assumed a despotic power when they should rather have conceived of a power ordered by the most perfect wisdom." Leibniz, *Theodicy*, 54–55 (Preface).

28. Ibid., 53.

29. "I have already said that insight must be joined to fervour, that the perfecting of our understanding must accomplish the perfecting of our will. . . . When virtue is reasonable, when it is related to God, who is the supreme reason of things, it is founded on knowledge. One cannot love God without knowing his perfections, and this knowledge contains the principles of true piety." Ibid., 54 (Preface).

30. On this point, Leibniz and Hobbes could not be more different. See Riley, *Leibniz' Universal Jurisprudence*; Miller, *Mortal Gods*.

31. Riley, *Leibniz' Universal Jurisprudence*.

32. Hobbes, *Lev.*, 32.2.

33. Ibid., 32.3.

34. Leibniz, *Theodicy*, Reflexions, 400 [sec. 8] (on Hobbes, Freedom, Necessity and Chance [sec. 8]). Cf. Hobbes, *Lev.*, 31.28, 33; 32.3.

35. Leibniz will agree with Hobbes that all that happens happens by necessity, but he finds in Hobbes an unsatisfying concept of necessity. For Hobbes, that fact that one thing or its opposite might happen (the dice may come up 7 or 11) can be of little moment. He calls both outcomes "necessary." His notion of necessity is not, therefore, one of determinate necessity. Hobbes's concept, Leibniz stressed, also excludes moral necessity. In *Theodicy* Leibniz claimed that all that happens in the universe happens according to God's plan and that it all unfolds, determinately, by *moral necessity*. Ibid., 397 (ibid. [sec. 3]). He also faults Hobbes for failing to approve punitive justice: there is, according to Leibniz, a satisfaction to be had in the "the fitness of things" reflected in punishments that may not amend or alter the future conduct of bad persons, but which both victims and the wise appreciate in seeing the guilty punished as per the punishment promised either by God or "those who are entitled to govern" (164–65 [secs. 73–74]).

36. Leibniz, "Second Letter to Clarke," sec. 2; Leibniz, "Against Barbaric Physics," 319; Leibniz, "Two Sects." For a discussion of Leibniz's attack on Hobbes's materialism that also illustrates the former's will to inquire where he finds Hobbes unwilling, see Duncan, "Leibniz on Hobbes's Materialism."

37. Leibniz, *Theodicy*, 299 [sec. 276].

38. Pope, "Essay on Man," sec. 1, ll. 34–51:

Presumptuous Man! The reason wouldst though find,
Why form'd so weak, so little, and so blind!
First, if thou canst, the harder reason guess, . . .
Of System's possible, if 'tis confest
That Wisdom infinite must form be best,
Where all must full or not coherent be,
And all that rises, rise in due degree;
Then, in the scale of reas'ning life, 'tis plain
There must be, somewhere, such a rank as Man;
And all the question (wrangle e'er so long)
Is only this, if God has plac'd him wrong?

39. Voltaire, *Candide*, 8.

40. Ibid., 5.

41. Bayle's interest in the prosperity of the wicked was substantial. See note § D in *Brutus*, and of the biblical David, esp. in the sections deleted from the 1702 *Dictionary*. Bayle, *Political Writings*. See also Hobbes, *Lev.*, 236.

42. Bayle, *Miscellaneous Reflections*, 459–60. Leibniz, *Theodicy*, 256–58.

43. Hobbes, *On the Citizen*, 13.1 (Silverthorne's translation). The absolute and ordinary powers distinction was at the center of Frances Oakley's criticism of MacIlwain's view of "constitutionalism."

44. Hobbes, *Lev.*, 18.20; 19.8 (favorites and flatterers); 19.9, 23; 20.18.

45. Ibid., 13.6; 21.7.

46. Ibid., 20.18.

47. Hobbes, *On the Citizen*, preface to the readers, 20, strikes such a tone. See also Hobbes and Bramhall, *Liberty, Necessity, and Chance*, 176.

48. Hobbes, *Lev.*, Introduction: 1; see Miller, *Mortal Gods*.

49. This is not to suggest that Hobbes does not do much to flatter his would-be mortal god, that is, the soon to be Charles II (see Miller, chap. 8, passim), nor that Leibniz does not sometimes insult and criticize mortal gods not his own. Having subscribed to a universal jurisprudence, Leibniz's philosophy sits uneasily with absolutism, and so it is perhaps unsurprising that when he wished to criticize Louis XIV, he mocked him as a grossly deficient deity in Leibniz, "Mars Christianissimus 1683."

50. Hobbes, *On the Citizen*, 13.4; cf. Hobbes, *Lev.*, 30.1; *Elements of Law*, 28.1.

51. Hobbes, *On the Citizen*, 7.4.

52. Under some circumstances, however, Hobbes may have had good reason to know that allowing antagonists to prosper might present itself as a necessity, or at least tempting possibility—especially for those who either possessed or sought to regain sovereignty in times of conflict. The evidence in Malcolm, "Unknown Policy Proposal," suggests an intriguing possibly. Even if one might wish to resist Malcolm's assertion that it was Hobbes's own policy proposal rather than a sign of his involvement in the scheme, there is good evidence that Hobbes knew the temptation to let the wicked prosper firsthand. Malcolm argues that the undated letter (written between December 1643 and April 1645) advises that the royalist side attempt to buy off an important man from the enemy's side, Robert Rich, the second Earl of Warwick. It asserts that Robert Rich—known to both Hobbes and his patron William Cavendish through conflicts with him in the 1620s as members of the Virginia Company—should be lured by money, pride, and the promise of pardons for himself and his friends and family to abandon the rebels' cause. The proposal falsely predicts that Warwick might be willing to do so for the above reasons, but also because England was going to be conquered by the Scots in combination with the Swedes in the very near future. It suggests that Warwick, at that moment lord high admiral of the navy controlled by Charles I's successful domestic foes, might find it better to become famous as England's savior from a foreign foe than infamous for assisting the side that delivered it over to Swedish/Scottish rule. In addition to his instrumental role in fomenting rebellion in England and Scotland, Hobbes and Cavendish would have had additional reasons for thinking the earl particularly wicked, not least his use of court connections in 1623 to have

Cavendish placed under house arrest, and later scuffles in a meeting of the Somer's Island Company that resulted in Cavendish challenging Warwick to a (unrealized) duel. This kind of favor for troublemakers might have left a bad taste in Hobbes's mouth, as it certainly did Cavendish and other royalists. For a treatment of civil war that emphasizes Warwick's role and Charles I's allies' and Privy Council's understanding of his and other rebellious noblemen's defiance of royal authority as motivated by a desire for preferment, see Adamson, *Noble Revolt*, esp. 63. For an *ex-post* account of Cavendish's resentments toward noblemen favored for their disobedience, see Newcastle, *Life of William Cavendish*, 178–79. Cf. *Lev.*, 30.24.

53. Hobbes, *On the Citizen*, 13.3.

54. Hobbes, *Lev.*, 18.2; 29.14; 30.14; 46.35–36; also see him fling "tyrant" at Cromwell in the Latin *Leviathan*, 47 (OL).29. Cf. Erasmus, *Erasmus*, 27–29.

55. Hoekstra, "Hobbes and the Foole."

56. See also Latin edition, p. 193.

57. Strauss, *Political Philosophy of Hobbes*; Thomas, "Social Origins."

58. In the 1668 Latin edition, Hobbes differentiates the great (the rich, those already in authority, or the popular) from the poor (*Lev.*, 195). The poor can only expect immunity "in concealment or opportunities for flight" whereas these others have more. Historical records suggest impunity was more widespread than this, although even with a system of common nonenforcement, Hobbes might have been able to refer to two tiers of forgiveness.

59. Ibid., 195–96.

60. Cf. ibid., 23–34.

61. Ibid., 227–28. The Beggars' Revolt was, in fact, a rising spearheaded by Protestant lower nobility against Hapsburg efforts to centralize religious authority and to achieve unity by destroying heretical religion. The aforesaid nobles presented their petition to Philip II's regent, Margaret of Parma, and were dubbed "the beggars" (*les gueux*) by a nobleman advising her. Although ultimately defeated by Hapsburg armies, this was the first revolt of what became the Eighty Years' War.

62. Hobbes, *Lev.*, 228n9.

63. Justinian, *Institutes* 4.4.7.

64. Hobbes does not voice complaint with the potential insufficiency of capital, or corporal punishment, or imprisonment. He signals that he knew, however, of their potential insufficiency. Severity was counted a virtue among traditional leaders, and even capital punishment may be done with or without torment (*Lev.*, 28.17). He was concerned with the potential insufficiency of exile, because it is more like "escape" and "the mere change of air is no punishment." Hobbes, *Lev.*, 28.21. Transportation as a widely used form of punishment started in the early eighteenth century. Cf. Beattie, *Crime and the Courts*.

65. See also *Lev.*, 30.21. On owning the sovereign representatives' words and actions, see *Lev.*, 16.4, 14; 17, 13. For a reading of Hobbes that connects good law and good law making with equality, largely through a discussion of Hobbes's views on the obligation to the principle of equity, see May, *Limiting Leviathan*, 67–84.

66. Fox, *Monopolies and Patents*, 127–39.

67. The Great Britain money-trap laws served the centralized state. In contemporary America, something of an inversion of Hobbes's predicated disaster, "money-trap" laws and enforcement rules and guidelines have recently been exposed as the willful substitute for tax revenues in the now infamous Ferguson, Missouri; police practices have demonstrated a bias against an impoverished minority community. United States Department of Justice, "Investigation," 9–15, 54–79.

68. A traditional justification for grants of monopolies, for example, was to protect the purity of products. It was a concept of the regulation of trade that legitimized guild monopolies within towns. The charge against the egregious monopolies was that their ability to deprive manufactures of an authorized seal (as proof that it met the standards of the patent holder) was not being used to maintain the quality of the products produced for the market, but to extort payments to the monopoly holders, to price-gouge, or to drive competitors out

of business. Fox, *Monopolies and Patents*, 127–39; W. Price, *English Patents of Monopoly*.

69. Bayle, *Dictionary*, 2:605–16 (David); esp. 607, note D, 608. Following criticism from the Church of Rotterdam, Bayle removes many of the criticisms of David (ibid., 612ff.).

70. 1 Samuel 8–12.

71. 2 Samuel 11.

72. Curley notes that Hobbes falsely attributes this act to Samuel, when it was God who commanded that Samuel anoint David. Cf. Hobbes, *Lev.*, 40.13 and n9, 1 Samuel 15–16. This said, Hobbes does trace God's direct responsibility for David's kingship in Hobbes, "Answer," 331.

73. Although the ancient Hebrews demanded that they have kings, even in the knowledge that they would be the slaves of those kings (says Hobbes, *Lev.*, 20.16), it seems an open question as to how they authorized their kings, as God himself appointed them. See note 72.

74. Hobbes, *Lev.*, 20.16, ref. 1 Samuel 24:9.

CHAPTER 6

1. For a discussion of the centrality of office-centered thinking in that era, see Condren, *Argument and Authority*.

2. Lewis, "End of Sovereignty"; Krasner, "Sovereignty"; Ward, "End of Sovereignty."

3. Miller, *Mortal Gods*.

4. See esp. Xenophon, *Cyropaedia* 8.2.

5. Ibid., 8.2.3–4.

6. Cicero, "Against Verres." Cicero painted a damning picture of a lawless regional governor (of Sicily), a man who openly flouted the law and popular, republican, notions of justice, who made clear that his vast fortune and the capacity to bribe his judges was the best protection against prosecution, and a Senate at risk of further ruining its reputation by permitting such a person, and especially one of their own rank, to continue his vicious ways with impunity. For a discussion of Cicero's ongoing conceptual, and contextual, change on questions of clemency as it related to the people and Caesar's

clemency, see Dowling, *Clemency and Cruelty*, 6–7, 17–24, 31–38.

7. Cicero, *De Officiis* 1.20, 22, 42–43. For a discussion of Seneca's relation to his predecessors on the question of giving and receiving benefits, see Griffin, *Seneca on Society*, 15–25; on Cicero's relation to Seneca, ibid., passim, but esp. 7–14. For a discussion of the predecessors and precursors of *De Clementia*, see Braund, "Introduction." For a wide-ranging account, centered on clemency, see Dowling, *Clemency and Cruelty*.

8. Seneca, *De Clementia* 1.5.4. Here, I have substituted Kaster's translation; Seneca, "On Clemency." Unless marked, I will be using Braund's translation. She translates this passage as "To kill in defiance of the law is open to anyone. To preserve life is open to no one except for me." Kaster's translation correctly carries through in the single sentence the notion that the prince is defying the law when he kills *and* when he saves life. If this does not carry through past Seneca's comma, we open the door to the false, and quite unlikely, inference that Seneca is not discussing the emperor's extralegal power to save a life contrary to a lawful lethal punishment. This likewise opens the door to the absurd notion that the emperor, in general, is the only person capable of saving lives.

9. Stacey, *Roman Monarchy*; Braund, *Seneca*, Commentary, 154.

10. Seneca, *De Clementia* 1.1.1, see also Braund, "Commentary," 155. That pleasure will issue from his virtue.

11. Thus, he may, "say to oneself: 'Have I of all mortals proved good enough and been chosen to act as the god's representative on earth? I make decisions of life and death for the world. The prosperity and condition of each individual rests in my hand.'" *De Clementia* 1.1.1–2. As Braund notes, the text cleverly permits Seneca to dress the prescriptive as a form of description, and thus the goal remains encouragement to close a gap between the real and ideal Nero, a gap whose very existence it can also erase if need be. Finding an emperor deficient is a dangerous thing to do, and so, of course,

Nero always already answered to his virtuous image.

12. Braund, "Introduction," 16–17. For reasons that will become evident, Braund mentions that some Seneca scholars have been reluctant to set the date of this text as late as 55–56, as this puts the text that declares Nero's (fictional) innocence after his murder of Britannicus. Both morally and historically, the consensus, which includes Braund, is that the contradiction between the actual Nero and the one young man mirrored in the text of *De Clementia* is best explained by Seneca's own compromised morality. Seneca's willingness to praise Nero in spite of the murder, rather than attempts to find the text's origins in a period that preceded the killing, best explain its content. For an analysis that questions the neat division into periods of the *quinquennium* and of the decline, see Griffin, *Nero*, 83–99. She finds reasons to blur the distinction as well as larger structural questions of the relationship between the *princeps* and the Senate, which must widen the focus beyond Nero's personal degeneracy. On the question of structural sources that caused emperors to be drawn toward lethal solutions to succession questions, see Veyne, *Seneca*, 7–9.

13. This is the picture of Seneca that emerges, in part, from Tacitus, but the adequacy of this picture has been questioned by readers of Seneca's tragedies who see a man working under morally challenging tensions between his own life and ideals. Henry and Walker, "Tacitus and Seneca." Scholiast commentary on Juvenal suggested that Seneca knew from the start that Nero had been born an inherent savage, and that they did their best to keep him, not unlike a wild animal, from tasting blood for fear of what would follow. Cited in Braund, "Introduction," 3n5. For a very different, recent, view see Drinkwater, *Nero*.

14. For a reading of Seneca that suggests that he was attempting to redefine republican hopes toward a princely republic, one in which Seneca augments in his use of Stoicism a claim like Augustus's that he restored liberty from a people made subordinate to faction and the self-

destruction of factional fighting, see Stacey, "Princely Republic." Stacey is interested in the defense of the princely governance, "if the Roman *princeps* does, in fact, embody the moral personality which Seneca depicts in the mirror" (141). The approach taken here is to consider what this beatific vision of good governance, or even freedom, might mean when the *princeps* does not, and prefers—as Neroes, then and now, very clearly did—false praise instead.

15. Nero had applause crews trained in rhythmic clapping that followed him as he submitted audiences to his singing performances. Tacitus, *Annals* 14.15; Suetonius (1914), Nero, 20. The leaders of these crews, or claques, were rewarded in gold.

16. There are, of course, parallels between Seneca's praise for clemency in this work and Cicero's praise for this same virtue in the person of Caesar in speeches like the *Pro Marcello*. Cicero, "Speech . . . in Behalf of Marcus Claudius Marcellus (Pro Marcello)." There are also important distinctions. Cicero allowed himself to praise Caesar, after honoring the unanimous Senate request made to him to show his clemency to Marcello—as he had to many other supporters of Pompey, like Cicero himself—after his victory in civil war. He praises Caesar's clemency as a general in war, and his unwillingness to give into anger against his opponents or in promoting the suffering of his defeated enemies. Not unlike Seneca, he even imagines that Rome going forward would require the further services of its foremost member, Caesar, including his clemency. Nonetheless, the text is quite different than Seneca's on the political register. Whereas Cicero allows himself to praise Caesar in this speech as the one who, after his victory in the civil war, would restore the republic, even if as its first citizen and leading light he does not countenance praising Caesar as Rome's clement king: "This, then, is the part which remains to you—this is the cause which you have before you; this is what you must now labour at,—to settle the republic, and to enjoy it yourself, as the first of its citizens, in the greatest tranquility and peacefulness" (ibid., 466).

17. Dowling, *Clemency and Cruelty*.

18. Cassius Dio, *Roman History* 59.18.7–8. For a discussion of Seneca's popularity at court during Caligula's rule, see Veyne, *Seneca*, 6–7.

19. Suetonius (1914), Claudius, 29; Dio, *Roman History* 60.8.5; Griffin, *Seneca*, 52, 59–60.

20. We know of the death sentence from the Senate and Claudius's alteration of the sentence from Seneca himself. Seneca, *De Consolatione Ad Polybium*, secs. 13, 2.

21. On his connections with Agrippina and the particular charge of adultery with Julia Livilla, see Griffin, *Seneca*, 52, 59–60. For his career both for, and later against, Agrippina's designs, see ibid., passim. For the order to bring back Seneca at Agrippina's request, and also the reason for the inference of Agrippina's earlier intercession, see Tacitus, *Annals* 12.8.

22. Tacitus, *Annals* 12.64–69.

23. Griffin summarizes the position this way: "When the Emperor called someone his friend, it was virtually a title bestowing . . . high social cachet, the attentions of people seeking favours though his influence, and the expectation of being asked from time to time to advise the Emperor." Even among Nero's other friends, Seneca had a special position in the early years of Nero's reign, and was counted as particularly influential and close. Griffin, *Nero*, 71–72.

24. Tacitus, *Annals* 13.42.

25. Ibid., 14.52–6. As his influence waned, Seneca offered much of what he received back to Nero, who in turn refused Seneca's offer. Thereafter, Tacitus records, Seneca kept a much lower profile. He kept what had been customary crowds of visitors to his immense holdings (parks, palaces, etc.) at bay, and he avoided being seen almost entirely in Rome, or at least avoided an entourage (which, Tacitus implies, had been usual).

26. Braund, "Introduction," 16–17.

27. Ibid., 38–40.

28. *De Clementia*'s opening description of Nero's power was particularly authoritative with Bodin, but also with many before in the Middle Ages. Stacey, "Sovereign Person."

29. For example, "in his own eyes he seems abundantly blessed if he can share with his people his good fortune. He . . . is well disposed to requests that are reasonable, and not harsh to ones that are not. He is loved, protected, and revered by the whole state. People say the same things about him in secret as they do openly. . . . An emperor like this [clement and generous] is protected by his own good deeds and has no need of a bodyguard." *De Clementia* 1.13.4–5.

30. The fatherhood trope is developed at length in ibid., 1.14.1–1.16.3. This begins: "So what is his duty? It is that of good parents, who as a rule scold their children sometimes gently, sometimes with threats, and on some occasions even chastise them with a flogging. Does anyone in their right mind disinherit a son for his first offense?"

31. Double negatives that yield a positive, used in classical Latin, could cause confusion in late Latin (conforming to Romance languages' [e.g., *ne . . . pas*] concordance). This, combined perhaps with a desire to make Seneca an authoritative defender of a just and equitable sovereign, resulted in noteworthy variations in the way this passage was misquoted, and translated, in later centuries. Hugo Grotius, for example, converts the passage into a blanket prohibition against killing contrary to law: "Occidere contra Legem nemo potest, sevare nemo, praeter me" (or "Kill contrary to the law, no man can, and save, none can, besides myself"). This he stated in support of extralegal pardon powers after sentencing in book 2, chap. 20 (On Punishment), sec. 24; cited in Grotius, *Three Books*, 377. (We see the same "nemo potest" in the Latin Blau edition of 1633, p. 234.) Two more examples of this omission are Taylor et al., *Whole Works*, 183 and note. And on the title page of Brydall, *New-Years-Gift*, Brydall wrote "in Defense of [Charles II's contested] Power-Royal, of granting Pardons, as he pleases," and specifically the pardon of the Earl of Danby, Sir Thomas Osbourne.

32. See note 31. *De Clementia* 1.5.4 refers not to just any household's exercise of clemency, but the palace's.

33. Suetonius (1914), Claudius, 29, 37, 44.

34. For a partial defense of Nero, including a refutation of the notion of his indifference toward Romans during the fire, see Champlin, *Nero*. He draws upon Josephus to cast doubt on the historical witnesses against Nero, and argues against the relatively low, if nonetheless prevalent, view that asserts that Nero was a monster. He remains, in this account, a tyrant. Suspicion and skepticism toward Tacitus, Suetonius, and Cassius Dio (as class antagonists) form a near invitation to praise by the curator of a recent exhibit at the British Museum. Bologna, "Who Was Nero?" See also Drinkwater, *Nero*.

35. Tacitus, *Annals* 13.14–17; Suetonius (1914), Nero, 33; Dio, *Roman History* 61.1.1; 61.7.4.

36. Tacitus, *Annals* 14.3–13 [AD 59]; Suetonius (1914), Nero, 34; Dio, *Roman History* 61.5.3; 61.9.2–4.

37. Griffin, *Nero*, 83–99. Veyne, *Seneca*, 7–9.

38. Tacitus, *Annals* 13.25 [AD 56]; Suetonius (1914), Nero, 26; Dio, *Roman History* 61.5.3; 61.9.2–4. Cf. Seneca, *De Clementia* 2.4.1–2. Like the highwaymen or pirates who kill and rob strangers, Nero was guilty of brutality. Cruelty, says Seneca, is the opposite of clemency, but only in the context of one who exacts punishment. Since the victims of pirates are not, strictly speaking, punished, clemency is not the virtue that opposes their particular vice.

39. Suetonius (1914), Nero, 29. Suetonius also notes, however, that Nero held that no one could remain chaste, and that if anyone confessed to obscenity he "pardoned all other faults in those who confessed to him their lewdness."

40. Ibid., 26, 28–29, 34. Tacitus, *Annals* 13.25. For the using of Christians as human torches, ibid., 15.44. After a sufficient number of confessions, Christians were burned, says Tacitus, not so much for arson as for their "hatred of mankind" ("odio generi humanis"). There is speculation, without evidence, that Nero's second wife and former mistress, Poppaea, interceded on behalf of the Jews at the time of the fire and was able to keep this otherwise blamable target community safe from becoming the

scapegoat in this instance. Williams, "'Θεοσεβὴς γὰρ ἦν,'" 98n5; Griffin, *Nero*, 133.

41. For a recent summary of analysis along these lines, see Braund, "Introduction," 11–16. A part of the optimism, as Wiseman argues, was that Claudius's rule seemed a threat to the peace of a constant Julian line of succession. Claudius's reign was cast by Calpurnius Siculus as a return to civil war. Nero's lineage was welcome as a return to an order Claudius had disrupted. Wiseman, "Calpurnius Siculus."

42. This, most recently, in the engaging biography by Romm, *Dying Every Day*. See also Griffin, *Seneca*.

43. For an exception, although one still very much in orbit around the hostile sovereignty concepts of Schmitt that it also critiques, see Sitze, "Keeping the Peace."

44. Tuckness and Parrish, *Decline of Mercy*, 72–83.

45. Alex Tuckness and John M. Parrish describe Seneca as defending mercy in the broad development of Stoic and ancient thought, but largely spurn an approach that situates Seneca within Nero's reign. Ibid., 72–84.

46. Dio, *Roman History* 44.6.4. Roman coins were also likely to pair the goddess with Caesar. On the propaganda of the late Republic and after, see Dowling, *Clemency and Cruelty*, 20–26, 126–68. Dowling argues, persuasively, that the Senate's desire to shape the propaganda of a clement Caesar was its own feeble way of both acknowledging their subordination and their efforts, from weakness, to shape the actions of the *princeps* so that he would become clement in a manner that best suited them.

47. Stacey, *Roman Monarchy*, 32.

48. Griffin, *Nero*, 95, 77–78; Griffin, *Seneca*.

49. Dowling, *Clemency and Cruelty*, 16–18.

50. Cicero, "Speech . . . in Behalf of Marcus Claudius Marcellus (Pro Marcello)"; Cicero, "Speech . . . in Defense of Quintus Ligarius (Pro Ligario)."

51. *De Clementia* 1.14.1–1.15.2.

52. Braund, "Introduction," 32. Tracing the development of the concept, which had no equivalent in Greek (*pace* Tuckness and

Parrish, *Decline of Mercy*), clemency was a distinctly Roman notion. It was relatively rare, notes Braund, in the republican period, and then begins to take a much more prominent role as that form gave way to rule by *princeps*: "What under the Republic was the *clementia populi Romani*, directed towards defeated peoples or provincial subjects and dispensed by individual generals or governors, became a political slogan during the civil wars as Julius Caesar expands the concept of *clementia*, and ultimately morphs into a more or less standard attribute of the *princeps*, so that by the fourth century an emperor might readily be addressed as *Clementia Tua*." Braund, "Introduction," 34. This last appellation she compares to "Your Majesty," a term for royalty that has become so commonplace that it has lost its connection with the greatness normally associated with the majestic.

53. Wirszubski, *Libertas*, 151.

54. Ibid., 151–53.

55. Braund, "Introduction," 42.

56. Seneca thus "equate[d] the *princeps* with the heroic figure of the Stoic *vir sapiens*, whose state of perfected rationality, and therefore of perfect *virtus*, made him such a pivotal figure of moral reflection and emulation in Stoic and Senecan ethics. And since the prince is identifiable as just such a wise man, he will understand that he is 'born to assist the community and promote the common good'. He will therefore always ensure that the *bonum commune* and never a partisan interest is upheld by his government. This point helps to validate Seneca's description of the monarchy as *a res publica*, now extensively restructured along universal lines." Stacey, *Roman Monarchy*, 33. Stacey, "Princely Republic."

57. Stacey, *Roman Monarchy*, 31:

> In *De clementia*, Seneca makes Stoic *ratio* the governing principle of his political community, which thereby comes to share the same rationality, law and justice as the cosmic city. The two *res publicae* begin to be identified at a theoretical level. Although it is by no means a smooth or stable alignment, the

manoeuvre enables Seneca to ground the Roman imperial ideology of *virtus* upon a strictly Stoic notion of reason. He can then immediately inscribe a principle of universal law and justice upon the person of the prince in order to justify the emperor's lack of any formal obligation in terms of the human, positive law or agency or constitutional requirement at a local level. The virtue of Seneca's *princeps* explains and legitimates his absolutism: by definition, the prince is bound only to a higher, universal moral law.

See also ibid., 34.

58. *Lev.*, 29.1.

59. Wirszubski, *Libertas*, 124–29. A tension needs exploration: If the nondomination concept of freedom was still operative in the minds of Romans, but also considered politically impractical for a collective, why (and for whom, one might ask Stacey) would Seneca wish to propose a Stoic liberty concept as a replacement?

60. Skinner, *Liberty Before Liberalism*.

61. Wirszubski, *Libertas*, chap. 5.

62. Stacey, "Princely Republic," 146–53.

63. Stacey, *Roman Monarchy*, 51.

64. Seneca, *De Clementia* 1.1.8.

65. Against Stoics (and Epicureans, of which he numbered Hobbes), Leibniz claimed that he was preserving God's choice of the morally best and perfect world. Against these thinkers, as well as Spinoza, he would maintain that he protected the moral integrity of a providential God. He was nonetheless criticized for coming too close to determinism. Leibniz, "Two Sects"; Voltaire, *Candide*; Rutherford, "Leibniz and the Stoics"; Forman, "Free Will."

66. Berlin, "Two Concepts of Liberty," 135–41. We can, of course, come full circle. A former critic of negative liberty concepts, Quentin Skinner, has argued that Hobbes also redefined liberty in a way that undermined the (neo-Roman) republican conceptions. Skinner, *Hobbes and Republican Liberty*.

67. A principal target in the contemporary debate has been Murphy, "Mercy and Legal Justice."

CHAPTER 7

1. Wirszubski, *Libertas*, 125–26.

2. Some of these tensions, including the notion that it is only the Stoic sage himself who is free and the ironies of attempting to move readers toward moral choices in a determinist universe are explored, although not justified, in Stacey, *Roman Monarchy*, e.g., 49–50.

3. Dowling, *Clemency and Cruelty*, 126–68.

4. "In his youth Caesar's heir [i.e., the future 'Augustus'], the revolutionary adventurer, won Pompeian support by guile and coolly betrayed his allies, overthrowing the Republic and proscribing the Republicans: in his mature years the statesman stole their heroes and their vocabulary." Syme, *Roman Revolution*, 317. According to Syme, it is not that they did not know it; it is that they refused for many years to speak the truth: that they were, in fact, under a dictator or king. Ibid., 324.

5. Griffin, *Nero*, 59–60, 89–90. While the Senate's consent was often needed, she notes, it was, in fact, had by the overwhelming authority of the prince. Princes therefore needed to maintain an appearance of deference for an authority they could, nonetheless, overwhelm.

6. For this they earned the repeated scorn of Tacitus and later historians. Syme, *Roman Revolution*, 294–330. On Tiberius and Augustus as princely, i.e., despotic legal authorities and how criminalization of libel against the emperor was good grounds for doubting republican pretenses, see Tacitus, *Annals* 1.72–74. For a briefer account of the construction of the principate, see Griffin, *Nero*, 18–20. For Augustus's own account of how he "restored liberty to the republic" from the "tyranny of faction" and against those who unlawfully slew his father, Julius Caesar, see Velleius Paterculus, "Res Gestae Divi Augusti." Here Augustus boasts of the offices, contrary to the republican constitution, that he declined, but nevertheless makes clear that he was indeed the preeminent power in the state.

7. "It early became evident that one man held all the power and authority. And it was not long before a theory developed, to save appearances and permit the senator to maintain his dignity: precisely the ideal of the middle path, liberty but not licence, discipline but not enslavement. It suited Senate and senator. Like the claim or pretext of 'res publica,' that ideal might be equivocal or fraudulent. The honest name of compromise lent itself to deceit or abasement. It was captured and paraded by bland intriguers, subtle careerists, or avowed agents of autocracy." Syme, *Tacitus*, 548. See also Griffin, *Nero*, 89–90.

8. Veyne, *Seneca*, 7–8:

Although the Julio-Claudian family seized control of the state, those of its members who became emperors were considered simply the preeminent magistrates of Rome, and the first among their equals, the senators. They were kings without a title, to whom the sincere monarchist sentiment of the people was directed; they were objects of a genuine cult, just like the potentates of the ancient Middle East (for example, [their] portraits . . . were, like icons, sacred). Caesar's own role was so ambiguous it provoked his own madness. . . . Comrade Stalin and the first magistrate of Rome developed the same psychosis of blame and suspicion against their peers, whom they had effectively ousted while maintaining them in their posts. Hence the purges in the ranks of the old Bolsheviks and in those of Rome's senatorial families.

9. Syme, *Roman Revolution*.

10. Augustus, *Res Gestae* 1.1. Eder, "Augustus."

11. Veyne, *Bread and Circuses*, 296.

12. Eder, "Augustus," 21–24. Augustus, *Res Gestae*, 34.

13. A part of Augustus's strategy for solidifying power, if not a lasting and reliable one, was to allow the competition for power to reemerge among the nobles and ride back into Rome to rescue the state and reestablish law and order once again. Eder, "Augustus," 27.

14. Veyne, *Bread and Circuses*, 340. Under Julius Caesar, Romans were the recipients of numerous benefits. According to Suetonius,

these included gladiatorial contests, stage plays in every quarter of Rome in several languages, chariot races in the Circus, athletic competitions, and a mock naval battle. Caesar's legion infantrymen earned 240 gold pieces as war gratuity on top of a prior 20 paid at the outbreak of hostilities. They were also each given a farm. Plebs: 10 pecks of grain, 10 pounds of oil, 3 gold pieces, paid with interest after a four-year delay to total 5. He gave a popular banquet, "and a distribution of meat," and two victory dinners celebrating triumph at Munda in five days, the second followed the first because it was thought insufficiently splendid. Suetonius (1914), Julius Caesar, 38–39.

For a broad synthetic approach mediated through artworks, see Starobinski, *Largesse*.

15. Eder, "Augustus," 26. The consuls, the highest magistrates in Rome, were meant to rotate annually, and two were appointed. Augustus held his well beyond the normal limits (his third from 31 BC to 23 BC), although maintained, as would most other Roman autocrats, the tradition of having two consuls; however, his counterparts held much shorter terms than those outlined in the constitution.

16. Ibid.

17. Ibid., 27. Augustus, *Res Gestae*, 34. Syme, *Roman Revolution*, 523.

18. Augustus, *Res Gestae*, 34. For an image of the shield, see Wallace-Hadrill, "Emperor and His Virtues," plate I. On the primacy of Augustus's clemency, and its transition from a mere conqueror's mercy to a "global" clemency that approached a universal virtue, see Dowling, *Clemency and Cruelty*, 163–66.

19. Syme, *Roman Revolution*, 510. This observation, published in 1939, sounds like a meditation on the decline of the twentieth-century British aristocracy. Nevertheless, if this inverted Cinderella's shoe—that turned their carriages into pumpkins—fit the Roman nobles' feet just as well as those of some of Syme's near contemporaries, then his own preoccupations need not matter.

20. Griffin, *Nero*, 87–94.

21. Wallace-Hadrill, "Civilis Princeps."

22. Griffin, *Nero*, 87–94.

23. Wirszubski, *Libertas*, 126. Dio, *Roman History* 60.1.

24. Suetonius (1914), Claudius, 11, 12; Dio, *Roman History* 60.5.3–7.

25. Syme, *Tacitus*, 459–550.

26. Ibid., 552; see also 547ff.

27. Seneca, *De Clementia* 1.4.2–3.

28. According to Griffin, the spirit of *De Clementia* was "resigned acceptance of the Principate on historical grounds combined with a frank attempt to infuse into the institution the qualities of ideal kingship [esp. those inherited from Greek sources on kingship, like Xenophon] to which all the philosophical schools paid tribute." Against the now-abandoned promise of the speeches to restore "proper forms" of relations between Nero and the Senate, the "major aim" of *De Clementia* "recommends concentration on reality [i.e., monarchy] rather than the forms." Griffin, *Seneca*, 147, 141–54, 191, 194, 202.

29. Griffin, *Seneca*, 143–46, 147–48. For a more recent survey of literature relating *De Clementia* to Greek sources, especially Plato's *Statesman* and Xenophon's *Cyropaedia*, and transmission of Greek kingship concepts through Cicero and Philodemus that may not have been available to him, but in which Seneca's concepts of good kingship are said to be deeply embedded, see Braund, "Introduction," 24–30.

30. Sallust, *War with Catiline*, sec. 52. Seneca registers other traditional Stoic sources of opposition to clemency in *De Clementia* 2.5.2–3. On Greek Stoics, see Braund, "Introduction," 66–68. Dowling notes the innovation in contrast with the Stoics, who refused to pity and who followed, in many cases, republican affinities for severity. She also credits Seneca with having made clemency a widely admired virtue, and not merely among emperors. Dowling, *Clemency and Cruelty*, 202–5. Especially after the failure of Julius Caesar's clemency, clemency was itself spurned by republicans (including Cicero) and of course Octavian (the avenger of his adopted father) until Pompey deploys the strategic uses of shelter

and mercy for those threatened or harmed by rival triumvirs. Ibid., 34–75.

31. For a contrary view, although one that refrains from generalizing on the meaning of clemency during the De Clementia's period, see Konstan, "Clemency as a Virtue." Cf. Braund, "Introduction," sec. 5, esp. p. 32; Dowling, Clemency and Cruelty.

32. Dio, Roman History 43.10.3–5. For Konstan, see above; the rejection of "pity" is not a rejection of clemency. Given that Cato is also said to allow his son, as already brought up in servitude, to accept Caesar's offer, what is clear is that republican liberty is allergic to accepting the kind of kindnesses that Seneca is here gathering under his rather capacious concept of "clemency." See also Cato's rejection of Caesar's "grace" in Plutarch, Cato the Younger 66.1–3. "'For if,' said he, 'I were willing to be saved by grace of Caesar, I ought to go to him in person and see him alone; but I am unwilling to be under obligations to the tyrant for his illegal acts. And he acts illegally in saving, as if their master, those over whom he has no right at all to be lord.'"

33. Seneca, On Benefits 2.20.3. Cf. Cicero, "Second Philippic."

34. Dowling, Clemency and Cruelty, 166–68.

35. Suetonius (1914), Nero, 22–24. For a sympathetic treatment of Nero's artistic endeavors—no small part of how he conceived of his rule—see Champlin, Nero, 53–83. See also Griffin, Nero, 119–63.

36. Dowling sees the didactic aspects of Seneca's De Clementia as a part of a longer history of attempts by Rome's elite to tame their emperors. As such, that which is "for Nero" is perhaps slightly less a work designed to aid Nero in his own propaganda than a part of a longer effort to achieve tranquility under submission, which, in turn, converts clemency from a tactical or wise opportunity for the victorious into a sublime quality and "an ethic essential to the nature of a good man." Dowling, Clemency and Cruelty, 195–205.

37. Veyne, "What Was a Roman Emperor?"; Wallace-Hadrill, "Emperor and His Virtues."

38. Griffin, Seneca, 133–71, esp. 137. See also the more recent discussion in Braund, "Commentary," 51–64. See also Stacey, Roman Monarchy, 37ff.

39. Wirszubski, Libertas, 130–33.

40. Tacitus, Annals 15.62.

41. Suetonius allows his Seneca a premonition about Nero's bad behavior: he dreams Nero is Caligula. Tacitus makes a general claim about the need to keep Nero's indulgences within bounds, and a concrete example: substituting the ex-slave Acte as an object of desire so as to prevent incest with Agrippina. Suetonius (1914), Nero, 7; Tacitus, Annals 13.2, 12. On Nero's public singing and chariot racing, see ibid., 14.4.

42. Cassius Dio (AD 220), whom we only have through his epitomizers, not the original, stands as one of least sympathetic views of Seneca. Dio, Roman History 61.4–5; 61.12; 61.20. In Dio's moralizing account, Seneca looks to his own advantage by indulging Nero's bad behavior. Dio's Seneca is shortsighted (as is Agrippina; cf. 61.2.) Their indulgence of Nero's vices allowed Seneca and Burrus to rule in the irresponsible youth's stead, but the decision comes back to bite them. Nero first insincerely acknowledges his flaws but over time openly spurns all authority and moral limitations. On Seneca in the eyes of historians and their lost sources, see Griffin, Seneca, 421–44.

43. Tuckness and Parrish, Decline of Mercy, 75–84. Tuckness and Parrish tend to emphasize instrumental reasons over and above all others.

44. Seneca, De Clementia 1.3.3–4.

45. Ibid., 1.5.5.

46. Ibid.

47. We lack the text of these speeches. Tacitus and Dio report that Seneca wrote Nero's speeches during the first year of his reign: for Claudius's funeral, the accession speeches before the praetorian guard and the Senate, and speeches to the Senate specifically on clemency. Clemency, therefore, was a major theme, accompanied by clement acts. Tacitus, Annals 13.3–4, 10–11; Dio, Roman History 61.3. Words were accompanied by deeds: the recuperation of

Plautius Lateranus. Tacitus, *Annals* 13.11. About which more below.

48. Tacitus, *Annals* 13.3.

49. *Apocolocyntosis* or "Pumpkinification," or perhaps more literally "gourdification," is likely a pun on ἀποθέωσις (apotheosis), linking it with the Greek for a gourd, in Latin the *cucurbita*, or κολοκύντη, hence "Apo-colocynt-osis." Scholars continue to discuss the precise connotation; for a recent review and discussion, see James and Braund, "Quasi Homo," 298–301. Griffin, *Seneca*, 129n3.

50. It was obviously not the first, but Menippus's work is lost, so *Apocolocyntosis* is considered the earliest surviving intact example of Menippean satire. Paschalis, "Afterlife of Emperor Claudius"; Eden, "Introduction," 13–17.

51. "Under Augustus the *consul* began to take cases involving the same offense by members of the upper classes in the Senate itself. It was a pernicious development, turning legal into political issues and infringing laws designed to protect Roman citizens against condemnation on capital charges into courts not established by the people. It went unchallenged because it seemed to make the senators masters in their own house." Levick, *Claudius*, 115.

52. Suetonius (1914), Claudius, 15.

53. Levick, *Claudius*, 116–19; Tacitus, *Annals* 11.5.

54. Seneca, *Apocolocyntosis*, sec. 12, subsec. 3.

55. Ibid., sec. 10, subsec. 4.

56. Ibid., secs. 14, 1–2.

57. Suetonius (1914), Nero, 10. Griffin, *Seneca*, 105–28. As Griffin notes, there was no making good on speeches that seemed to promise to share authority with the Senate, but in matters of correcting Claudius's bad practices, including the delegation of power and honors to freedmen, expansive juridical roles for the emperor in trying ordinary cases, a lack of clemency in handing out punishments, and a kinder style of beneficence toward senators in need, Nero's alterations were real and were greeted with approval by senators for a time in the period before 62, when Seneca lost influence.

58. Tacitus reports that in his accession speech to the Senate, he declared that the judicial institution would be respected again in its "ancient tasks" and that the "long silence of the laws" would be broken. Tacitus, *Annals* 13.4. Notably, Seneca does not promise returned authority for the Senate in *De Clementia*. "Seneca's adoption of [the] metaphysical description of the Principate [in *De Clementia*] . . . refuted the partnership with the Senate urged in the [accession] speech." Griffin, *Seneca*, 141. Nevertheless, the tract puts forward an image of Nero as a restorer of justice and a restorer of law, summoning the laws "from their neglect and darkness into the light." Seneca, *De Clementia* 1.1.4.

59. Tacitus, *Annals* 13.4.

60. Ibid., 13.11. This in AD 55.

61. Ibid., 11.1–7; 13.42–43. Tacitus notes that Sullius was unhumbled by Claudius's fall, and then charged in the Senate for violating the Cinian law against those who had pleaded in court for hire—a law passed in response to his own abuses during Claudius's reign. Griffin notes Sullius may well have been Seneca's Claudian era accuser. More on this below. Griffin, *Seneca*, 97–98.

62. Substantial steps were taken, even if Dio is now thought to have made claims that exaggerate the influence of Seneca and Burrus in terms of legislation. Suetonius acknowledges the salutary changes under Nero, though does not mention Seneca or Burrus as responsible. Suetonius (1914), Nero, 10, 12, 16. Tacitus discusses a number of changes, from the more humane treatment of slaves and relief for regional authorities from undue burdens to the mandate that neither slaves nor animals be killed in games. He is in places, however, dismissive. Tacitus, *Annals* 13.5, 26–34. For a detailed discussion of the initial reversals of Claudian abuses by Nero and the role of Seneca and Burrus, see Griffin, *Nero*, 50–82. After 62, and Nero's (likely) murder of Burrus, says Tacitus, Seneca's influence is at an end. Tacitus, *Annals* 14.51–53, 57.

63. Griffin, *Seneca*, 128, 133, 138–43, 146–51, 169–71, and passim.

64. He ought, for example, to be forgiving of slights done to himself, but ought not to permit wrongs to others go unpunished with the same leniency (*De Clementia*, 1.20.2–3). Clemency, a disposition of the wise and unperturbed judge (who may become properly so if guided by Stoic philosophy, says Seneca) is not pity, which is distressed and gloomy and consumed by a sadness for the fate of others. Ibid., 1.4.4–5, 2.5.4–6, 3.

65. Ibid., 1.7.3–4.

66. Seneca, "On Clemency" 1.8.6; 1.11.24.

67. Seneca, *De Clementia* 1.7.1–3.

68. Ibid., 1.13.4.

69. "What difference is there between a king and tyrant—after all, the appearance of their position and the extent of their power are the same—except that tyrants are ferocious in accordance with their whims, but kings only for a reason and when they have no choice?" Ibid., 1.11.4. The question, of course, is who will call a tyrant a tyrant within earshot rather than a "good king"? Insofar as Seneca's understanding of kings and tyrants carries forward to the seventeenth century, this passage might serve the revisionist view of seventeenth-century politics, wherein the self-restraint of kings, rather than the constitutional prerogatives, differentiates kings from tyrants in the minds of subjects. Cf. Burgess, *Absolute Monarchy*.

70. Seneca, "On Clemency" 1.12.4–13, 4.

71. Seneca, *De Clementia* 1.13.2.

72. [Seneca the Younger], *Octavia*, ll. 440–532. We do not know the actual author. For an argument that the play dates to the late Flavian period, see Ferri, "Introduction," 5–30. Nero's recent biographer Champlin considers *Octavia* deeply unfair. Champlin, *Nero*, 9, 306 n65.

73. [Seneca the Younger], *Octavia*, ll. 454–457.

74. This was an issue for Suetonius who, in spite of recognizing some of the good acts of Nero's early reign, leaves us with a picture of a vicious youth, born of a vicious mother, who could never truly depart from his horrible self. Suetonius (1914), Nero, passim, and 10–11, 16, 19, and esp. 26.

75. After first offering loud praise of the proposal, senators (and this would have included advisors like Seneca) were compelled to explain the disastrous consequences of taking this step; the ultimate result was reforms to check the rapacity of the tax farmers. Tacitus, *Annals* 13.50–51. Tacitus gives these reforms his approval.

76. Griffin, *Nero*, 211. For this he was celebrated as liberator of the Greeks. Ibid., and Champlin, *Nero*, 25–26.

77. Suetonius (1914), Nero, 10. On the felon's execution, cf. Seneca, De Clementia 2.1.2.

78. In 62 he is said by Tacitus to have likely pursued a charge of *maiestas* (harming the dignity of the state) against a senator, Antistius, with the idea that the Senate would vote a severe deserved punishment. He would then step in, veto the harsh punishment, and receive credit for clemency. When the Senate opted to exercise its own clemency by lessoning the punishment from death to exile and property confiscation, Nero could only agree with the lesser punishment, with expressions of clear displeasure. Tacitus, *Annals* 14.48–49.

79. Veyne, "What Was a Roman Emperor?"

80. Veyne, *Bread and Circuses*, 406; Veyne, *Seneca*, 22–24. Suetonius (1914), Nero, 10–11. See also Dowling, *Clemency and Cruelty*.

81. Being seen and interacting with the people at public spectacles such as games, however, was also a way in which the people sometimes communicated their dissatisfactions to (if not about) the emperor. This was also true for Nero. Griffin, *Nero*, 110.

82. Suetonius (1957), Nero, 20.

83. Kyle, "Greek Athletic Competitions."

84. Suetonius (1914), Nero, 23–24.

85. Although she is less interested in *De Clementia* as propaganda than as a text that helped transform clemency into a universal virtue, Dowling notes the prior history and reception of a clement Caesar as propaganda and its expanding place among Romans, especially after reconciliation with Augustus's dominance. Dowling, *Clemency and Cruelty*, 126–218, esp. 196.

86. Suetonius (1914), Claudius, 21.

87. Julius Caesar had done so, so had Sulla, and Augustus boasts of three Greek athletic competitions. H. Lee, "Greek Sports in Rome." Augustus, *Res Gestae*, 22.

88. Augustus, *Res Gestae*, 1, 3ff. For example, "in my eleventh consulship I made twelve distributions of food from grain bought at my own expense, and in the twelfth year of my tribunician power I gave for the third time four hundred sesterces to each man. These largesses of mine reached a number of persons never less than two hundred and fifty thousand. In the eighteenth year of my tribunician power, as consul for the twelfth time, I gave to three hundred and twenty thousand of the city plebs sixty denarii apiece" (ibid., 1.15). The list goes on and on.

89. Suetonius (1957), Claudius, 21.

90. Ibid., 21.

91. Seneca, *De Clementia* 1.8.1, 3.

92. Dowling, *Clemency and Cruelty*, 166–68.

93. Nisbet, "Dating of Seneca's Tragedies."

94. Seneca, *Thyestes*, ll. 204–8.

95. Ibid., ll. 211–12. This inversion was noted by Calvin, *Calvin's Commentary*, 116, 117. For a recent illuminating discussion of flattery, both ancient and modern, see Kapust, *Flattery*.

96. Seneca, *Thyestes*, ll. 213–19.

97. Wiedemann, "Tiberius to Nero," 198–99.

98. Seneca, *De Clementia* 1.1.4.

99. Wallace-Hadrill, "Civilis Princeps."

CONCLUSION

1. Murphy, "Mercy and Legal Justice."

2. Plutarch, *Cato the Younger*, secs. 4.16–17, 23.

3. Seneca, "On Providence," sec. 2.

4. Dowling, *Clemency and Cruelty*, 202–5; Braund, "Introduction," 64–73; Tuckness and Parrish, *Decline of Mercy*, 75–84.

5. Seneca, "On Providence," p. 14.

6. This did not mean that Stoicism, as a moral or philosophical doctrine, dictated a preference for monarchical forms. One found Stoics situated on opposite sides of that debate. Brunt, "Stoicism and the Principate."

7. "Terrarum orbis tandem destituit." Suetonius (1914), Nero, 40. Not unreasonably, especially where Suetonius purports to describe Nero's internal state of mind, this account has been suspected of a certain fantastic quality. Given some of its duplication in Dio (Dio, *Roman History* 63), it has been argued that a common mythology, based upon Plato's Myth of Er, was at the root of a common gloss on Nero's demise. Sansone, "Nero's Final Hours."

8. Dio has him learning the news at the event, and displaying his indifference, upon learning of the revolt, by opting to test his prowess in the ring with the athletes. Dio, *Roman History* 63.26.

9. For a historical treatment that describes coordination between Vindex and Galba and the propaganda of the revolt—against Nero's objectional conduct at court, and for restoring Roman liberties, and to govern with clemency, see Brunt, "Revolt of Vindex."

10. Suetonius (1914), Nero, 40–42.

11. Nero had been falsely accused of setting Rome's great fire in 64. Suetonius's implicit assertion here may have been that if Nero wasn't actually guilty, he was as blameworthy in character, if not in fact, as his accessors had believed.

12. Stacey, "Princely Republic."

13. Brunt, "Stoicism and the Principate."

14. Seneca himself seems to approve of such a censor in his criticism of Brutus in Seneca, *On Benefits* 2.20.

15. Hobbes, *Lev.*, 29.1.

16. Stacey, *Roman Monarchy*.

17. Seneca's purpose in *On Benefits* was to pen an ethical lesson for the Roman elite—in how to give and receive benefits with the right frame of mind—but Seneca occasionally used emperors, notably Caligula, as negative exemplars. For example, Seneca, *On Benefits* II, 12.1. In the seventeenth century, Seneca's text helped shape the vocabulary used to condemn court corruption and could inform critiques of greedy favorites or even

the monarch himself. Peck, *Court Patron-age*, esp. 12–14.

18. De Tocqueville, *Old Regime*.

19. Hobbes, *On the Citizen*, dedicatory, 1–3. Plutarch, *Cato the Elder*, 8.13.

20. Locke, *Two Treatises*, 2.93.

21. Xenophon, *Cyropaedia* 8.2.

22. See Daumier, "Very Humble, Very Obedient, Very Submissive, and Most of All, Very Voracious Subjects," February 9, 1832, in The Daumier Register, Digital Work Catalogue, http://www.daumier-register .org/werkview.php?key=40.

23. Seneca, *De Clementia* 1.9; Dio, *Roman History* 55.14.3–16.2. Syme cast doubt, suggesting that because the conspiracy is not recorded by other historians it did not occur. Syme, *Roman Revolution*, 414n1, although cf. 420. This not the view of some recent (and some past) scholars who focus more on attempting to reconcile the conflicts between Seneca's and Dio's accounts. See Seneca, *De Clementia*, 263–64; Adler, "Cassius Dio's Livia"; Dowling, *Clemency and Cruelty*, 66.

24. Seneca, *De Clementia* 1.9.8.

25. Dio, *Roman History* 55.15.4–6.

26. Adler, "Cassius Dio's Livia."

27. Dio, *Roman History* 55.17.4.

28. Adler, "Cassius Dio's Livia."

29. Montaigne, *Complete Essays*, chap. 24.

30. Viallaneix, *La Voie Royale*, 149; Michelet and Quinet, *Jesuits*, 61.

31. Aronica, "Corneille entré dans l'Histoire." For Dumas, following but adding to Michelet, Corneille can be seen as a tool of pro-Spanish factions at court, including Marie de Medici, the Queen Mother (of Anne of Austria, and Henrietta Marie, queen of Charles I). *Le Cid* becomes a way to signal the nobility's favor for Spain and for the ethos of dueling. Richelieu had been working to banish all of the above. Dumas, *Souvenirs dramatiques*, 1:83–126, esp. 95 98. For Michelet, as Aronica notes, Corneille is both a poor man against the state (a distortion given his standing as a judge) but also the creative genius that symbolizes the French people's embrace of the poet's embrace of Spanish passion and a desacral-ization of the monarchy by making, in effect, Corneille's play the true father of

Louis XIV for its having fostered the rapprochement between Anne of Austria and Louis XIII. Michelet, *Histoire de France*, 12:187–200.

32. Van Roosbroeck, "Corneille's 'Cinna.'" The play of Louis's justice in punishing La Rochelle, and his mercy, was very much a part of accounts offered not long after in England. See, for example, Mervault, *Last Famous Siege*, 170–84.

33. Michelet, *Histoire de France*, 12:190.

34. Ibbett notes that pedagogues of the nineteenth century invented what the French called "classism" and drew upon a tradition, beginning with anti-Mazarines, and which at times described French culture as a perfect balance that smoothed out the excesses of others. Thus Spain was full of braggarts (and duelists), and Italy of Machiavels. She singles out Nicolas Boileau's *Art poetique* of 1674 as particularly important. Ibbett, "Italy Versus France," esp. 184. Dumas wished to supplement what he saw as Michelet's analysis of Italian corrupting influences at work in France, its manners, and its court, in the course of his discussion of Corneille. Dumas, *Souvenirs dramatiques*, 1:119–20.

35. Ibbett, "Italy Versus France," 387.

36. Cf. Shklar, *Ordinary Vices*, 169–71. She sees in Augustus's pardon—accepted with pride by compromised aristocrats in service to an absolutist—a domestication of Machiavelli. Looking behind Corneille's *Cinna* to Montaigne, she does not go further back to Seneca, for whom clemency was the opposite of cruelty.

37. Corneille, "Cinna," ll. 1210–16.

38. Bilis, "Corneille's Cinna." Bilis links Augustus's decision with Agamben's appropriation of the exception. Augustus's decision, and perhaps even Richelieu's dictates, could be understood, as she explains, as extralegal. Augustus's decision to show Cinna and the conspirators clemency is, as she notes, the instauration on stage of an absolutist sovereign, immune from justice. I think she has underestimated how the inclusion of Corneille's Augustus's clemency stands as a counter-example to the hostile exceptions

that are the rule in Agamben's understanding of sovereignty.

39. See Jacques Stella's *Liberality of Titus (Allegory of the Liberality of Louis XIII and Cardinal Richelieu)*, ca. 1637–38, Fogg Museum, Harvard University, http://www .harvardartmuseums.org/art/227880. For how that liberality, especially after putting down a rebellion in Corneille's native Rouen (and with regard to Corneille himself) may have been at work, see van Roosbroeck, "Corneille's 'Cinna.'" Unlike later readers like Bilis, van Roosbroeck took the forgiveness and generosity of Augustus in *Cinna* not as a critique or regret but as a gracious acknowledgment of what the Cardinal had done for him and the nobles who, after having their capacity to represent the region suspended by Richelieu, were reunited with the state.

40. Suetonius, *Augustus*, described Toranius as his guardian, and his death under proscription as an example of Octavia's severity while a member of the Truimvirate. Perhaps Corneille's re-description of Toranius as his tutor is a nod to Seneca. As a young man, Augustus was tutored by Stoics. Richelieu had ennobled Corneille's father.

41. Corneille, "Cinna," ll. 1696–1701.

42. For a contrast between Corneille and Hobbes on sovereigns as representatives, see Herzog, "Hobbes and Corneille."

43. Corneille, "Cinna," l. 1713.

44. Ibid., ll. 1715–24.

45. His parade passed through a series of triumphal arches; the first saluted him as a triumphant Augustus having defeated a rebellion. Ogilby and Knowles, *Entertainment*, introduction, 18–26; 12–42 [main].

46. "Charles II, 1660: An Act of Free and Generall Pardon Indempnity [*sic*] and Oblivion," in *Statutes of the Realm: Volume 5, 1628–80*, ed. John Raithby (Great Britain Record Commission, 1819), 226–34, 226–34. In anon., *Musa Præsica the London Poem*, 13: "Thou now ascends the Throne, / Not like a Nero or Domitian, / But like Augustus Great and Wise, / Forgiving and forgetting Injuries."

Adler, Eric. "Cassius Dio's Livia and the Conspiracy of Cinna Magnus." *Greek, Roman, and Byzantine Studies* 51, no. 1 (2011): 133–54.

Ackerman, Bruce. *The Decline and Fall of the American Republic*. Cambridge: Belknap Press, 2010.

Adamson, John. *The Noble Revolt: The Overthrow of Charles I*. London: Weidenfeld & Nicolson, 2007.

Agamben, Giorgio. *Homo Sacer: Sovereign Power and Bare Life*. Translated by Daniel Heller-Roazen. Meridian. Stanford: Stanford University Press, 1998.

———. *State of Exception*. Chicago: University of Chicago Press, 2005.

Allen, Gay W. "Walt Whitman and Jules Michelet." *Études Anglaises* 1 (1937): 230–37.

Anderson, Frank M. "The Constitutional Charter of 1814." In *Constitutions and Documents Illustrative of the History of France, 1789–1901*, edited by Frank M. Anderson, 456–64. Minneapolis: H. W. Wilson, 1904.

Anon. *Musa Præsica the London Poem, or, An Humble Oblation on the Sacred Tomb of Our Late Gracious Monarch King Charles the II, of Ever Blessed and Eternal Memory / by a Loyal Apprentice of the Honourable City of London*. London, 1685.

Arendt, Hannah. *The Human Condition*. 2nd ed. Chicago: University of Chicago Press, 1998.

———. "What Is Freedom?" In *Between Past and Future*, 143–71. New York: Viking Press, 1968.

Aronica, Claire. "Corneille entré dans l'Histoire. Michelet lecteur du *Cid*." *Les Lettres Romanes* 68, nos. 3–4 (2014): 511–23. https://doi.org/10.1484/J.LLR.5.103659.

Augustine. *The City of God*. Translated by Henry Bettenson. Harmondsworth, UK: Penguin, 1984.

Augustus. *Res Gestae*. Translated by Frederick W. Shipley. Cambridge: Harvard University Press, 1924.

Baker, Peter, Maggie Haberman, and Sharon LaFraniere. "Trump Commutes Sentence of Roger Stone." *New York Times*, July 10, 2020. https://www.nytimes.com/2020/07/10/us/politics/trump-roger-stone-clemency.html.

Balakrishnan, Gopal. *The Enemy: An Intellectual Portrait of Carl Schmitt*. London: Verso, 2000.

Baranger, Denis. "The Apparition of Sovereignty." In Kalmo and Skinner, *Sovereignty in Fragments*, 47–63.

Bartelson, Jens. *A Genealogy of Sovereignty*. Cambridge: Cambridge University Press, 1995.

Barthes, Roland. *Michelet*. Translated by Richard Howard. New York: Hill and Wang, 1987.

Bayle, Pierre. *The Dictionary Historical and Critical . . . The Second Edition*. Vol. 2. London, 1734.

———. *Miscellaneous Reflections, occasione'd by the comet which appear'd in December 1680*. Vol. 2. 1708.

———. *Political Writings*. Edited by Sally Jenkinson. Cambridge: Cambridge University Press, 2000.

Beattie, J. M. *Crime and the Courts in England, 1660–1800*. Princeton: Princeton University Press, 1986.

Bellamy, Richard Paul. *Liberalism and Modern Society: A Historical Argument*. University Park: Penn State University Press, 1992.

Berlin, Isaiah. "Two Concepts of Liberty." In *Four Essays on Liberty*, 118–72. Oxford: Oxford University Press, 1969.

Bilis, Hélène. "Corneille's Cinna, Clemency, and the Implausible Decision." *Modern Language Review* 108, no. 1 (2013): 68–89.

Birdsall, Paul. "Non Obstante: A Study of the Dispensing Power of English Kings." In *Essays in History and Political Theory in Honor of Charles Howard McIlwain*, 37–76. Cambridge: Harvard University Press, 1967.

Blackstone, William. *Commentaries on the Laws of England*. Edited by George Sharswood. Vol. 2. Philadelphia: J. B. Lippincott, 1893.

Blanc, Louis. *History of the French Revolution of 1789*. Philadelphia: Lea and Blanchard, 1848.

Bloch, Marc. *The Royal Touch: Monarchy and Miracles in France and England*. Translated by J. E. Anderson. New York: Dorset Press, 1989.

Bodin, Jean. *The Six Bookes of a Common-weale: A Facsimile Reprint of the English Translation of 1606, Corrected and Supplemented in the Light of a New Comparison with the French and Latin Texts*. Translated by Richard Knolles. Cambridge: Harvard University Press, 1962.

Bolingbroke, Henry St. John. "A Dissertation upon Parties." In *Political Writings*, edited by D. Armitage, 1–191. Cambridge: Cambridge University Press, 1997.

Bologna, Francesca. "Who Was Nero?—British Museum Blog." *British Museum Blog*, April 22, 2021, accessed July 22, 2021. https://blog.british museum.org/who-was-nero/.

Braddick, Michael. *God's Fury, England's Fire: A New History of the English Civil Wars*. London: Penguin, 2009.

Braund, Susanna. "Commentary." In Seneca, *De Clementia*, 153–422.

———. "Introduction." In Seneca, *De Clementia*, 1–91.

Brown, Wendy. *Walled States, Waning Sovereignty*. New York: MIT Press, 2010.

Brunt, P. A. "The Revolt of Vindex and the Fall of Nero." *Latomus* 18, no. 3 (1959): 531–59.

———. "Stoicism and the Principate." *Papers of the British School at Rome* 43 (1975): 7–35.

Brydall, John. *A New-Years-Gift for the Anti-Prerogative-Men*. Early English Books, 1641–1700. London: John Fish, 1682.

Buchez, Ph., and P. C. Roux. *Histoire Parlementaire de La Révolution Française*. Vol. 1. Paris: Paulin, 1834.

Burgess, Glenn. *Absolute Monarchy and the Stuart Constitution*. New Haven: Yale University Press, 1996.

Butler, Judith. *Precarious Life: The Powers of Mourning and Violence*. London: Verso, 2004.

Caldwell, Peter C. *Popular Sovereignty and the Crisis of German Constitutional Law: The Theory and Practice of Weimar Constitutionalism*. Durham: Duke University Press, 1997.

Caldwell, Peter C., and William E. Scheuerman. "Introduction." In *From Liberal Democracy to Fascism*, edited by Peter C. Caldwell and William E. Scheuerman, 1–19. Boston: Humanities Press, 2000.

Calvin, Jean. *Calvin's Commentary on Seneca's De Clementia*. Leiden: E. J. Brill, 1969.

Cassirer, Ernst. *The Question of Rousseau*. Translated by Peter Gay. New Haven: Yale University Press, 1989.

Champlin, Edward. *Nero*. Cambridge: Harvard University Press, 2003.

Cicero, Marcus Tullius. "Against Verres." In *The Orations of Marcus Tullius Cicero*, translated by C. D. Yonge, 132–545. London: George Bell & Sons, 1903.

———. *De Officiis*. Translated by Walter Miller. New York: Macmillan, 1903.

———. "Second Philippic." In *The Orations of Marcus Tullius Cicero*, vol 4., translated by C. D. Yonge, 19–68. London: Henry G. Bohn, 1852.

———. "The Speech of M. T. Cicero in Defense of Quintus Ligarius (Pro Ligario)." Translated by C. D. Yonge, vol. 3, 469–83. London: George Bell & Sons, 1891.

———. "The Speech of M.T. Cicero in Behalf of Marcus Claudius Marcellus

(Pro Marcello)." In *The Orations of Marcus Tullius Cicero*, translated by B. A. Youge, 457–68. London: George Bell & Sons, 1891

Collingham, H. A. C. *The July Monarchy: A Political History of France 1830–1848*. Edited by R. S. Alexander. London: Longman, 1988.

Colliot-Thélène, Catherine. "Carl Schmitt Versus Max Weber: Juridical Rationality and Economic Rationality." In *The Challenge of Carl Schmitt*, edited by Chantal Mouffe, 138–54. New York: Verso, 1999.

Condren, Conal. *Argument and Authority in Early Modern England: The Presupposition of Oaths and Offices*. Cambridge: Cambridge University Press, 2006.

Corneille, Pierre. "Cinna or the Clemency of Augustus." In *The Cid; Cinna; The Theatrical Illusion*, translated by John Cairncross, 23–110. Harmondsworth, UK: Penguin, 1975.

Cressy, David. *Charles I and the People of England*. Oxford: Oxford University Press, 2015.

Cristi, Renato. *Carl Schmitt and Authoritarian Liberalism: Strong State, Free Economy*. Cardiff: University of Wales Press, 1998.

Cromartie, Alan. "General Introduction to A Dialogue Between a Philosopher and a Student, of the Common Laws of England." In Thomas Hobbes, *Writings on Common Law and Hereditary Right*, edited by Alan Cromartie and Quentin Skinner, xiv–lxv. Oxford: Oxford University Press, 2005.

Crossley, Ceri. *French Historians and Romanticism: Thierry, Guizot, the Saint-Simonians, Quinet, Michelet*. London: Routledge, 1993.

Damrosch, Leo. *Jean-Jacques Rousseau: Restless Genius*. Boston: Houghton Mifflin, 2005.

Danner, Mark. "After September 11: Our State of Exception." *New York Review of Books*, August 13, 2011, 44–48.

Davis, Julie Hirschfeld, and Maggie Haberman. "Trump Pardons Joe Arpaio, Who Became Face of Crackdown on Illegal Immigration." *New York Times*, August 25, 2017. https://www.nytimes.com/2017/08/25/us/politics/joe-arpaio-trump-pardon-sheriff-arizona.html.

Derrida, Jacques. "Force of Law: The Mystical Foundation of Authority." In *Deconstruction and the Possibility of Justice*, 3–67. New York: Routledge, 1992.

———. *Politics of Friendship*. London: Verso, 2005.

———. *Rogues: Two Essays on Reason*. Stanford: Stanford University Press, 2005.

De Staël, Germaine. *Considerations on the Principal Events of the French Revolution*. Edited by Aurelian Craiutu. Indianapolis: Liberty Fund, 2008.

Dio, Cassius. *Roman History*. Translated by Earnest Cary and Herbert B. Foster. 9 vols. London, Heinemann, 1925.

Donne, John. *Pseudo-Martyr Wherein out of Certaine Propositions and Gradations, This Conclusion Is Euicted. That Those Which Are of the Romane Religion in This Kingdome, May and Ought to Take the Oath of Allegiance*. London: Printed by W. Stansby for Walter Burre, 1610.

Dougherty, M. Patricia. "The French Catholic Press and the July Revolution." *French History* 12, no. 4 (1998): 403–28.

Dowling, Melissa Barden. *Clemency and Cruelty in the Roman World*. Ann Arbor: University of Michigan Press, 2006.

Drinkwater, John F. *Nero: Emperor and Court*. Cambridge: Cambridge University Press, 2019.

Duguit, Leon, and Henry Monnier. *Les Constitutions et Les Principales Lois Politiques de La France Depuis 1789*. 3rd ed. Paris: Libraire General de Droit et de Jurisprudence, 1915.

Dumas, Alexandre. *Souvenirs dramatiques / par Alexandre Dumas*. Vol. 1. Paris: Librairie Nouvelle, 1868.

Duncan, Stewart. "Leibniz on Hobbes's Materialism." *Studies in History and Philosophy of Science* 41, no. 1 (2010): 11–18.

Dyzenhaus, David. "The Gorgon Head of Power: Heller and Kelsen on the Rule of Law." In *From Liberal Democracy to Fascism*, edited by Peter C. Caldwell and William E. Scheuerman, 20–46. Boston: Humanities Press, 2000.

———. "Kelsen, Heller and Schmitt: Paradigms of Sovereignty Thought." *Theoretical Inquiries in Law* 16, no. 2 (2015): 337–66.

———. *Legality and Legitimacy: Carl Schmitt, Hans Kelsen and Hermann Heller in Weimar*. Oxford: Oxford University Press, 1997.

Eames, Jane Anthony. *A Budget of Letters, Or, Things Which I Saw Abroad*. Boston: W. D. Ticknor, 1847.

Eden, P. T. "Introduction." In *Apocolocyntosis*, by Seneca, edited by P. T. Eden, 1–26. Cambridge Greek and Latin Classics. Cambridge: Cambridge University Press, 1984.

Eder, Walter. "Augustus and the Power of Tradition." In *The Cambridge Companion to the Age of Augustus*, edited by Karl Galinsky, 13–32. Cambridge: Cambridge University Press, 2005.

Epicurus. *Epicurus: The Extant Remains*. Translated by Cyril Bailey. Oxford: Clarendon Press, 1926.

Erasmus, Desiderius. *The Education of a Christian Prince*. Edited by Lisa Jardine. Translated by Neil M. Cheshire and Michael J. Heath. Cambridge: Cambridge University Press, 1997.

Ferri, Rolando. "Introduction." In *Octavia: A Play Attributed to Seneca*, edited by Rolando Ferri, 1–82. Cambridge: Cambridge University Press, 2003.

Fielding, Henry. *An Enquiry Into the Causes of the Late Increase of Robbers, &c.* London: Printed for A. Millar, 1751.

Figgis, John Neville. *The Divine Right of Kings*. New York: Harper and Row, 1965.

Forman, David. "Free Will and the Freedom of the Sage in Leibniz and the Stoics." *History of Philosophy Quarterly* 25, no. 3 (2008): 203–19.

Fortescue, William. "Morality and Monarchy: Corruption and the Fall of the Regime of Louis Philippe in 1848." *French History* 16, no. 1 (2002): 83–100.

Foucault, Michel. *"Society Must Be Defended": Lectures at the Collège de France, 1975–1976*. Translated by David Macey. New York: Picador, 2003.

Fox, Harold G. *Monopolies and Patents: A Study of the History and Future of the Patent Monopoly*. Toronto: University of Toronto Press, 1947.

Franke & Heidecke. *Success Alone Decides*. Braunschweig: Franke & Heidecke, 1938. http://www.cameramanuals .org/rolleiflex/rolleiflex_success.pdf.

Furet, François. *Revolutionary France 1770–1880*. Translated by Antonia Nevill. Oxford: Blackwell, 1992.

Gardiner, Samuel Rawson. *The Personal Government of Charles I*. London: Longmans, Green, 1877.

Geffen, Arthur. "Walt Whitman and Jules Michelet—One More Time." *American Literature* 45, no. 1 (1973): 107–14.

Gildea, Robert. *The Past in French History*. New Haven: Yale University Press, 1996.

Goldie, Mark. "The Ancient Constitution and the Languages of Political Thought." *Historical Journal* 62, no. 1 (2019): 3–34.

Gossman, Lionel. "Jules Michelet and Romantic Historiography." In *Scribner's European Writers*, edited by Jacques Barzun and George Stade, 571–606. New York: Charles Scribner's Sons, 1985.

Griffin, Miriam T. *Nero: The End of a Dynasty*. London: Routledge, 2013.

———. *Seneca: A Philosopher in Politics*. Oxford: Clarendon, 1992.

———. *Seneca on Society: A Guide to De Beneficiis*. Oxford: Oxford University Press, 2014.

Grotius, Hugo. *Three Books Treating of the Rights of War and Peace*. Translated by William Evats. London: Thomas Basset, 1682.

Guizot, François. *History of the Origin of Representative Government in Europe [Lectures of 1820–22]*. Translated by Andrew Scoble. London: Henry G. Bohn, 1861.

Haberman, Maggie, and Michael S. Schmidt. "Trump Gives Clemency to More Allies, Including Manafort, Stone and Charles Kushner." *New York Times*, December 24, 2020. https://www.nytimes.com/12/23/us/politics/trump-pardon-manafort-stone.html.

———. "Trump Pardons Two Russia Inquiry Figures and Blackwater Guards." *New York Times*, December 23, 2020. https://www.nytimes.com/2020/12/22/us/politics/trump-pardons.html.

Habermas, Jürgen. "The Horrors of Autonomy: Carl Schmitt in English." In Habermas, *The New Conservatism: Cultural Criticism and the Historians' Debate*, edited by Shierry W. Nicholsen, 128–39. Cambridge: MIT Press, 1989.

Hansen, Thomas Blom, and Finn Stepputat. "Sovereignty Revisited." *Annual Review of Anthropology* 35 (2006): 295–315.

Harris, Tim. "Anti-Catholicism and Anti-Popery in Seventeenth-Century England." In *Against Popery: Britain, Empire, and Anti-Catholicism*, edited by Evan Haefili, 26–43. Charlottesville: University of Virginia Press, 2020.

———. *Restoration: Charles II and His Kingdoms, 1660–1685*. London: Penguin, 2006.

———. *Revolution: The Great Crisis of the British Monarchy, 1685–1720*. London: Penguin, 2007.

Hay, Douglas. "Property, Authority and the Criminal Law." In *Albion's Fatal Tree: Crime and Society in Eighteenth-Century England*, by Douglas Hay et al., 17–63. London: Verso, 2011 [1975].

Hegel, Georg Wilhelm Friedrich. *Hegel's Philosophy of Right*. Translated by Thomas Malcolm Knox. Oxford: Oxford University Press, 1967.

———. *The Philosophy of History*. Translated by J. Sibree. New York: Dover, 1956.

Heller, Hermann. "The Essence and Structure of the State." In *Weimar: A Jurisprudence of Crisis*, edited by Arthur J. Jacobson and Bernhard Schlink, 265–71. Berkeley: University of California Press, 2000.

Henry, Denis, and B. Walker. "Tacitus and Seneca." *Greece and Rome* 10, no. 2 (1963): 98–110.

Herrup, Cynthia. *The Common Peace: Participation and the Criminal Law in Seventeenth-Century England*. Cambridge: Cambridge University Press, 1987.

Herzog, Annabel. "Hobbes and Corneille on Political Representation." *European Legacy* 14, no. 4 (2009): 379–89.

Hibbard, Caroline M. *Charles I and the Popish Plot*. Chapel Hill: University of North Carolina Press, 1983.

Hill, Christopher. *The Century of Revolution, 1603–1714*. London: Routledge, 2002.

Hirst, Paul. "Carl Schmitt's Decisionism." In *The Challenge of Carl Schmitt*, edited by Chantal Mouffe, 7–17. London: Verso, 1999.

Hobbes, Thomas. "An Answer to [Bishop Bramhall's] 'Catching of the Leviathan.' Together with an Historical Narration Concerning Heresy, and the Punishment Thereof." In *The English Works of Thomas Hobbes*, vol. 4, edited by William Molesworth, 279–408. London: John Bohn, 1840.

———. *Leviathan*. Edited by Edwin Curley. New ed. Indianapolis: Hackett, 1994.

———. *On the Citizen*. Edited by Richard Tuck. Translated by Michael

Silverthorne. Cambridge: Cambridge University Press, 1998.

———. "A Dialogue Between A Philosopher and a Student, of the Common Laws of England." In *Writings on Common Law and Hereditary Right*, edited by Alan Cromartie and Quentin Skinner, 1–147. Oxford: Oxford University Press, 2005.

Hobbes, Thomas, and Bishop Bramhall. *Questions Concerning Liberty, Necessity, and Chance*. Vol. 5 of *The English Works of Thomas Hobbes*. London: J. Bohn, 1841.

Hoekstra, Kinch. "Hobbes and the Foole." *Political Theory* 25, no. 5 (1997): 620–54.

Holmes, Stephen. "Does Hobbes Have a Concept of the Enemy?" *Critical Review of International Social and Political Philosophy* 13, nos. 2–3 (2010): 271–389.

The House of Commons. "The Grand Remonstrance, with the Petition Accompanying It." In *The Constitutional Documents of the Puritan Revolution*, edited by Samuel R. Gardiner, 202–32. Oxford: Clarendon Press, 1906.

Ibbett, Katherine. "Italy Versus France; or, How Pierre Corneille Became an Anti-Machiavel." *Renaissance Drama* 36/37 (2010): 379–95.

James I. *Basilicon Doron*. In King James VI and I, *Political Writings*, edited by Johann P. Sommerville, 1–61. Cambridge: Cambridge University Press, 1991.

———. *A Declaration of His Majesties Royall Pleasure, in What Sort He Thinketh Fit to Enlarge, or Reserve Himself in Matter of Bounty*. London: Robert Baker, 1610.

James, Paula, and Susanna Morton Braund. "Quasi Homo: Distortion and Contortion in Seneca's *Apocolocyntosis*." *Arethusa* 31, no. 3 (1998): 285–311.

James, William. *Pragmatism and Other Writings*. New York: Penguin Random House, 2000.

Jolley, Nicholas. "Leibniz on Hobbes, Locke's Two Treatises and Sherlock's Case of Allegiance." *Historical Journal* 18, no. 1 (1975): 21–35.

Jurecic, Quinta. "What's New in the Unredacted Mueller Report?" Lawfare, July 2, 2020. https:// www .lawfareblog.com/whats-new -unredacted-mueller-report.

Justinian. *The Institutes of Justinian*. Translated by Thomas C. Sandars. Chicago: Callaghan, 1876.

Kalmo, Hent, and Quentin Skinner. "Introduction: A Concept in Fragments." In Kalmo and Skinner, *Sovereignty in Fragments*, 1–25.

———, eds. *Sovereignty in Fragments: The Past, Present, and Future*. Cambridge: Cambridge University Press, 2010.

Kalyvas, Andreas. *Democracy and the Politics of the Extraordinary: Max Weber, Carl Schmitt, and Hannah Arendt*. Cambridge: Cambridge University Press, 2008.

Kant, Immanuel. "To Perpetual Peace: A Philosophical Sketch (1795)." In *Perpetual Peace and Other Essays*, translated by Ted Humphrey, 107–44. Indianapolis: Hackett, 1983.

Kaplan, Edward K. *Michelet's Poetic Vision: A Romantic Philosophy of Nature, Man, and Woman*. Amherst: University of Massachusetts Press, 1977.

Kapust, Daniel J. *Flattery and the History of Political Thought: That Glib and Oily Art*. Cambridge: Cambridge University Press, 2018.

Karni, Annie. "President Trump Grants Pardon to Conrad Black." *New York Times*, May 15, 2019. https://www .nytimes.com/2019/05/15/us/politics /conrad-black-pardon.html.

Kelsen, Hans. "Legal Formalism and the Pure Theory of Law." In *Weimar: A Jurisprudence of Crisis*, edited by Arthur J. Jacobson and Bernard Schlink, 76–83. Berkeley: University of California Press, 2000. http://ark .cdlib.org/ark:/13030/kt209nc4v2/.

Kennedy, Ellen. *Constitutional Failure: Carl Schmitt in Weimar.* Durham: Duke University Press, 2004.

Keohane, Oisín. "Bodin on Sovereignty: Taking Exception to Translation?" *Paragraph* 38, no. 2 (2015): 245–60.

Kesselring, K. J. *Mercy and Authority in the Tudor State.* Cambridge: Cambridge University Press, 2003.

King, Peter. "Decision-Makers and Decision-Making in the English Criminal Law, 1750–1800." *The Historical Journal* 27, no. 1 (1984): 25–58.

Kipper, Stephen A. *Jules Michelet: A Study of Mind and Sensibility.* Albany: SUNY Press, 1981.

Kishlansky, Mark. *A Monarchy Transformed: Britain 1603–1714.* London: Penguin, 1996.

———. "Tyranny Denied: Charles I, Attorney General Heath, and the Five Knights' Case." *Historical Journal* 42, no. 1 (1999): 53–83.

Konstan, David. "Clemency as a Virtue." *Classical Philology* 100, no. 4 (2005): 337–46.

Koselleck, Reinhart. *Critique and Crisis: Enlightenment and the Pathogenesis of Modern Society.* Cambridge: MIT Press, 1988.

Koskenniemi, Martti. "Conclusion: Vocabularies of Sovereignty— Powers of a Paradox." In Kalmo and Skinner, *Sovereignty in Fragments,* 222–42.

———. *The Gentle Civilizer of Nations: The Rise and Fall of International Law 1870–1960.* Cambridge: Cambridge University Press, 2004.

Krabbe, Hugo. *The Modern Idea of the State.* Translated by George Sabine and Walter Shepard. New York: D. Appleton, 1922.

Kracauer, Siegfried. "The Revolt of the Middle Classes." In *The Mass Ornament: Weimar Essays,* translated by Thomas Levin, 107–27. Cambridge: Harvard University Press, 1995.

Krasner, Stephen D. *Sovereignty.* Princeton: Princeton University Press, 1999.

———. "Sovereignty." *Foreign Policy,* no. 122 (January 1, 2001): 20–29.

Krause, Sharon R. *Freedom Beyond Sovereignty: Reconstructing Liberal Individualism.* Chicago: University of Chicago Press, 2015.

Kyle, Donald G. "Greek Athletic Competitions." In *A Companion to Sport and Spectacle in Greek and Roman Antiquity,* edited by Paul Christesen and Donald G. Kyle, 17–35. West Sussex, UK: John Wiley & Sons, 2013.

Lake, Peter. "Anti-Popery: The Structure of a Prejudice." In *Conflict in Early Stuart England: Studies in Religion and Politics 1603–1642,* edited by Richard Cust and Ann Hughes, 72–106. Harlow, UK: Longman, 1989.

Lamartine, Alphonse. *Atheism Among the People.* Translated by Edward Hale and Francis Le Baron. Boston: Phillips, Sampson, 1850.

Landler, Mark. "Trump to Invite Putin to Washington, Blindsiding His Intelligence Chief." *New York Times,* July 19, 2018. https://www.nytimes.com/2018/07/19/us/politics/trump-putin-browder-mcfaul.html.

Langbein, John H. "Albion's Fatal Flaws." *Past & Present,* no. 98 (1983): 96–120.

Larmore, Charles. *The Morals of Modernity.* Cambridge: Cambridge University Press, 1996.

Laski, Harold Joseph. *Studies in the Problem of Sovereignty.* New Haven: Yale University Press, 1917.

Lee, Daniel. "'Office Is a Thing Borrowed': Jean Bodin on Offices and Seigneurial Government." *Political Theory* 41, no. 3 (2013): 409–40.

Lee, Hugh M. "Greek Sports in Rome." In *A Companion to Sport and Spectacle in Greek and Roman Antiquity,* edited by Paul Christesen and Donald G. Kyle, 533–42. West Sussex, UK: John Wiley & Sons, 2013.

LeFort, Claude. "Edgar Quinet: The Revolution That Failed." In *Democracy and Political Theory*, translated by David Macey, 115–34. Minneapolis: University of Minnesota Press, 1988.

———. "The Permanence of the Theologico-Political?" In *Democracy and Political Theory*, translated by David Macey, 213–25. Minneapolis: University of Minnesota Press, 1988.

Leibniz, Gottfried Wilhelm. "Against Barbaric Physics." In Leibniz, *Philosophical Essays*, 312–20.

———. "Mars Christianissimus 1683." In *Leibniz: Political Writings*, edited by Patrick Riley, 121–45. Cambridge: Cambridge University Press, 1988.

———. *Philosophical Essays*. Edited by Roger Ariew and Daniel Garber. Indianapolis: Hackett, 1989.

———. "Second Letter to Clarke." In Leibniz, *Philosophical Essays*, 321–24.

———. *Theodicy: Essays on the Goodness of God and the Freedom of Man and the Origin of Evil*. Edited by Austin Marsden Farrer. Translated by E. M. Huggard. New York: Open Court, 1985.

———. "Two Sects of Naturalists (1677–80)." In Leibniz, *Philosophical Essays*, 281–84.

Levick, Barbara. *Claudius*. London: Batsford, 1990.

Lewis, Flora. "The End of Sovereignty." *New York Times*, May 23, 1992.

The Livre Rouge, or the Red Book. 8th ed. London: G. Kearsley, 1790.

Locke, John. *Two Treatises of Government*. Student edition. Edited by Peter Laslett. Cambridge: Cambridge University Press, 1988.

Machiavelli, Niccolò. *The Discourses on Livy*. Translated by L. J. Walker and B. Richardson. Harmondsworth, UK: Penguin, 1974.

———. *The Prince*. Translated by Harvey C. Mansfield. 2nd ed. Chicago: University of Chicago Press, 1998.

MacLean, Nancy. *Democracy in Chains: The Deep History of the Radical Right's Stealth Plan for America*. New York: Knopf, 2017.

Magalhães, Pedro T. "A Contingent Affinity: Max Weber, Carl Schmitt, and the Challenge of Modern Politics." *Journal of the History of Ideas* 77, no. 2 (2016): 283–304.

Malcolm, Noel. "An Unknown Policy Proposal by Thomas Hobbes." *Historical Journal* 55, no. 1 (2012): 145–60.

Mali, Joseph. "Jules Michelet: Vico and the Origins of Nationalism." In *The Legacy of Vico in Modern Cultural History: From Jules Michelet to Isaiah Berlin*, 12–70. Cambridge: Cambridge University Press, 2012.

Mandeville, Bernard. *The Fable of the Bees or Private Vices, Public Benefits*. Vol. 2. Indianapolis: Liberty Fund, 1988.

Maritain, Jacques. *Man and the State*. Chicago: University of Chicago Press, 1951.

Marx, Karl. "The Eighteenth Brumaire of Louis Bonaparte." Translated by Ben Fowkes. In *Surveys from Exile*, edited by David Fernbach, vol. 2, 143–249. New York: Random House, 1974.

———. "The June Revolution [29 June, 1848, Neue Rheinische Zeitung]." In *The Revolutions of 1848*, edited by David Fernbach, 129–34. New York: Random House, 1974.

———. "Manifesto of the Communist Party." In *The Marx-Engels Reader*, 2nd ed., edited by Robert Tucker, 469–500. New York: Norton, 1978.

———. "Review of Guizot's Book on the English Revolution." Translated by Paul Jackson. In *Surveys from Exile*, edited by David Fernbach, vol. 2, 250–55. New York: Random House, 1974.

———. "Speeches on Poland 22 February 1848." In *The Revolutions of 1848*, edited by David Fernbach, 102–5. New York: Random House, 1974.

Maurras, Charles. *Trois idées politiques: Chateaubriand, Michelet, Sainte-Beuve*. Paris: Champion, 1912.

Maus, Ingeborg. "The 1933 'Break' in Carl Schmitt's Theory." In *Law as Politics: Carl Schmitt's Critique of Liberalism*, edited by David Dyzenhaus, 196–216. Durham: Duke University Press, 1998.

May, Larry. *Limiting Leviathan: Hobbes on Law and International Affairs*. New York: Oxford University Press, 2013.

Mayer, J. P. *Max Weber and German Politics: A Study in Political Sociology*. London: Faber and Faber, 1943.

McCormick, John P. *Carl Schmitt's Critique of Liberalism: Against Politics as Technology*. Cambridge: Cambridge University Press, 1997.

———. "Fear, Technology, and the State: Carl Schmitt, Leo Strauss, and the Revival of Hobbes in Weimar and National Socialist Germany." *Political Theory* 22, no. 4 (1994): 619–52.

Meier, Heinrich. *Carl Schmitt and Leo Strauss: The Hidden Dialogue; Including Strauss's Notes on Schmitt's Concept of the Political and Three Letters from Strauss to Schmitt*. Translated by J. Harvey Lomax. Chicago: University of Chicago Press, 1995.

———. *The Lesson of Carl Schmitt: Four Chapters on the Distinction Between Political Theology and Political Philosophy*. Translated by Marcus Brainard. Chicago: University of Chicago Press, 1998.

Mellon, Stanley. *The Political Uses of History: A Study of Historians in the French Restoration*. Stanford: Stanford University Press, 1958.

Mervault, Pierre. *The Last Famous Siege of the City of Rochel Together with the Edict of Nantes / Written in French by Peter Meruault, a Citizen of Rochel Who Was in the City from the Beginning of the Siege Until the Rendition of It*. London, 1680.

Michelet, Jules. *France Before Europe*. Boston: Roberts Brothers, 1871.

———. *Histoire de France*. Vol. 10. New ed. Paris: A. Lacroix, 1880.

———. *Histoire de France*. Vol. 12, *Richelieu et la fronde*. Paris: Chamerot, 1858.

———. *Histoire de la Révolution française*. Vol. 1. Paris: C. Marpon et E. Flammarion, 1879.

———. *Historical View of the French Revolution, from Its Earliest Indications of the Flight of the King in 1791*. Translated by C. Cocks. London: G. Bell & Sons, 1888.

———. *History of the French Revolution*. Vol. 7 (books 14–17). Translated by Keith Botsford. Wynnewood, PA: Kolokol Press, 1973.

———. "Introduction to World History." In *On History*, translated by Flora Kimmich, 23–118. New York: Open Book Publishers, 2013. https://books.openbookpublishers.com/10.11647/obp.0036.pdf.

———. *Love*. Translated by John W. Palmer. New York: Rudd & Carleton, 1860.

———. *Oeuvres complètes*. Edited by Paul Vialleneix. Vol. 21. Paris: Flammarion, 1982.

———. *The People*. 3rd ed. Translated by C. Cocks. London: A. Spottiswoode, 1848.

———. "Preface of 1869 to the History of France." In Kaplan, *Michelet's Poetic Vision: A Romantic Philosophy of Nature, Man, and Woman*, 143–68.

———. *Priests, Women, and Families*. Translated by C. Cocks. London: Longman, Brown, Green and Longmans, 1845.

Michelet, Jules, and Edgar Quinet. *Jesuits and Jesuitism*. Translated by G. H. Smith. London: Whittaker, 1846.

Mill, John Stuart. "On Liberty." In *Mill: Texts and Commentaries*, edited by Alan Ryan, 41–131. New York: Norton, 1997.

Miller, Ted H. *Mortal Gods: Science, Politics, and the Humanist Ambitions of Thomas Hobbes*. University Park: Penn State University Press, 2011.

Mitzman, Arthur. "Michelet and Social Romanticism: Religion, Revolution, Nature." *Journal of the History of Ideas* 57, no. 4 (1996): 659–82.

———. *Michelet, Historian: Rebirth and Romanticism in Nineteenth-Century France*. New Haven: Yale University Press, 1990.

Mommsen, Wolfgang J. *Max Weber and German Politics, 1890–1920*. Translated by Michael S. Steinberg. Chicago: University of Chicago Press, 1984.

Montaigne, Michel de. *The Complete Essays of Montaigne*. Translated by Donald M. Frame. Stanford: Stanford University Press, 1958.

Moreau, Thérèse. "Revolting Women." *Clio* 6, no. 2 (1977): 167–79.

Morrill, John. "The Attack on the Church of England in the Long Parliament." In *The Nature of the English Revolution*, 69–90. London: Taylor & Francis, 1993 [1985].

———. "Charles I, Tyranny and the English Civil War." In *The Nature of the English Revolution*, 285–306. London: Taylor & Francis, 1993 [1990].

———. "The Religious Context of the English Civil War." In *The Nature of the English Revolution*, 45–68. London: Taylor & Francis, 1993 [1984].

Moyn, Samuel. "Hannah Arendt on the Secular." *New German Critique*, no. 105 (Fall 2008): 71–96.

Mueller, Robert S., III. *Report on the Investigation into Russian Interference in the 2016 Presidential Election*. 2 vols. Washington, DC: US Department of Justice, 2019.

Murphy, Jeffrie G. "Mercy and Legal Justice." In *Forgiveness and Mercy*, by Jeffrie G. Murphy and Jean Hampton, 162–86. Cambridge: Cambridge University Press, 1988.

Newcastle, Margaret Cavendish, Duchess of. *The Life of the Thrice Noble, High and Puissant Prince William Cavendishe, Duke, Marquess and Earl of Newcastle* . . . London: A. Maxwell, 1667.

New York Times. "At Long Last, a Measure of Justice for Some Drug Offenders." Editorial. June 11, 2019. https://www .nytimes.com/2019/06/11/opinion /first-step-act-drug-offenders.html.

———. "The President and His Power to Pardon." Editorial. May 19, 2019.

https://www.nytimes.com/2019/05 /19/opinion/trump-pardon-conrad -black-patrick-nolan.html.

Nisbet, R. G. M. "The Dating of Seneca's Tragedies, with Special Reference to Thyestes." *Papers of the Leeds International Latin Seminar* 6 (1990): 95–114.

Norris, Andrew, ed. *Politics, Metaphysics, and Death: Essays on Giorgio Agamben's "Homo Sacer."* Durham: Duke University Press, 2005.

Ogilby, John, and Ronald Knowles. *The Entertainment of His Most Excellent Majestie Charles II in His Passage Through the City of London to His Coronation*. Binghamton, NY: Medieval & Renaissance Texts & Studies, 1988.

Paine, Thomas. *The Rights of Man*. In *The Complete Writings of Thomas Paine*, edited by Philip S. Foner, 1:243–458. New York: Citadel Press, 1945.

Pankakoski, Timo. "Conflict, Context, Concreteness: Koselleck and Schmitt on Concepts." *Political Theory* 38, no. 6 (2010): 749–79.

Paschalis, Michael. "The Afterlife of Emperor Claudius in Seneca's *Apocolocyntosis*." *Numen* 56, no. 2 (2009): 198–216.

Passavant, Paul A. "The Contradictory State of Giorgio Agamben." *Political Theory* 35, no. 2 (2007): 147–74.

Peck, Linda Levy. *Court Patronage and Corruption in Early Stuart England*. London: Routledge, 1993.

Pettit, Philip. *Republicanism*. Oxford: Oxford University Press, 1997.

Philipps, Dave. "Trump's Pardons for Servicemen Raise Fears That Laws of War Are History." *New York Times*, November 16, 2019. https://www .nytimes.com/2019/11/16/us/trump -pardon-military.html.

Pilbeam, Pamela M. *Republicanism in Nineteenth-Century France, 1814–1871*. London: Macmillan, 1995.

Pincus, Steve. *1688: The First Modern Revolution*. New Haven: Yale University Press, 2011.

Pinkney, David H. *The French Revolution of 1830*. Princeton: Princeton University Press, 1972.

Plato. *Republic*. Translated by G. M. A. Grube and C. D. C. Reeve. Indianapolis: Hackett, 1992.

Plutarch. *Cato the Younger*. In *Lives*, vol. 8, *Sertorius and Eumenes. Phocion and Cato the Younger*, translated by Bernadotte Perrin, 235–411. Cambridge: Harvard University Press, 1919.

———. *Plutarch's Lives*. Translated by Bernadotte Perrin. Vol. 2. Loeb Classical Library. Cambridge: Harvard University Press, 1917.

Pocock, J. G. A. *The Ancient Constitution and the Feudal Law: A Study of English Historical Thought in the Seventeenth Century*. Cambridge: Cambridge University Press, 1987.

Pope, Alexander. "An Essay on Man." In *The Poems of Alexander Pope*, edited by John Butt, 501–47. New Haven: Yale University Press, 1963.

Price, Munro. *The Perilous Crown: France Between Revolutions, 1814–1848*. London: Macmillan, 2007.

Price, William Hyde. *The English Patents of Monopoly*. Boston: Houghton, Mifflin, 1906.

Prynne, William. *The Sovereign Power of Parilaments and Kingdomes Divided into Foure Parts*. London: For Michael Sparke, Sr., 1643.

Raspa, Anthony. "John Donne on Royal Mercy and Pardon." *ESC: English Studies in Canada* 25, no. 2 (1999): 157–67.

Rétat, Claude. "Jules Michelet, l'idéologie du vivant." *Romantisme*, no. 130 (2005): 9–22.

Riley, Patrick. *Leibniz' Universal Jurisprudence: Justice as the Charity of the Wise*. Cambridge: Harvard University Press, 1996.

Ristroph, Alice. "Sovereignty and Subversion." *Virginia Law Review* 101, no. 4 (2015): 1029–54.

Romm, James. *Dying Every Day: Seneca at the Court of Nero*. New York: Knopf, 2014.

Roosbroeck, Gustave L. van. "Corneille's 'Cinna' and the 'Conspiration Des Dames.'" *Modern Philology* 20, no. 1 (1922): 1–17.

Rosanvallon, Pierre. *Democracy Past and Future*. Edited by Samuel Moyn. New York: Columbia University Press, 2007.

———. "The Market, Liberalism, and Anti-Liberalism." In *Democracy Past and Future*, edited by Samuel Moyn, 147–59. New York: Columbia University Press, 2006.

———. *La monarchie impossible*. Paris: Fayard, 1994.

Rousseau, Jean-Jacques. *Discourse on the Origin and Foundations of Inequality Among Men*. In *The Basic Political Writings*, translated by Donald A. Cress, 27–120. Indianapolis: Hackett, 2011.

———. *Emile: or On Education*. Translated by Allan Bloom. New York: Basic Books, 1979.

———. *Letter to Beaumont, Letters Written from the Mountain, and Related Writings*. Hanover: University Press of New England, 2013.

———. *Oeuvres complètes*. Edited by Marcel Raymond and Bernard Gagnebin. 4 vols. Paris: Gallimard, 1959.

———. *On the Social Contract*. In *The Basic Political Writings*, translated by Donald A. Cress, 155–252. Indianapolis: Hackett, 2011.

———. *"The Reveries of the Solitary Walker," Botanical Writings, and Letter to Franquières*. Edited by Christopher Kelly. Translated by Charles Butterworth. The Collected Writings of Rousseau 8. Hanover: University Press of New England, 2000.

Rubini, Rocco. "The Vician 'Renaissance' Between Giuseppe Ferrari and Jules Michelet." *Intellectual History Review* 26, no. 1 (2016): 9–15.

Rutherford, Donald. "Leibniz and the Stoics: The Consolations of Theodicy." In *The Problem of Evil in Early Modern Philosophy*, edited by Elmar J. Kremer and Michael J. Latzer, 138–64. Toronto: University of Toronto Press, 2001.

Sallust. *The War with Catiline*. Translated by J. C. Rolfe. Cambridge: Harvard University Press, 2013.

Sansone, David. "Nero's Final Hours." *Illinois Classical Studies* 18 (1993): 179–89.

Sarat, Austin. *Mercy on Trial: What It Means to Stop an Execution.* Princeton: Princeton University Press, 2005.

Savage, Charlie. "Trump Pardons Michael Flynn, Ending Case His Justice Dept. Sought to Shut Down." *New York Times*, November 25, 2020. https://www.nytimes.com/2020 /11/25/us/politics/michael-flynn -pardon.html.

Scheuerman, William E. "Carl Schmitt and the Road to Abu Ghraib." *Constellations: An International Journal of Critical and Democratic Theory* 13, no. 1 (2006): 108–24.

———. *Carl Schmitt: The End of Law.* Lanham, MD: Rowman & Littlefield, 1999.

———. "Emergencies, Executive Power, and the Uncertain Future of US Presidential Democracy." *Law & Social Inquiry* 37, no. 3 (2012): 743–67.

———. "Hermann Heller and the European Crisis: Authoritarian Liberalism Redux?" *European Law Journal* 21, no. 3 (2015): 302–12.

Schmidt, Michael S., Jo Becker, Mark Mazzetti, Maggie Haberman, and Adam Goldman. "Trump's Lawyer Raised Prospect of Pardons for Flynn and Manafort as Special Counsel Closed In." *New York Times*, March 28, 2018. https://www.nytimes.com /2018/03/28/us/politics/trump -pardon-michael-flynn-paul-mana fort-john-dowd.html.

Schmidt, Michael S., and Kenneth P. Vogel. "Prospect of Pardons in Final Days Fuels Market to Buy Access to Trump." *New York Times*, January 17, 2021. https://www.nytimes.com/2021 /01/17/us/politics/trump-pardons .html.

Schmitt, Carl. "The Age of Neutralizations and Depolitizations (1929)." In Schmitt, *The Concept of the Political: Expanded Edition*, 80–96.

———. *The Concept of the Political: Expanded Edition.* Translated by Matthias Konzett and John P. McCormick. Chicago: University of Chicago Press, 2007.

———. *Constitutional Theory.* Translated by Jeffrey Seitzer. Durham: Duke University Press, 2008.

———. *The Crisis of Parliamentary Democracy.* New York: MIT Press, 1988.

———. *Dictatorship.* Translated by Michael Hoelzl and Graham Ward. Cambridge: Polity, 2014.

———. *The Guardian of the Constitution: Hans Kelsen and Carl Schmitt on the Limits of Constitutional Law.* Translated by Lars Vinx. Cambridge: Cambridge University Press, 2015.

———. *The Leviathan in the State Theory of Thomas Hobbes: Meaning and Failure of a Political Symbol.* Translated by George Schwab. Chicago: University of Chicago Press, 2008.

———. *Political Romanticism.* Translated by Guy Oakes. Studies in Contemporary German Social Thought. Cambridge: MIT Press, 1986.

———. *Political Theology: Four Chapters on the Concept of Sovereignty.* Translated by George Schwab. Chicago: University of Chicago Press, 2005.

———. *Roman Catholicism and Political Form.* Translated by G. L. Ulmen. Westport, CT: Greenwood Press, 1996.

Schröder, Peter. "Carl Schmitt's Appropriation of the Early Modern European Tradition of Political Thought on the State and Interstate Relations." *History of Political Thought* 33, no. 2 (2012): 348–71.

Seneca, Lucius Annaeus. *Apocolocyntosis.* Edited by P. T. Eden. Cambridge Greek and Latin Classics. Cambridge: Cambridge University Press, 1984.

———. *De Clementia.* Edited by Susanna Braund. Oxford: Oxford University Press, 2009.

———. *On Benefits.* Translated by Miriam T. Griffin and Brad Inwood. Complete

Works of Lucius Annaeus Seneca. Chicago: University of Chicago Press 2011.

———. "On Clemency." Translated by Robert A. Kaster. In Seneca, *Anger, Mercy, Revenge*, translated by Robert A. Kaster and Martha C. Nussbaum, 132–94. Chicago: University of Chicago Press, 2010.

———. "On Providence: To Lucilius." In *Seneca: Dialogues and Essays*, translated by John Davie, 3–17. Oxford: Oxford University Press, 2007.

———. *Thyestes*. Translated by John G. Fitch. Cambridge: Harvard University Press, 2004.

[Seneca the Younger]. *Octavia*. Translated by John G. Fitch. Cambridge: Harvard University Press, 2004.

Shapiro, Kam. *Carl Schmitt and the Intensification of Politics*. Lanham, MD: Rowman & Littlefield, 2008.

Sharpe, James A. *Crime in Early Modern England, 1550–1750*. 2nd ed. London, New York: Routledge, 1998.

Sharpe, Kevin. *The Personal Rule of Charles I*. New Haven: Yale University Press, 1992.

Shear, Michael D. "Obama's 78 Pardons and 153 Commutations Extend Record of Mercy." *New York Times*, December 19, 2016. https://www.nytimes.com /2016/12/19/us/politics/obama -commutations-pardons-clemency .html.

Shklar, Judith N. *Ordinary Vices*. Cambridge: Harvard University Press, 1984.

Sidney, Algernon. *Discourses Concerning Government*. Edited by Thomas G. West. Indianapolis: Liberty Fund, 1996.

Sieyès, Emmanuel Joseph. "What Is the Third Estate?" In *Political Writings*, translated by Michael Sonenscher, 92–162. Indianapolis: Hackett, 2003.

Sitze, Adam. "Keeping the Peace." In *Forgiveness, Mercy, and Clemency*, edited by Austin Sarat and Nasser Hussain, 156–224. Stanford: Stanford University Press, 2007.

Skinner, Quentin. *Hobbes and Republican Liberty*. Cambridge: Cambridge University Press, 2008.

———. "Hobbes and the Purely Artificial Person of the State." In *Hobbes and Civil Science*. Vol. 3, 177–208, of *Visions of Politics*. Cambridge: Cambridge University Press, 2002.

———. "The Sovereign State: A Genealogy." In Kalmo and Skinner, *Sovereignty in Fragments*, 26–46.

———. *Liberty Before Liberalism*. Cambridge: Cambridge University Press, 1998.

Slomp, Gabriella. *Carl Schmitt and the Politics of Hostility, Violence and Terror*. New York: Macmillan, 2009.

Sommerville, J. "Absolutism and Royalism." In *The Cambridge History of Political Thought 1450–1700*, edited by J. H. Burns and Mark Goldie, 347–73. Cambridge: Cambridge University Press, 1994.

———. "The Ancient Constitution Reassessed: The Common Law, the Court, and the Languages of Politics in Early Modern England." In *The Stuart Court and Europe*. Cambridge: Cambridge University Press, 1996.

———. *Royalists and Patriots: Politics and Ideology in England, 1603–1640*. 2nd ed. New York: Routledge, 1999.

Sorell, Tom. "Schmitt, Hobbes and the Politics of Emergency." *Filozofski Vestnik* 24, no. 2 (2003): 223–41.

Sparling, Robert. "Political Corruption and the Concept of Dependence in Republican Thought." *Political Theory* 41, no. 4 (2013): 618–47.

Stacey, Peter. "The Princely Republic." *Journal of Roman Studies* 104 (November 2014): 133–54.

———. *Roman Monarchy and the Renaissance Prince*. Cambridge: Cambridge University Press, 2007.

———. "The Sovereign Person in Senecan Political Theory." *Republic of Letters: A Journal for the Study of Knowledge, Politics, and the Arts* 2, no. 2 (2011): 15–73.

Stark, Werner. *The Sociology of Religion.* Vol. 1. London: Routledge, 2013.

Starobinski, Jean. *Largesse.* Chicago: University of Chicago Press, 1997.

Stein, Lorenz von. *The History of the Social Movement in France 1789–1850.* Translated by Kaethe Mengelberg. Totowa, NJ: Bedminster Press, 1964.

Strauss, Leo. "Notes on Carl Schmitt, *The Concept of the Political.*" Translated by J. Harvey Lomax. In *The Concept of the Political*, by Carl Schmitt, 82–107. Chicago: University of Chicago Press, 1996.

———. *The Political Philosophy of Hobbes: Its Basis and Its Genesis.* Chicago: University of Chicago Press, 2014.

Strong, Tracy B. *Politics Without Vision: Thinking Without a Banister in the Twentieth Century.* Chicago: University of Chicago Press, 2012.

Suetonius. *Suetonius.* London: Harvard University Press, 1970.

———. *Suetonius.* Translated by John Carew Rolfe. Cambridge: Harvard University Press, 1979 [1914].

———. *The Twelve Caesars.* Translated by Robert Graves. Harmondsworth, UK: Penguin, 1957.

Sullivan, Eileen. "What We've Learned from Hill's and Holmes's Impeachment Testimonies." *New York Times*, November 21, 2019. https://www.nytimes.com/2019/11/21/us/politics/impeachment-hearings-day-five.html.

Syme, Ronald. *The Roman Revolution.* Oxford: Oxford University Press, 2002.

———. *Tacitus.* Oxford: Oxford University Press, 1958.

Tacitus, Cornelius. *Annals.* New York: Penguin, 2012.

Taylor, Jeremy, Charles Page Eden, Reginald Heber, and Alexander Taylor. *The Whole Works of the Right Rev. Jeremy Taylor . . . : Ductor Dubitantium, Part II, Books III and IV.* London: Longman, Brown, Green, and Longmans, 1855.

Thierry, Augustin. *The Formation and Progress of the Tiers Etat.* Translated by Francis Ballard Wells. London: H. G. Bohn, 1859.

Thomas, Keith. "The Social Origins of Hobbes's Political Thought." In *Hobbes Studies*, edited by K. C. Brown, 185–236. Oxford: Blackwell, 1965.

Thomsen, Jacob Als. "Carl Schmitt: The Hobbesian of the 20th Century?" *Social Thought and Research* 20, nos. 1–2 (1997): 5–28.

Tocqueville, Alexis de. *Democracy in America.* Edited by J. P. Mayer. Translated by George Lawrence. New York: Harper, 2006.

———. *The Old Regime and the Revolution.* Edited by François Furet and François Melonio. Translated by Alan S. Kahan. Chicago: University of Chicago Press, 1988.

———. *Recollections (Souvenirs).* Edited by J. P. Mayer. Translated by George Lawrence. Garden City: Doubleday, 1971.

Tuchscherer, Emmanuel. "Le décisionnisme de Carl Schmitt: Théorie et rhétorique de la guerre." *Mots: Les langages du politique*, no. 73 (2003): 25–42.

Tuckness, Alex, and John M. Parrish. *The Decline of Mercy in Public Life.* Cambridge: Cambridge University Press, 2014.

Twain, Mark. *Life on the Mississippi.* Boston: James R. Osgood, 1883.

United States Department of Justice. Civil Rights Division. "Investigation of the Ferguson Police Department." US Department of Justice, March 4, 2015.

Varouxaks, Georgios. "French Radicalism Through the Eye of John Stuart Mill." *History of European Ideas* 30, no. 4 (2004): 433–61.

Veblen, Thorstein. *Absentee Ownership: Business Enterprise in Recent Times; The Case of America.* Piscataway, NJ: Transaction Publishers, 1945.

Velleius Paterculus (ca. 19 BC–ca. AD 30). "Res Gestae Divi Augusti." In *Compendium of Roman History*, translated by Frederick W. Shipley, 332–405. London: Harvard University Press, 1924.

Veyne, Paul. *Bread and Circuses: Historical Sociology and Political Pluralism.* Translated by Brian Pearce. London: Penguin, 1992.

———. *Seneca: The Life of a Stoic.* New York: Routledge, 2002.

———. "What Was a Roman Emperor? Emperor, Therefore a God." *Diogenes* 50, no. 3 (2003): 3–21.

Viallaneix, Paul. "Jules Michelet, évangéliste de La Révolution française." *Archives de Sciences Sociales des Religions* 66, no. 1 (1988): 43–51.

———. *La Voie Royale: Essai sur l'idée de peuple dans l'œuvre de Michelet.* Paris: Flammarion, 1971.

Vinken, Barbara. "Wounds of Love: Modern Devotion According to Michelet." *Clio* 36 (2007): 155–76.

Voltaire. *Candide.* Translated by Robert M. Adams. 2nd ed. New York: Norton, 1991.

Wallace-Hadrill, Andrew. "Civilis Princeps: Between Citizen and King." *Journal of Roman Studies* 72 (1982): 32–48.

———. "The Emperor and His Virtues." *Historia: Zeitschrift Für Alte Geschichte* 30, no. 3 (1981): 298–323.

Walton, Benjamin. "'Quelque Peu Théâtral': The Operatic Coronation of Charles X." *19th-Century Music* 26, no. 1 (2002): 3–22.

Ward, Ian. "The End of Sovereignty and the New Humanism." *Stanford Law Review* 55, no. 5 (2003): 2091–112.

Weber, Max. *Economy and Society: An Outline of Interpretive Sociology.* Edited by Guenther Roth and Claus Wittich. 2 vols. Berkeley: University of California Press, 1978.

———. "Politics as a Vocation." In *From Max Weber,* translated by Hans H. Gerth and C. Wright Mills, 77–128. New York: Oxford University Press, 1946.

White, Hayden. *Metahistory: The Historical Imagination in Nineteenth-Century Europe.* Baltimore: Johns Hopkins University Press, 1973.

Wiedemann, T. E. J. "Tiberius to Nero." In *The Cambridge Ancient History,* edited by Alan K. Bowman, Edward Champlin, and Andrew Lintott, 2nd ed., 198–255. Cambridge: Cambridge University Press, 1996.

Williams, Margaret H. "'Θεοσεβὴς γὰρ ἦν' —The Jewish Tendencies of Poppaea Sabina." *Journal of Theological Studies* 39, no. 1 (1988): 97–111.

Wirszubski, C. *Libertas as a Political Idea at Rome During the Late Republic and Early Principate.* Cambridge: Cambridge University Press, 1950.

Wiseman, T. P. "Calpurnius Siculus and the Claudian Civil War." *Journal of Roman Studies* 72 (1982): 57–67.

Xenophon. *Cyropaedia: Books 5–8.* Loeb Classical Library. Cambridge: Harvard University Press, 1989.

Yourish, Karen, and Troy Griggs. "8 U.S. Intelligence Groups Blame Russia for Meddling, but Trump Keeps Clouding the Picture." *New York Times,* July 16, 2018. https://www.nytimes.com/interactive/2018/07/16/us/elections/russian-interference-statements-comments.html.

on Sullius, 205n61
suspicion of, 205n34
Tarquin kings, 143
tax farmers, 154, 211n75
technicity, 94–98, 196n36
Terror. *See* Robespierre and the Terror
theodicy, 81–82, 102–13, 121–22, 198n6,
  199n35
Theodicy (Leibnitz), 199n35
Thierry, Augustine, 183n7, 189n4
Thiers, Adolphe, 56, 187n80
Thirty Years' War (1648), 24
Thomas, Keith, 115
Thyestes (Seneca), 158–59, 163
Tiberius, 143, 152, 173, 207n4
Tocqueville, Alexis de, 40, 53, 57, 60, 67, 170,
  189n96
"To Perpetual Peace" (Kant), 29–30
Toranius, C., 174–75, 214n40
Trump, Donald, abuse of office, 12–13, 36,
  179n26
Tuckness, Alex, and John M. Parrish, 52,
  198n15, 205n45, 209n43, 212n4
Turgot, Anne Robert Jacques, 60

ultraroyalistes (Ultras), 53, 55, 183n18
United Nations, 36
United States, Constitution, 181n32

Veyne, Paul, 144, 155, 203n12, 207n8
Viallaneix, Paul, 182n3, 186n66, 189n100
Vico, Giambattista, 44, 185n35
Virginial Company, 200n52
Voltaire, 73, 110–11, 183n3, 186n47, 192n39,
  192n41

Walpole, Robert, 185n43
War on Terror, 9
Warwick, Earl of, 200n52
wealthy *versus* the poor, judgements on,
  115–17, 201n58
Weber, Max, 5, 31, 79, 80, 95, 97, 193n51,
  196n34
Weidemann, T. E. J., 159
Weimar Republic, 32, 93, 178n16, 181n41,
  182n1, 182n56, 193n45
Weinberger, Caspar, 179n26
"What Is Freedom?" (Arendt), 27
Whitman, Walt, 70, 191n24
will/general will, 26–29, 41, 180n30,
  181n31
Windebanck, Francis, 178n20
Wirszubski, C., 137–38
Wiseman, T. P., 205n41
wolves, 3, 171

Xenophon, 126–27, 171

Milton Keynes UK
Ingram Content Group UK Ltd.
UKHW021546050924
447875UK00004B/282